"Immersed in militarism sinc[...] pill of aggression and self-righteousness disguised as fostering democracy and freedom, or the red pill of truth. Coyne and Hall offer us the red pill and a path to freeing ourselves from the military machine. They believe we can handle the truth. Prove them right. Read this book."

—William J. Astore, Lieutenant Colonel, USAF (Ret.), and author of *Hindenburg: Icon of German Militarism*

"This book brilliantly analyzes one of the deepest problems of American democracy: the role of mass media in reinforcing government propaganda that promotes war, intervention, and militarism. From Washington to Hollywood, from Iraq to American sports stadiums, the order of the day is inflating threats, inventing enemies, and fanning the flames of fear and xenophobia. *Manufacturing Militarism* explains why the world that Americans see is so different from the world that actually exists."

—Stephen Kinzer, Watson Institute, Brown University, columnist for *The Boston Globe*, and author of *Poisoner in Chief*

"In *Manufacturing Militarism* Christopher Coyne and Abigail Hall offer both a vital rejoinder to uncritical American exceptionalism and this dirty secret: democracies, too, peddle in propaganda. Blending analyses of recent history, politics, and culture, they chronicle a narrative game long rigged—the U.S. government's ceaseless post-9/11 campaign to sell wars we don't need, that people don't otherwise want. Their disturbing conclusions ring as collective alarm bells for a republic in its long night of peril."

—Major (Ret.) Danny Sjursen, senior fellow at the Center for International Policy and the author of *Patriotic Dissent* and *Ghostriders of Baghdad*

"*Manufacturing Militarism* is a timely and far-reaching study of the role state-sponsored propaganda has played and continues to play in 21st century American life. Coyne and Hall show how, since 9/11, successive administrations held back relevant information and deliberately misled journalists and the public, damaging America's democracy, national security, and international reputation."

—David C. Unger, Johns Hopkins University SAIS Europe
and author of *The Emergency State*

"You can't handle the truth! At least that's what your government thinks. *Manufacturing Militarism* shows how democratic governments utilize their monopoly on classified information to propagandize their citizens in order to enable government actions that benefit the politically elite at the expense of average citizens. Coyne and Hall superbly illustrate how we have been propagandized by the U.S. government throughout the war on terror."

—Benjamin Powell, executive director,
Free Market Institute, Texas Tech University

"In *Manufacturing Militarism*, Christopher Coyne and Abigail Hall document the pernicious effects of the government's control and dissemination of information. They describe the "threat inflation" that characterizes government propaganda, facilitating citizen compliance and shifting power away from citizens and to the political elite who control public policy. More than just a tool that enables government policymakers to enact policies they prefer, Coyne and Hall make a persuasive case that government propaganda is a real threat to a free society."

—Randall Holcombe, professor of economics, Florida State University

"Rich with maddening examples, *Manufacturing Militarism* demonstrates that the U.S. government constantly emits lies and half-truths meant to shore up public support for endless wars against an endless stream of enemies, real and imaginary. And Coyne and Hall show us what to do about it. Read this book: Democracy is hanging in the balance."

—Roger Koppl, professor of finance, Syracuse University,
and author of *Expert Failure*

MANUFACTURING MILITARISM

MANUFACTURING MILITARISM

U.S. Government Propaganda in the War on Terror

Christopher J. Coyne and Abigail R. Hall

Stanford University Press
Stanford, California

Stanford University Press
Stanford, California

Printed in the United States of America on acid-free, archival-quality paper

Library of Congress Cataloging-in-Publication Data

Names: Coyne, Christopher J., author. | Hall, Abigail R., author.
Title: Manufacturing militarism : U.S. government propaganda in the
War on Terror / Christopher J. Coyne and Abigail R. Hall.
Description: Stanford, California : Stanford University Press, 2021. |
Includes bibliographical references and index.
Identifiers: LCCN 2020045727 (print) | LCCN 2020045728 (ebook)
| ISBN 9781503628359 (cloth) | ISBN 9781503628366 (paperback) |
ISBN 9781503628373 (ebook)
Subjects: LCSH: Militarism—United States. | Propaganda—United
States. | Propaganda, American. | Terrorism—Prevention—Government
policy—United States. | United States—Military policy. | United
States—History, Military—21st century. | United States—Politics and
government—21st century.
Classification: LCC E897 .C69 2021 (print) | LCC E897 (ebook) | DDC
303.3/750973—dc23
LC record available at https://lccn.loc.gov/2020045727
LC ebook record available at https://lccn.loc.gov/2020045728

Cover design: Kevin Barrette Kane

To F. A. "Baldy" Harper
A peacemonger in search of peace

"Among the calamities of war may be jointly numbered the diminution of the love of truth, by the falsehoods which interest dictates and credulity encourages."
—Samuel Johnson (1758)

Contents

Acknowledgments

This book has benefitted greatly from detailed comments from Yahya Alshamy, Diana Thomas, and two anonymous referees. We thank Alan Harvey and Caroline McKusick at Stanford University Press for their guidance on this project.

Portions of this book were presented at the Free Market Institute at Texas Tech University, the Mercatus Center at George Mason University, the Institute for Economic Inquiry at Creighton University, and Bellarmine University. Parts of this manuscript were also presented at the Southern Economic Association and the Association of Private Enterprise Education Annual Conferences as well as a special meeting of the Mont Pelerin Society. We are grateful to the organizers and participants for their feedback, comments, and suggestions, which undoubtedly improved the work.

We would like thank Jordan Hurwitz for research assistance and Matthew Alford and Tom Secker for correspondence related to chapter 7.

Chris would like to thank his wife, Rachel, and daughters, Charlotte and Cordelia, for their love and support. He also thanks his colleagues in the F. A. Hayek Program for Advanced Study in Philosophy, Politics, and Economics at the Mercatus Center at George Mason University for creating a supportive intellectual environment. Finally, he would like to express gratitude to the Institute for Humane Studies, where he was a Senior Fellow during the final stages of this project.

Abby would like to thank her husband Edgar and her daughter Elizabeth for their support and encouragement. She would also like to thank Jerod Hassell, whose interest and queries into the project provided a wonderful source of motivation. She is grateful to her former colleagues at the University of Tampa for their support.

The Afghanistan Papers: Decades of Deceit

In December 2019, *The Washington Post* released an in-depth report titled "At War With the Truth."[1] The report based its findings on a trove of internal documents from the Special Inspector General for Afghanistan Reconstruction (SIGAR) regarding the status of the U.S. government's war in Afghanistan. Among other things, the Afghanistan Papers highlighted that high-ranking U.S. leaders held the view that the war was unwinnable and took steps to keep this information from the American public and Congress. As John Sopko, the head of SIGAR put it, the Afghanistan Papers showed that "the American people have constantly been lied to."[2]

This was consistent with prior warnings regarding deception by the U.S. government regarding the Afghanistan War. Over a decade ago, Lieutenant Colonel Daniel Davis, a veteran of the Afghanistan War, wrote the following:

Senior ranking US military leaders have so distorted the truth when communicating with the US Congress and American people in regards to conditions on the ground in Afghanistan that the truth has become unrecognizable. This deception has damaged America's credibility among both our allies and enemies, severely limiting our ability to reach a political solution to the war in Afghanistan. It has likely cost American taxpayers hundreds of billions of dollars Congress might not otherwise have appropriated had it known the truth, and our senior leaders' behavior has almost certainly extended the duration of this war. The single greatest penalty our Nation has suffered, however, has been that we have lost the blood, limbs and lives of tens of thousands of American Service Members with little to no gain to our country as a consequence of this deception.[3]

What Davis and the Afghanistan Papers highlight is the systematic use of propaganda by the U.S. government. Propaganda involves the dissemination of biased or false information to promote a political cause championed by the propagandist. Its purpose is to manipulate the beliefs of the recipients to align with the aims of the propagandist even if those goals are at odds with the interests of the target audience.

The purpose of this book is to explain how propaganda operates in democratic politics and why it matters for citizens. Our focus is on government-produced propaganda targeting the domestic populace within the United States in the post-9/11 period. We show that the U.S. government has purposefully provided partial and misleading information about the actual threats to the security of U.S. persons while contributing to a broader culture of militarism, which holds that a powerful military apparatus is necessary to protect and promote freedom and order at home and abroad.[4]

Government propaganda is a direct threat to freedom and liberty because it empowers a small political elite who wields awesome discretionary powers to shape policies while keeping citizens in the dark about the underlying realities and the array of alternative options available. In doing so, propaganda aims to shift the relationship between the citizenry and the state. Instead of the consent of the governed being the driving force behind the state's operations, private citizens are viewed as opposition that must be manipulated to achieve the propagandists' goals. As we will discuss, these issues are especially pertinent in matters of national security, where the government jealously guards its monopoly on privileged access to information. This monopoly on information enables those in power to present information to the public in a manner conducive to achieving their desired ends in the name of the "public interest."

As the Afghanistan Papers remind us, the dissemination of war-related propaganda by the U.S. government is alive and well. In what follows we explore how the government's propaganda machine operates and the threat it poses to a free society.

MANUFACTURING MILITARISM

CHAPTER I

Propaganda

Its Meaning, Operation, and Limits

AMERICAN WAR PROPAGANDA: A HISTORY

Since America's earliest days, war and propaganda have been intimately connected. Before the Revolutionary War, propaganda was used to shape public opinion in order to unite the colonists against the British. Among the most famous propaganda pieces from this time period is Paul Revere's 1770 engraving titled "The Bloody Massacre Perpetrated in King Street," which depicted events from the Boston Massacre and was intended to galvanize support against the British. The engraving shows British Captain Thomas Preston standing behind an orderly line of seven Red Coats with his sword raised to indicate an order to fire at the colonists standing before them. The colonists are depicted with looks of fear and sadness on their faces, some lying on the ground in pools of blood. The British soldiers, in contrast, are depicted as enjoying inflicting harm on the colonists.

The image was meant to present the British as the violent aggressors against the passive colonists. Moreover, the massacre was presented as a coordinated and planned effort carried out by the British soldiers at the superior officer's order. In reality, the Boston Massacre began as a disorderly street fight between American colonists and a single British soldier who called for reinforcements. The situation escalated into bloodshed after colonists antagonized and assaulted the soldiers. A soldier fired into the crowd, and several other soldiers followed suit, killing five colonists and wounding several others. However, there is no formal evidence that Captain Preston ever ordered his men to fire, and all but two of the men involved were acquitted of any wrongdoing. While Revere's engraving misrepresented the realities of the events surrounding the Boston Massacre, it had the desired effect of rousing anti-British sentiments among the colonists.

I

Propaganda appeared throughout the revolutionary period and was used during the American Civil War. While the specific content varied, the defining feature of propaganda during this period was that it was highly decentralized. There was no coordinated government effort to develop and disseminate propaganda. Instead, propaganda was produced by a variety of government and private organizations in an uncoordinated and ad hoc manner.[1] This changed during the world wars, when propaganda became an institutionalized aspect of the U.S. government's arsenal.

Soon after entering World War I, President Woodrow Wilson signed Executive Order 2594 on April 13, 1917, which established the Committee on Public Information (CPI), also known as the Creel committee. The purpose of the CPI was to systematically influence domestic public opinion in support of the U.S. government's participation in World War I.[2] The reach of the CPI spanned numerous media outlets, including newspapers, movies, radio, posters, and short four-minute public talks by trained volunteer orators—the "Four Minute Men." Its purpose was to frame conscription, economic rationing, war bonds, victory gardens, and other wartime measures in a positive light with the aim of convincing citizens that the various aspects of the government's war effort, and the sacrifice they entailed, were crucial to the maintenance and extension of America's core principles.[3]

The CPI was officially disbanded by executive order in August 1919. A growing backlash against its operations led many in government to make public claims about abandoning the use of war propaganda in the future. This criticism was short lived, however, with the onset of World War II. Over the course of the war, a multipronged apparatus disseminated government-approved information despite an official policy indicating that the government was not to issue propaganda.

On June 13, 1942, President Franklin D. Roosevelt signed Executive Order 9182, which authorized the Office of War Information (OWI).[4] The purpose of the OWI was to consolidate and distill information related to the war effort. Specifically, the executive order declared that the OWI should "formulate and carry out, through the use of press, radio, motion picture, and other facilities, information programs designed to facilitate the development of an informed and intelligent understanding, at home and abroad, of the status and progress of the war effort and of the war policies, activities, and aims of the Government."[5] The OWI, which was split into domestic and international branches, had near monopoly control over the dissemination of war-related information. Through its various operations, the OWI sought not just to provide information to American citizens but to do so in a manner that would encourage public support for the government's war activities.

A separate but related part of the wartime propaganda apparatus was the Writer's War Board (WWB), established in December 1941 at the urging of the U.S. Treasury Department. The board was privately organized and operated, meaning it did not have a formal government budget (although the government subsidized the writer's offices and staff). This private civilian status, however, should not be mistaken for independence from government influence. The WWB operated through the OWI and served as a "liaison between American writers and U.S. government agencies seeking written work that will directly or indirectly help win the war."[6] Indeed, the WWB "received governmental funding and functioned, according to one member, as 'an arm of the government.'"[7] In total, the WWB leveraged the skills of around five thousand writers who sought to influence public opinion through a wide range of media outlets, including newspapers, magazines, books, and radio.[8]

The operations of the OWI and WWB were complemented by other government-sponsored propaganda. For example, the U.S. government commissioned Academy Award–winning filmmaker Frank Capra to direct a series of documentaries, under the general title *Why We Fight*, to justify America's involvement in the war to soldiers and the general public. Following the end of World War II, the operations of the OWI and WWB ceased. But that was not the end of U.S. government propaganda.

In 1948 Congress passed the U.S. Information and Educational Exchange Act (Public Law 80-402), also known as the Smith-Mundt Act, which institutionalized the U.S. government's foreign propaganda efforts, including Voice of America, the largest U.S. international multimedia broadcasting institution. Those concerned with the negative consequences of government propaganda were partially placated by the insertion of a stipulation in the bill that information produced for foreign broadcast was not to be disseminated domestically.

During the Cold War and the Vietnam War the U.S. government operated, and publicly acknowledged, the United States Information Agency (USIA), which was established in 1953 by order of President Eisenhower. The mission of the USIA was "to understand, inform and influence foreign publics in promotion of the national interest, and to broaden the dialogue between Americans and U.S. institutions, and their counterparts abroad."[9] The activities of the USIA were split into four categories. The first dealt with the dissemination of information including taking over the operations of the Voice of America program, that had been approved as part of the aforementioned Smith-Mundt Act. The second dealt with exhibits and cultural products, and the third focused on the publication of print media. The final division focused on motion pictures. The activities of the USIA were subject to the ban on domestic dissemination established under the Smith-Mundt Act. This, however, is not meant to suggest that there was no domestic government propaganda.

Starting in the early 1950s, the U.S. government, under the auspices of the Central Intelligence Agency (CIA), began Operation Mockingbird. This large-scale international initiative recruited leading journalists and reporters to serve as spies and to actively disseminate propaganda in support of the American government's anticommunist efforts at home and abroad.[10]

The reach of Operation Mockingbird was extensive, with connections in at least twenty-five American news outlets and wire agencies—including the *New York Times*, the *Washington Post*, and *Time* magazine—and control over fifty foreign newspapers.[11] The program also sought to influence the content of commercial film productions. Operation Mockingbird was a covert operation, meaning that it was not subject to congressional oversight. Similarly, members of the public were unaware of its operations until a series of reports starting in the late 1960s revealed the government's secretive propaganda efforts to manipulate public opinion.

Also during this time, the Department of Defense (DOD) engaged in a wide range of domestic propaganda activities under the guise of "public relations," including such things as locating news crews in Southeast

Asia to produce newsreels for distribution in the United States, a domestic speakers bureau to facilitate speeches by military and civilian officers in support of the war effort, a publications division to assist with the creation and dissemination of pro-military materials written by members of the armed forces, and a "Projects Division" responsible for providing and coordinating military-related personnel for public events, such as fairs and parades.[12] The DOD also ran programs for American civilians to tour and actively participate in interactive demonstrations at its facilities with the aim of connecting with the general public to foster support. The agency also held "freedom forums" throughout the country to "educate" the public regarding threats and U.S. war efforts to address them.[13]

The propaganda activities of the DOD were unchecked by Congress and not subject to the stipulations of the Smith-Mundt Act banning the domestic dissemination of propaganda. As Senator William Fulbright wrote,

It is interesting to compare [the] American government's only official propaganda organization, the U.S. Information Agency with the Defense Department's apparatus. USIA is so circumscribed by Congress that it cannot, with the rarest of exceptions, distribute its materials within this country. . . . But the Department of Defense, with more than twice as many people engaged in public relations as USIA has in all its posts abroad, operates to distribute its propaganda within this country and without control other than the executive, and floods the domestic scene with its special, narrow view of the military establishment and its role in the world.[14]

It was this expansive, institutionalized propaganda apparatus that so concerned Fulbright. His concerns remain relevant, as what he called the "Pentagon propaganda machine" is alive and flourishing.

A recent report by American Transparency found that over the seven-year period from 2007 to 2014, the U.S. government spent over $4.3 billion on public relations.[15] Further, the report indicates that, based on the number of employees, the U.S. government is the second largest PR firm on the globe. Of the ten federal agencies who spend the most on external PR services, the Army ranked second, spending $255 million, and the Department of the Navy ranked seventh, spending some $80 million. The Department of Veterans Affairs, Department of the Air Force, U.S.

Coast Guard, and the Missile Defense Agency also ranked in the top fifty contracting agencies.[16]

While the specific details regarding how this money was spent are not publicly known, what is clear is that the U.S. government continues to spend a significant amount of taxpayer dollars promoting itself to the American public. In addition, as we will discuss throughout this book, the U.S. government's approach satisfies the distinctive features of the "firehose of falsehood" model of propaganda. This approach consists of a "high numbers of channels and messages and a shameless willingness to disseminate partial truths or outright fictions."[17] As such, Senator Fulbright's concern that few Americans "have much cognizance of the extent of the military sell or its effects on their lives" remains as valid today as when first raised decades ago.[18]

THE MEANING, TECHNIQUES, AND FUNCTIONS OF PROPAGANDA

Propaganda Defined

The term *propaganda* can be traced back to the 1620s with the establishment of the Congregatio de Propaganda Fide (Congregation for the Propagation of Faith) by the Roman Catholic Church to train missionaries. The favorable religious usage of the term, which was not yet part of the popular vernacular, continued through the eighteenth century and into the nineteenth century.[19] This changed with World War I, where the usage of the term *propaganda* became widespread and took on an unfavorable connotation. As journalist Will Irwin notes, "propaganda, before the World War [World War I], meant simply the means which the adherent of a political or religious faith employed to convince the unconverted. Two years later, the word had come into the vocabulary of peasants and ditchdiggers and had begun to acquire its miasmic aura. In loose, popular usage it meant the next thing to a damned lie."[20] Today, this negative connotation remains.

According to the Lexico, propaganda refers to "information, especially of a biased or misleading nature, used to promote a political cause or point of view."[21] Philosopher Randal Marlin defines propaganda as "the organized attempt through communication to affect belief or action or inculcate attitudes in a large audience in ways that circumvent or suppress an individual's adequately informed, rational, reflective judgement."[22] Similarly, communications scholars Garth Jowett and Victoria O'Donnell emphasize that "propaganda is the deliberate, systematic attempt to shape perceptions, manipulate cognitions, and direct behaviors to achieve a response that furthers the desired intent of the propagandist."[23]

As these definitions suggest, the purpose of propaganda is to shape the views, beliefs, and actions of the target audience so that they align with the goals of the propagandist even if they are at odds with the interests of the recipients.[24] As philosopher Jason Stanley argues, "propaganda is characteristically part of the mechanism by which people become deceived about how best to realize their goals, and hence deceived from seeing what is in their own best interests."[25] Propaganda is characterized by its lack of commitment to objective truth and accuracy. "Propaganda's preoccupation," write communication scholars Richard Nelson and Foad Izadi, "is with efficiency and not truthfulness."[26] This means that the propagandist may employ half-truths and outright lies as necessary to achieve their ends in the most efficient way possible. While there is a distinction between outright lying, framing information provided in a knowingly biased manner, and providing selective information, each of these actions falls under the broader category of deception. As international relations scholar John Mearsheimer notes, "lying, spinning and withholding information are all forms of deception, and all three can be contrasted with truth telling."[27] It is within this context that propaganda is best understood.

So, while propaganda has numerous definitions,[28] for our purposes, the term encapsulates three key characteristics. First, propaganda is purposefully biased or false. Its purpose is to deter people from having access to truthful information. Second, propaganda is used to promote a political cause. Third, propaganda is bad from the perspective of those targeted by the propagandist's message because it limits their ability to make an informed judgment.

We are fully aware that the use of propaganda extends well beyond matters pertaining to foreign policy, national security, and the military.[29] Nonetheless, we limit our focus to U.S. government-produced propaganda related to national security and foreign affairs with a particular focus on the post-9/11 period. We do so for three reasons.

First, those in government are in a privileged position of power. As legal scholar Helen Norton indicates, "the [United States] government is unique among speakers because of its coercive power, its substantial resources, its privileged access to national security and intelligence information, and its wide variety of expressive roles as commander-in-chief, policymaker, educator, employer, property owner, and more."[30] These distinct features create opportunities for those in power to deceive and manipulate the citizenry.

Second, as discussed, propaganda has been intertwined with the U.S. national security state since its earliest days. Historian Susan Brewer notes, "to rally Americans around the flag, officials have manipulated facts, exaggeration, and misinformation" with the aim of persuading people to their position.[31] Similarly, in his review of government propaganda, Senator William Fulbright noted that "there have been too many instances of lack of candor and of outright misleading statements. . . . Too often we have been misled by the very apparatus that is supposed to keep us factually informed or, in the very strictest sense, honestly guided."[32] Similar tactics continue to be used by the U.S. government, as we discuss in subsequent chapters.

Third, propaganda has played a central role in the U.S. government's "war on terror." We therefore take the opportunity to catalog this propaganda and to use it to illuminate the operation of propaganda in democratic political institutions. This exercise offers insight into both key aspects of the ongoing war on terror as well as future efforts by the U.S. government in matters of national security and foreign affairs. The observable costs of the war on terror are significant. According to the Costs of War Project at Brown University, the U.S. government has, through fiscal year 2020, appropriated $5.4 trillion and is obligated to spend at least another $1 trillion on post-9/11 war efforts.[33]

Our analysis of propaganda in the post-9/11 period explains how the U.S. government took active steps to convince the American public of the need for this massive spending despite a highly questionable return in terms of increased safety and security.[34] In doing so, we make clear how the government's use of propaganda threatens the efficacy of liberal democratic institutions as a check on political opportunism—actions by those in positions of political power to pursue their own goals at the expense of citizens whose interests they purport to represent.

Propaganda Techniques

There are four common devices employed in the production of government propaganda.[35] These techniques aim to appeal to certain beliefs, conditions, attitudes, and emotions in order to persuade the target audience to support and adopt the propagandist's point of view and desired course of action. In doing so, they attempt to foster unquestioning acceptance by the target audience of the message being communicated by the propagandist.

Appeal to Authority

Propaganda typically includes markings of government authority. This technique is intended to bring credibility to the message being communicated while reinforcing the importance of government as *the* solution to the threat. For example, government propaganda typically includes images of official seals, names of agencies and political officials, and the nation's flag as signals of expert authority.

Appeal to Patriotism

Propaganda attempts to foster widespread and vigorous support for the government that, in turn, represents "the country." This technique links support for a cause or activity to the "common good" of "the country." Support is associated with advancing the "national interest" while, either directly or indirectly, the absence of support indicates a lack of support for the common good. This device seeks to foster public support for the nation's armed forces and attempts to create a link to broader support for the government, nation, and war effort. One example of this technique is the Four Minute Men, a group of volunteers authorized by the president who during World War I would speak at public venues to encourage support for the war, including promoting the purchase of "Liberty Bonds" as a way for citizens to demonstrate their patriotism for the government's war effort. More recently, in 2015, it was revealed that the Pentagon had spent close to $7 million to pay for public patriotic displays during professional sports events to foster national pride among the American populace and to aid in recruitment efforts.

Appeal to "Us versus Them"

This device entails identifying clear, black-and-white distinctions between "in groups"—the nation and its allies—and "out groups"—enemies and their allies.[36] It presents the target audience with a simple and clear choice between two conflicting sides with no recognition of nuance or other intricacies. As President George W. Bush bluntly stated in the wake of the 9/11 attacks, "every nation, in every region, now has a decision to make. Either you are with us, or you are with the terrorists."[37] He made similar statements elsewhere, saying, "Every nation . . . across the world now faces a choice. Nations that choose to support terror are complicit in a war against civilization. . . . Nations that choose to fight terror are defending their own safety and the safety of free people everywhere."[38]

This technique also reinforces notions of patriotism, since the in group is "the nation" and the out group refers to "others" who threaten the lives and well-being of insiders. During the two world wars, for instance, government-produced propaganda posters depicting evil "Huns" as a direct threat to Americans were ubiquitous and had the purpose of arousing anti-German sentiment while reinforcing American patriotism in support of the war effort.

Appeal to Simple Slogans and Images

Propaganda typically contains simple slogans and images intended to be memorable and to appeal to the emotion of the target audience. In May 2003, the Bush administration staged a dramatic television event involving the president arriving on the USS *Abraham Lincoln* aircraft carrier via fighter jet. This was followed by a public declaration of the end of major combat operations by the president standing under a massive "Mission Accomplished" banner and to the applause of the sailors on the ship.

In simplifying complex foreign affairs, this device reinforces themes of patriotism and "us versus them." Further, because slogans and images are overly simple relative to the complexities they represent, propaganda avoids meaningful nuance. The simple "Mission Accomplished" motif, for instance, left no room for the many challenges that lay ahead in Iraq since, by definition, the government's goals had been achieved.

In general, propaganda seeks to present information as if it is simple, objective, clear cut, and static. As journalism scholar Jay Black notes, "while creative communication accepts pluralism and displays expectations that its receivers should conduct further investigations of its observations, allegations, and conclusions, propaganda does not appear to do so." In doing so, propaganda attempts to limit contestability over information and ideas.

The Functions of Propaganda

Producers of propaganda employ the aforementioned techniques in varying combinations and ways to achieve three main purposes. First, propaganda is a means of transmitting and framing information from the government to citizens. "Wartime presidents and propagandists understand that at any given moment a range of competing frames or opinions about war are in fact possible."[39] Propaganda can attempt to persuade the recipient both within a given frame of acceptable activities and over the frame itself by shifting the range of what is considered appropriate activities by the recipient. As political scientist William Jacoby notes, "the ability to frame issues—that is, define the way that policy controversies will be presented to the public—is undoubtedly one of the most important 'tools' that political elites have at their disposal."[40] This is certainly the case during war, where propaganda has historically played an important role in the U.S. government's military efforts.[41]

Second, propaganda serves as a coordination device. In this role, propaganda generates common knowledge to coordinate citizens around the government's objectives and goals. The key characteristic of common knowledge is that it is public—those who are exposed to information know that others are exposed to the same knowledge.[42] This allows for the creation of a shared set of expectations because each person can be confident that others know the same information. Propaganda is a tool for government to generate common knowledge among the populace around its national security activities.

Democratic governments need the support of a sufficient portion of the populace in order to execute their foreign policy. This not only requires informing citizens of policies but also creating shared public expectations around what is necessary for the government to do in order to succeed. In the context of war, success often requires significant sacrifice on the part of citizens. One way of incentivizing citizens to incur these costs is to create expectations that their fellow citizens are also aware of and are committed to making the sacrifices necessary for success. If people believe that their neighbors are likely to behave in a certain manner for the "good of the country," they are more likely to adopt similar behaviors to signal their patriotism. As political scientist Bruce Porter notes, "the exigencies of military conflict promote *internal rallying*: state and society unite in the common effort; economic and political cooperation increase; factionalism and partisanship are diminished; consonance reigns."[43] By creating common knowledge, propaganda serves the crucial function of facilitating this unification among the populace and, in the process, reducing opposition to the government's military activities.

The final purpose of propaganda is to instill or reinforce collective fear in the domestic citizenry. Public fear involves "people's felt apprehension of some harm to their collective well-being—the fear of terrorism, panic over crime, anxiety about moral decay—or the intimidation wielded over men and women by governments or groups."[44] Citizens' fear of some external threat and subsequent demands for government protection create space for state actors to expand the scale and scope of their power over the lives of citizens.[45] Indeed, economist Robert Higgs argues that the sustainability and growth of government require citizens to fear threats that require protection from the government. The result, he argues, is that governments "exploit it [fear], and they cultivate it. . . . They depend on fear to secure popular submission, compliance with official dictates, affirmative cooperation with the state's enterprises and adventures."[46]

Of course, fear might be justified in cases of a legitimate threat. However, fear can also be exaggerated and manipulated by those in government who benefit from the increased dependency of the citizenry on the state. In their study of the sociology of knowledge, Peter Berger and Thomas Luckmann note that those in positions of power may seek to protect their monopoly privileges through "intimidation, rational and irrational propaganda (appealing to the outsiders' interests and to their emotions), mystification, and, generally, the manipulation of prestige symbols."[47] This is especially relevant to the national security functions of the state, since a small group of elites possesses monopoly control over information and the tools of social control and violence.

General Douglas MacArthur recognized this possibility when he noted that "our government has kept us in a perpetual state of fear, kept us in a continuous stampede of patriotic fervor—with the cry of grave national emergency. Always there has been some terrible evil—to gobble us up if we would not blindly rally behind it by furnishing the exuberant funds demanded. Yet in retrospect, those disasters seem never to have happened, seem never to have been quite real."[48] More generally, the tendency of political actors will be to overstate threats because being biased in this direction is conducive to securing power and influence both within government and over the lives of citizens.

In building on people's fears, propaganda facilitates unification with the government by rallying citizens around a common threat that is the source of distress. It also primes the citizenry to tolerate behaviors by their government that they would not otherwise tolerate—for example, economic controls, military conscription, internment, increased domestic surveillance, and violations of a range of personal liberties—in the name of "national security." Propaganda does so by framing the costs of government actions as part of the broader sacrifice necessary for the effort being undertaken, an effort that is claimed to be necessary to protect individuals and prevent the erosion of social order.

Together, the three functions of propaganda aim to "sketch out a consistent system that is simple to grasp, one that both constructs and simultaneously provides an explanation for grievances against various out-groups."[49] In creating common knowledge around a shared, pro-state agenda, propaganda aims to nudge recipients toward supporting and accepting their government's national security policies, including expansions in the influence and power of the state over the citizenry. This is especially likely to be the case during instances where citizens perceive a crisis situation that demands a government solution.[50]

The Limits of Propaganda's Influence

Our argument is *not* that governments can deploy propaganda to manipulate and control citizens to do whatever those in power desire.[51] While political officials produce propaganda because they believe that it will persuade citizens, this belief, by itself, does not guarantee success. As Brian Anse Patrick, a communications scholar, and A. Trevor Thrall, a political scientist, emphasize, "propaganda must align with common beliefs for it to be effective; the propagandist becomes incredible when he swims upstream of popular culture norms and agendas; and this is why modern propaganda relies so heavily on polls and focus groups for guidance."[52] In line with this insight, our theory is recipient driven. Propagandists must act to either persuade recipients within the acceptable range of actions or persuade them to shift their frame of what they deem acceptable. In either case, the recipient's frame serves as a constraint on the influence of propaganda.[53]

Our position is that governments ultimately derive their power from the consent of the populace.[54] Citizens are not the passive pawns of government unless they choose to be. Instead, people possess significant agency, including the power to ignore or reject the messages being propagated. This power grants people the ability to curtail efforts by government agents to expand their domestic influence and power through the dissemination of propaganda. From this perspective, government propaganda is best understood as one of many influences on how people perceive both the specifics activities of their government and the appropriate overarching role of the state both in the broader world and in their own individual lives.[55] Within a given frame, or by convincing people to shift their frame, the propagandist can attempt to manufacture desired outcomes through the presentation of information in a certain manner. The magnitude and extent of this influence, however, ultimately rests with the members of the populace as recipients of government propaganda.

WHY PROPAGANDA MATTERS

Propaganda is important because it influences the behavior of the populace and the political elite that, in turn, affects a range of outcomes related to human well-being. This is especially important in matters of war because of the high costs that include devastating consequences for ordinary civilians. A study of the role of propaganda disseminated by radio in the Rwandan genocide against the Tutsi ethnic minority found that "broadcasts had a significant effect on participation in killings by both militia groups and ordinary civilians."[56] These effects were direct in terms of their influence on people's behaviors but also indirect in terms of those violent behaviors spilling over to other villages who observed the actions of their neighbors.

Discussing the role of deception by the American government in matters of war, journalist Jon Basil Utley recently noted that "Official Washington and those associated with it have misrepresented the facts numerous times in the service of military actions that might not otherwise have taken place. In the Middle East, these interventions have killed hundreds of thousands of innocent Arab civilians, brought chaos to Iraq and Libya, and led to the expulsion of a million Christians from communities where they have lived since biblical times."[57] As this indicates, effective propaganda can influence citizens to support misguided state violence with significant global costs for human welfare.

Understanding the nuances of propaganda also matters for those who value democracy and individual freedom. Government propaganda is often associated with totalitarian regimes, and while these regimes do disseminate propaganda, so, too, do democratic governments, despite their rhetorical commitment to transparency, accountability, and other liberal values. Appreciating the frequent use of propaganda by democratic governments raises crucial issues.

For one, state-produced propaganda highlights a potential flaw within democratic political institutions. As we document in the next chapter, the possibility for government propaganda emerges because of pathologies inherent in democratic politics. Appreciating the imperfections in political institutions is important for thinking about the scope and scale of powers granted to democratic governments. This is especially important in matters of national security, since significant power and secrecy is granted to government in the name of protecting citizens. Democratic pathologies, however, create the possibility that this power and secrecy will be used in a manner that does not comport with their intended purpose.

Further, while the creation and dissemination of state-produced propaganda are the result of democratic pathologies, the use of propaganda can also contribute to the intensification of these dysfunctions. Propaganda contributes to recipients receiving biased or overtly incorrect information that amplifies existing asymmetries between citizens and those in government who control information flows.

The cumulative result is that government-produced propaganda threatens the liberal aspects of democratic systems. As Jason Stanley argues, "the most basic problem for democracy raided by propaganda is the possibility that the vocabulary of liberal democracy is used to mask an undemocratic reality."[58] He goes on to note that when this happens, "the appearance of a liberal democracy would be merely the trappings of an illiberal, undemocratic reality."[59] From this perspective, one of the main threats from propaganda is that it facilitates government activities that undermine individual liberty and collective, yet voluntary, participation and deliberation—hallmarks of a self-governing liberal democracy.[60]

The use of propaganda changes the nature of the relationship between citizens and the state. Instead of viewing citizens as the driving force behind the actions of the state, the use of propaganda is grounded in the idea that citizens stand in opposition to the goals of political rulers. Propaganda aims to neuter this opposition by manipulating the views and opinions of citizens to comport with those of the elite. The relationship between citizens and the state shifts from one where the citizenry is viewed as the primary driver of political actions to one where a small number of state actors become the central source of control.

Propaganda further undermines liberalism by normalizing deception, which can spill over into other areas of political life. As John Mearsheimer writes, "once a country's leaders conclude that its citizens do not understand important foreign policy issues and thus need to be manipulated, it is not much of a leap to apply the same sort of thinking to national issues."[61] As we will discuss in the next chapter, one of the common justifications for the use of propaganda is the need for "noble deception." This view holds that benevolent political leaders can and should deceive the citizenry for their own good. One of the main problems with this justification for deception is that it views the citizenry as incapable of determining what is in their best interest. Moreover, once one adopts this position, it can be used to justify deception to accomplish a wide range of domestic and international policies. As state deception and power bleeds into more areas of life, individual liberty and democratic norms are quickly lost.

A final concern is that propaganda associated with national security and foreign affairs fosters a domestic culture of militarism. Colonel James Donovan noted that militarism "is defined as the tendency to regard military efficiency as the supreme ideal of the state, and *it subordinates all other interests to those of the military*."[62] Militarism creates an environment in which people "rank military institutions and ways above the ways of civilian life, carrying military mentality and modes of acting and decision into the civilian sphere."[63] Militarism threatens liberty and freedom as these values become subservient to the state and its national security goals and objectives in the name of protecting those very values.[64]

Senator William Fulbright warned that the "militarism that has crept up on us [the United States] is bringing about profound changes in the character of our society and government—changes that are slowly undermining democratic procedure and values."[65] Along similar lines, historian Andrew Bacevich observes that "today as never before in their history Americans are enthralled with military power."[66] He warns that the consequence of this militarism will be that "we will rob future generations of their rightful inheritance. We will wreak havoc abroad. We will endanger our security at home. We will risk the forfeiture of all that we prize."[67]

As these writers emphasize, militarism poses a unique threat to the foundations of a free society. While government-provided security is often viewed as being crucial for the maintenance of a free society, enabling government to provide security also empowers the state to subsume freedom in the name of safety. Militarism expedites this loss of freedom as the security functions of the government come to dominate society and subsume the very liberties the state purports to protect.[68]

Propaganda facilitates a culture of militarism by exaggerating the actual risks from external threats and framing the state as being the ultimate source of order and protection. This contributes to a culture emphasizing the primacy of the national security state as being necessary for the survival of domestic economic, political, and social institutions. In this role propaganda diverts the attention of citizens away from the fundamental and perpetual contest between domestic government power and liberty by focusing on external threats and the necessity of government to protect "the people." As George Orwell warned, political language, of which propaganda is one manifestation, "is designed to make lies sound truthful and murder respectable, and to give an appearance of solidarity to pure wind."[69] In this role, propaganda seeks to condition citizens to ignore the domestic threats from state power and instead accept increases in the government's scale and scope for their own good. These sacrifices are depicted as being necessary and temporary. However, expansions in state power rarely return to earlier levels and create a host of institutional possibilities for abuses in future periods.[70] A society defined by militarism is no longer a free society.

In the chapters that follow, we consider how propaganda can provide misleading information about specific current events while also contributing to a broader culture of militarism. Given the potential for propaganda to undermine liberal political institutions and to foster militarism, studying and appreciating its nuances is of central importance for the maintenance of a free society.

OUR CONTRIBUTION

Propaganda has been studied from a variety of interdisciplinary perspectives, including communications, economics, history, journalism, psychology, political science, and sociology.[71] These studies, which are both theoretical and applied in nature, explore propaganda in a number of contexts, settings, and time periods. We contribute to this literature by applying insights from political economy to understand the role that propaganda plays in democratic societies.

Political economy applies economics to nonmarket decision making, including politics.[72] Central to this approach is an appreciation of how different rules and organizational forms influence economic, legal, political, and social outcomes by producing varying incentives for those operating within these structures.[73] Our analysis focuses on the incentives created by democratic political institutions and how they influence policy as it pertains to national security.[74]

One of the many insights of political economy scholarship is that democratic governments often fail relative to a first-best scenario where various political actors—for example, elected officials and bureaucrats—represent the interests of "the people."[75] In contrast to the romantic view of democratic politics—where benevolent politicians seek to maximize some notion of the "public interest"—scholarship in political economy highlights that political institutions, just like private institutions, are populated by goal-driven individuals who respond to incentives. Further, the incentives created by political institutions often generate an array of frictions and imperfections that create room for political opportunism.

To date, the insights of political economy have been largely neglected in studies of government propaganda.[76] Likewise, scholars specializing in political economy have not studied the role that propaganda plays in democratic politics. Our analysis fills this gap. We explain how democratic institutions create space for the dissemination of propaganda and how this contributes to an environment conducive to political opportunism by those in power. In doing so, political propagandists produce two effects. First, propaganda creates bias around specific current policies. Second, propaganda erodes the liberal features of democratic political institutions by undermining the primacy of the citizenry living within those institutions. It does so by shifting emphasis from deriving genuine consent from citizens to the political elite manipulating citizens to achieve their desired ends.

We also contribute to the scholarship on "threat inflation," which refers to the overstatement of potential dangers to the well-being of the domestic populace.[77] Our analysis advances the "domestic political explanation" for threat inflation.[78] This explanation appreciates two realities. First, a variety of political actors—elected officials, bureaucrats, and members of special-interest groups—face incentives to overstate threats to the domestic populace in order to advance their interests. Second, the frictions inherent in domestic politics combined with the secrecy of the national security state intensify these incentives. Given these realities, members of the national security state will often misrepresent facts regarding threats in order to convince the populace that the political elite must "do something" to address the supposed problem. We explain how the production and distribution of propaganda are central to the process of threat inflation and provide solutions for weakening the incentive for political actors in democratic politics to mispresent facts in order to engage in narrow opportunism.

A final contribution is to catalog and analyze instances of U.S. government propaganda following the September 11, 2001, attacks on the World Trade Center and Pentagon. These cases illustrate how present-day propaganda operates in America. They are important for both understanding the operations of the U.S. government following the post-9/11 attacks and, more broadly, for better understanding the role of government propaganda in democratic politics and its deleterious effects on freedom, especially as it relates to the spread and entrenchment of militarism in American society.

A ROADMAP

The remainder of this book proceeds as follows. Chapter 2 provides an economic model of government propaganda. We begin with an ideal scenario where the interests of citizens and political actors are aligned. In this hypothetical world, there is no room for propaganda. The purpose of this ideal model to make clear how democratic institutions operate under first-best conditions. We then draw on the insights from political economy to explain why democratic governments deviate from this ideal model. The existence of information asymmetries in democratic institutions creates openings for propaganda. These openings are especially prevalent in the national security state because information asymmetries are intensified due to the secret nature of security and foreign affairs, which includes monopoly control over information by a small group of political elites.

The subsequent chapters analyze cases of government propaganda in the post-9/11 period. Their purpose is to illuminate the many ways that war-related propaganda permeates American life. The case-study method is appropriate for our topic of study given that "direct, 'smoking gun' evidence of deception is usually lacking."[79] This necessitates the study of indirect evidence focused on the gap between underlying realities and the public presentation of information.[80] Moreover, the precise form that propaganda takes varies greatly from case to case. Given this, delving into the details of specific cases is the most effective means of un-covering the realities and effects of propaganda. In each case we contrast the underlying realities of the specific situation with the (mis)information presented by U.S. government officials to identify gaps between the two and discuss the consequences.

The first two case studies consider the role of propaganda in the U.S. government's invasion of Iraq. Chapter 3 focuses on the creation and dis-semination of propaganda in the post-9/11 period by analyzing the lead up to the invasion of Iraq by the U.S. government in March 2003. We discuss the disconnect between what was known by U.S. officials in the months preceding the invasion and the information that was presented to the American public.

Continuing with Iraq, chapter 4 describes how U.S. government agen-cies and officials misled the public regarding the war in Iraq. We trace the intensive public relations campaign launched by the Bush administration following the invasion of Iraq. This includes deliberate efforts by officials to shape the narrative surrounding the war by working to control the flow of information to news agencies, crafting talking points for new agencies reporting on the war, and providing supposedly independent "experts" to appear on television.

Chapter 5 explores the use of propaganda in American sports. We dis-cuss how the U.S. government has utilized sports to normalize militarism for both enlisted personnel and civilians, rally support for U.S. military operations, and foster military unification. We then analyze "paid pa-triotism" following the 9/11 attacks, in which a variety of professional sports franchises accepted funds from the Department of Defense to en-gage in patriotic displays to garner support for the war in Iraq as well as the broader war on terror. Finally, we discuss the misleading and false information provided to the public surrounding the death of Pat Tillman, a former professional football player and army ranger, who was killed by fratricide while on deployment.

Chapter 6 examines the creation and operation of the Transportation Security Administration (TSA). We analyze how U.S. government officials consistently inflate the overall threat of terrorism as well as the threat of terrorism in aviation. We also consider several specific terror plots in the post-9/11 period, contrasting the known facts in each case with the official portrayals of each event.

The final case study (chapter 7) analyzes domestic war propaganda in the context of film. We discuss how mass entertainment is often significantly influenced and altered by U.S. government officials to shape the attitudes and opinions of the public regarding U.S. foreign policy. We examine the relationship between Hollywood film studios and the DOD and discuss how film studios cede editorial control to these agencies in exchange for the use of agency knowledge, personnel, and equipment.

Chapter 8 concludes with the implications of our analysis. We critically consider four potential solutions to overcoming the information asymmetries that allow those in government to use propaganda. These include self-policing by those in power, whistleblowing, the media, and citizen inoculation against propaganda. We consider the strengths and weaknesses of each alternative as well as the conditions under which each is likely to be effective in checking the deleterious effects of state-produced propaganda.

CHAPTER 2

The Political Economy of
Government Propaganda

THE IDEAL PROTECTIVE STATE

To understand a world with government-produced propaganda, we first consider a hypothetical situation where it does not exist. To do so, we begin with a baseline model of an ideal protective state. In this model, the property rights of citizens are well defined, and the purpose of the government is to protect and enforce these rights from internal and external threats.[1] This includes protection from domestic and external threats to individual rights through the operation of police, courts, and the national security state, which includes the military. This ideal model is also characterized by the existence of effective mechanisms allowing citizens to directly monitor, reward, or punish politicians for their actions.[2]

This first-best scenario is representative of how many economists, and social scientists more broadly, model the activities of democratic states, especially as it pertains to matters of national security. Discussing how economists model and study government military and defense activities, J. Paul Dunne notes that "the neoclassical approach to military expenditure . . . is based on the notion of a state with a well-defined social welfare function, reflecting some form of social democratic consensus, recognizing some well-defined national interest, and threatened by some real or apparent potential enemy."[3]

In this ideal model, elected politicians engage in protective activities only when it is in the interests of citizens. In doing so, elected officials employ, monitor, and reward or punish bureaucrats who serve as value-added inputs in the productive process of protecting citizens' person and property. There is no space for waste, fraud, corruption, or abuses of power because political actors are assumed to be ideal civil servants solely focused on advancing society's welfare. Further, in this first-best situation, it is assumed that the relevant information about the activities of the protective state is available to citizens, meaning that there is *symmetric* information between political actors and the citizenry. Citizens know what political actors are doing, and political actors know that citizens have this information. In addition to having access to the necessary information to monitor political actors, the ideal model assumes that people also have access to effective mechanisms to punish politicians by removing them from office if they fail to act to advance citizen interests.

Within the model of the ideal protective state, there is no room for political opportunism. Instead, politicians act in the public interest because, in the presence of symmetric information and effective punishment mechanisms, any deviations from advancing the public welfare will result in discipline by well-informed and motivated voters. This means that within the parameters of the ideal-state model, there is no government-produced propaganda because there is no space for deception due to the manipulation or concealment of information by politicians. Political actors do not need to persuade citizens through propaganda because they are already doing those activities—and only those activities—that advance social welfare.

Unfortunately, on closer inspection, it becomes clear that real-world democratic politics does not comport with the ideal baseline model presented above. In stark contrast, actual democratic politics is characterized by significant deviations from these ideal conditions, creating space for political opportunism. This space is especially expansive in matters of foreign affairs and national security because these state activities are highly centralized and a monopoly over information is tightly maintained by those in power. This allows political actors to expand their influence and power over citizens through the design and dissemination of propaganda. Instead of citizens being the main driver in political matters, members of the state become the driving force in politics.

DEVIATING FROM THE IDEAL:
THE REALITIES OF DEMOCRATIC POLITICS

The ideal model of the protective state assumes that political representatives have strong incentives to engage in activities producing outcomes aligning with the interests of citizens. In reality, this incentive is much weaker than suggested by the first-best model.[4] To see why, consider the well-known principal-agent problem.[5] This problem arises when ownership of an asset is separated from control of the asset. The principals, or owners, hire agents to represent their interests and manage their property. In an ideal situation, where incentives are perfectly aligned, the agents would appropriately represent the interests of the principal by being good stewards over their property.

A principal-agent problem emerges, however, when there are deviations from this ideal because agents may engage in opportunistic behaviors and exploit the principals rather than faithfully serve their interests. These types of problems occur frequently in a number of contexts. Publicly traded companies, for instance, are owned by shareholders who must rely on those hired to manage the firm to serve their interests. A lawyer hired by the firm to represent its interests (the "agent") may encourage additional legal procedures to increase their income even though it may not be in the best interest of their client (the "principal"). Similar problems potentially exist in medical situations between doctors and their patients.

Principal-agent problems also exist in democratic politics in which citizens are the principals and political actors—both elected and appointed—are the agents who are supposed to represent the interests of citizens. The problem can be mitigated if citizens have the incentive to acquire information and to act on that information to reward or punish their representatives. This, of course, assumes transparency—that the relevant information is available to principals if they choose to obtain it—and that effective punishment and reward mechanisms exist to appropriately incentivize agents. In practice, however, these conditions often fail to hold.

The reasons are provided by public choice economics—principal-agent interactions under democracy are characterized by the limited effectiveness of voting, rationally ignorant voters, vote-seeking politicians, special-interest groups, and a deep state that is beyond electoral accountability. These features of democratic politics weaken, if not entirely thwart, the potentially incentive-aligning features of democracy. A deeper consideration of the various groups of actors in democratic politics and the incentives they face will make the frictions, and the resulting space for propaganda, clear.

The Limits of the Voting Booth

In democratic politics, voting is seen as a central check on elected officials. The logic is simple. If those in office do not perform as voters expect, they can punish the official by electing someone else at the next election. There are two key factors that weaken the effectiveness of the voting booth as a disciplinary device and increase the payoff to state-produced propaganda.[6]

The first deals with the information possessed by voters. In order to solve the principal-agent problem in democratic politics, citizens must have the incentive to acquire the information necessary to monitor, reward, and punish elected officials. Unfortunately, this incentive is often weak. Since the chances of any one vote influencing the outcome of a federal election in a population the size of the United States are minuscule, citizens tend to remain rationally ignorant, or uninformed, of many of the behaviors of elected politicians.[7] This is because individual voters lack the incentive to gather the appropriate information to make highly informed choices about their representatives.[8]

This does not mean that voters are entirely ignorant of all aspects of politics, but rather that their incentive to obtain detailed information is often weak. American voters probably know that their government is engaged in a global "war on terror," but they are unlikely to know the specific details regarding the nuances of that war. Fully aware that voters are not attuned to the subtleties and details of foreign policy, political actors can use propaganda to influence what information is available to voters and how that information is framed. In the context of rational ignorance, the purpose of propaganda is to create systematic bias among voters in favor of the desired government policy by attempting to influence recipients to over- or underestimate certain details and likelihoods to advance the goals of the propagandists.[9]

The second factor is the substantial time between elections for federal offices (president, vice president, U.S. Congress). Each U.S. voter, over each six-year period, has a maximum of nine votes over four national elections.[10] The time between regular elections has two consequences.

First, even if voters identify clear links between specific elected officials and abuses of power, they might have to wait years to exert recourse for that behavior. Further complicating the situation is that in many cases it is difficult if not impossible for voters to identify a clear connection between a specific elected official and opportunistic behaviors given the internal complexities of the American government. Are failures in foreign policy due to the president, to members of Congress (and, if so, which ones), to some confounding factor outside of their control, or to some combination?

Second, assuming that voters are able to anticipate potential abuses of power or identify actual abuses of power by the time elections do arrive, it may be difficult if not impossible to undo the undesirable outcomes created by narrow self-interest in the interim period.[11] There was no way for voters who selected George W. Bush as the forty-third president of the United States during the 2000 presidential election to anticipate the September 11 attacks and the Bush administration's response, which included the use of widespread surveillance and torture. Voting during the 2000 election cycle could not serve as feedback regarding these unanticipated future activities, and there was no way for citizens to provide feedback through direct voting until the next presidential election in 2004.[12]

Even then, the various government activities that constitute the very broad and complex war on terror could not simply be undone if voters had so desired. Changes to the national security apparatus and the social and political fabric of domestic life tend to be sticky and hard to reverse.[13] The implication is that even *if* voting punishes a specific politician, it is an ineffective way to undo the harm caused by that politician's opportunism.[14] Various precedents and concrete changes to institutions will remain even if misbehaving politicians are removed from office.

Together, these factors weaken the voting booth as a disciplinary device to check undesirable behaviors by elected officials and the perverse consequences on domestic life. The result is that political leaders have space to pursue their narrow self-interest, including the use of propaganda to achieve their goals. Propaganda influences what voters know and how they perceive that information when making voting decisions. Moreover, given the substantial time between elections, voters are limited in their ability to punish or reverse the course set by those currently wielding political power.

SPECIAL INTERESTS

A special-interest group refers to a collection of voters who join together in the pursuit of a common cause. In contrast to individual voters, who often have an incentive to remain uninformed about the nuances of national security, special-interest groups have strong incentives to invest in collecting information regarding policies and the behavior of elected officials that affect their members. By banding together around a common cause, special interests are able to leverage their collective political power by exchanging their support—campaign contributions, endorsement, and block of votes—for policies and political favors that benefit their members.[15]

Special-interest groups pose a dilemma for the ideal model of democratic politics because they have the potential to influence policy to concentrate benefits on their members while dispersing costs across a large number of individual voters. This flies in the face of the conventional view that democratic politics is "for the people," which is meant to suggest that democratic outcomes advance some notion of the "national interest." In stark contrast, the logic of special-interest groups suggests that policies often reflect the interests of a small group of voters at the expense of the broader populace. The point is not that special interests have unilateral power to shape all policies as desired but rather that in democratic politics there are numerous margins where interest groups can influence policies in a way that narrowly directs benefits to group members while dispersing costs on the broader populace.

Examples of special interests abound in the national security state. Perhaps the most well known is the "military-industrial-congressional complex" (MICC), which refers to the interlinkages between the government's military apparatus, Congress, and private industry.[16] These connections create room for members of the private sector to influence and shape the government's security and military policies, which are supposed to align with and advance the interests of the populace.

One specific manifestation of the logic of special interests is what political scientist John Mueller refers to as the "terrorism industry," which includes members of the government, private industry, and the media involved in shaping the U.S. government's terrorism policy.[17] In order to secure resources, the members of the terrorism industry have the incentive to attempt to shape public opinion and government policy to inflate national security threats relative to their actual potential for harm. Where effective, this strategy results in a wedge between the policies adopted and the realities regarding actual threats.

In general, the existence of special interests creates room for political opportunism because political actors can cater to interest groups at the expense of the broader citizenry, which lacks the incentive to be informed of specific policies and the activities of special interests. As political scientist Murray Edelman notes, "not only does systematic research suggest that the most cherished forms of popular participation in government are largely symbolic, but also that many public programs universally taught and believed to benefit a mass public in fact benefit relatively small groups."[18] Propaganda is a crucial input into this process because it frames policies as serving "the nation" while, in reality, they benefit only a small segment of society with the costs borne by the broader citizenry, all under the guise of reflecting the "will of the people." In many cases, special-interest groups are active participants in influencing the content and distribution of propaganda to establish and entrench their position.

Vote-Seeking Politicians

In order to succeed in democratic politics, elected politicians must secure the votes necessary to win (re)election. Responding to the incentives inherent in democratic politics, elected officials will adopt policies that reflect some combination of the preferences of the median voter—the voter in the middle of the ideological distribution, which is critical in majority, winner takes all elections—and well-informed special-interest groups. The costs of these policies will be spread among the masses of taxpaying citizens.

Robert Gates, the former secretary of defense who served under both President George W. Bush and President Barack Obama, succinctly captures the dynamics of these incentives when summarizing his firsthand experience with Congress. He writes,

I was more or less continuously outraged by the parochial self-interest of all but a very few members of Congress. Any defense facility or contract in their district or state, no matter how superfluous or wasteful, was sacrosanct. I was constantly amazed and infuriated at the hypocrisy of those who most stridently attacked the Defense Department as inefficient and wasteful but fought tooth and nail to prevent any reduction in defense activities in their home state or district.[19]

As Gates's experience suggests, elected representatives respond to incentives, which in the national security sector include ensuring their narrow pool of constituents, as well as the special-interest groups who influence their re-election, are rewarded, even if those rewards come at the expense of "the nation's" well-being. As Gates highlights, each representative is looking out for the interests of those in their district or state even if those interests are at odds with the welfare of citizens residing in other areas of the country.

In general, compared with the ideal model of the protective state, democratic politics does not generate policies that maximize some notion of the "national interest." Instead, policies benefit some groups of voters at the expense of others. This reality is masked by government-produced propaganda that presents the state's national security activities in the opposite light. From the perspective of this propaganda, the state's national security activities put domestic political issues aside for the greater good of the whole in the name of patriotism and defending the rights of Americans. A careful review of the evidence, however, reveals that in practice, the experience described by Robert Gates, and not the hypothetical situation described by the ideal model of democratic politics, is reflective of reality, hence the importance of government propaganda to convince the masses otherwise.

Bureaucracy

Beyond voters and elected politicians, bureaucrats, or nonelected political actors, also play a crucial role in democratic politics. In the ideal model of politics, bureaucrats are disciplined by elected officials who, in turn, represent their constituents. In this model, there is a tight link between principals and agents throughout government operating as follows. Voters select elected officials as their agents and monitor and punish them accordingly through the voting booth. Elected officials, in turn, select bureaucrats to provide goods and services to voters and reward and punish them through the budgetary process and the passing and enforcement of laws that delineate agency powers. We have already discussed why the link between voters and elected officials is not as tight as represented in the ideal model of democratic politics. Similarly, there is reason to believe that the link between bureaucrats and elected officials contains significant slack, allowing for opportunism.

In order to understand the realities of bureaucracy, it is important to appreciate that a central feature of government agencies is that they, in contrast to private firms, do not sell their output on a competitive market to earn revenue. This means that bureaus cannot rely on the profit and loss mechanism to gauge effectiveness. Absent profit and loss as a gauge of performance, other metrics must be used as indicators of success. One alternative metric is the size of a bureau's discretionary budget, which refers to the budget beyond that necessary to satisfy the demands of budgetary gatekeepers (i.e., legislators).[20] A larger discretionary budget allows bureaus to exert influence and power by expanding the portfolio of activities undertaken to shape policy.[21] Absent constraints that limit how those in bureaus behave, there is a strong incentive to expand even if this growth does not provide voters with any added welfare.

In the ideal model of democratic politics, Congress serves as a constraint on the incentive for bureaus to engage in wasteful expansion. In this role, members of Congress monitor and discipline bureaus using some combination of budget allocations, administrative law, the political appointment process, congressional oversight, and the design of highly specific bills that limit space for discretion in implementation. There are, however, two factors that weaken the effectiveness of these checks in practice.

The first factor is information asymmetries between members of Congress and members of the agencies that they are tasked with monitoring. These asymmetries occur because the members of the bureau have context-specific knowledge of the agency's activities. Members of oversight committees must rely on this specialized knowledge when making their performance assessments. This, however, allows members of the agency being monitored to control the flow and content of the information available to members of Congress, creating space for opportunism.

To provide a concrete illustration of these dynamics, consider that a 2016 report by Craig Whitlock and Bob Woodward of the *Washington Post* revealed that the Pentagon hid an internal study that found $125 billion in potential savings through reductions in waste.[22] The reported motivation for this secrecy was that the leaders of the Pentagon were concerned that members of Congress would realize the magnitude of waste and reduce the Pentagon's budget. These types of asymmetries make it difficult for members of Congress to evaluate the activities of agencies and prevent abuses of power. As this example illustrates, bureaucrats can frame and filter the information presented to members of Congress in a manner that reduces the effectiveness of oversight.

The second factor limiting the efficacy of congressional oversight is that the members of Congress responsible for oversight are often demanders of the goods and services produced by the agency they are tasked with monitoring. Consider the U.S. Senate Committee on Armed Services, which is charged with overseeing the nation's military and defense policy. As was recently noted, "the Armed Services Committee has a tradition of uniting its members on both sides of the aisle, since many have a military background or home-state interests in defense."[23] Members of Congress tasked with oversight often have a strong interest in seeing the agencies and interests they oversee maintain their current status and further expand. This pro-bureau bias weakens the effectiveness of oversight and reinforces the bureau's incentive to grow. These dynamics exist across the agencies constituting the national security state and create significant space for political opportunism, which benefits the members of the agencies and those connected to its operations.

Precisely because bureaus possess information regarding their operations that is superior to that available to members of Congress and voters, they can reveal and frame information in a manner that serves the goals of those in the bureau and other areas of government. Effective propaganda creates a demand for government activities among voters. The issue is that given the control over information by specific government agencies, this demand can be cultivated and shaped even if those activities provide no additional value or even reduce citizen welfare.

Summing Up

The interaction between the actors discussed above reveals that democratic politics is, in practice, far from the ideal model discussed at the outset of this chapter. In contrast to the first-best view of democratic politics, the reality is that political interactions are often characterized by an intense competition to influence, secure, and wield power over others in the face of information asymmetries and perverse incentives. It is within this context that government propaganda plays a central role. Taking advantage of democratic pathologies, privileged political actors attempt to influence voters by justifying and legitimizing their actions through the strategic use of propaganda in the pursuit of their own goals.

THE SECRECY OF NATIONAL SECURITY: INFORMATION ASYMMETRIES AMPLIFIED

The information asymmetries that plague ordinary democratic politics are more severe in the realm of national security because of monopoly control of information and the prevalence of secrecy surrounding government activities in this area.[24] As John Mearsheimer recognizes, it is easy for policymakers to deceive the public in matters of national security because "they control the state's intelligence apparatus, which gives them access to important information that the public does not have and cannot get, at least in the short term."[25] Economist Roger Koppl summarizes the problematic features of this situation as follows:

The entangled deep state [Koppl's term for the national security state] produces the rule of experts. Experts must often choose for the people because the knowledge on the basis of which choices are made is secret, and the very choice being made may also be a secret involving, supposedly, "national security." . . . The phenomena intelligence experts report on are complex, uncertain, and indeterminate. And there is poor feedback between the global situation and any choices made on the basis of (possibly secret) expert opinions. The "intelligence community" has incentives that are not aligned with the general welfare or with democratic process. There is a problem of incentive alignment.[26]

This issue of incentive alignment is grounded in the principal-agent problem discussed above, which is intensified because of the opaqueness of the national security state. National security has always been associated with some degree of secrecy in order to keep critical information out of the hands of enemies. But in the United States, the secrecy associated with the government's national security activities expanded greatly during the two world wars and was institutionalized in the wake of World War II.

The culture of secrecy within the U.S. national security state is perhaps best illustrated by the overuse of the government's information classification system. The current system of classifying information was established in 1940 by the executive order (EO 8381) of President Franklin Delano Roosevelt. With the onset of World War II, its purpose was to enhance the ability of the government to protect information deemed crucial for the nation's security. The classification of information existed earlier, but before 1940 it covered a very limited amount of information related to a narrow range of military and diplomatic matters.

This changed with Roosevelt's executive order, which greatly expanded the scope of materials that could be classified.[27] Executive Order 8381 covered "all official military or naval books, pamphlets, documents, reports, maps, charts, plans, designs, models, drawings, photographs, contracts, or specifications which are now marked under the authority or at the direction of the Secretary of War or the Secretary of the Navy as 'secret,' 'confidential,' or 'restricted' and all such articles or equipment which may hereafter be so marked with the approval or at the direction of the President."[28] In addition to expanding the scope of materials that were subject to classification, EO 8381 also granted civilian employees the ability to classify information, since it stated that information could be classified with the approval of the president. A subsequent executive order (EO 10290) issued by President Harry Truman in 1951 extended the peacetime classification system to "all departments and agencies of the Executive Branch."[29] The ability of nonmilitary agencies to classify information further expanded the scope of secrecy in the government.

The increased scope of classification combined with the fear that information would fall into enemy hands incentivized government employees to default to classifying information. The tendency to overclassify information became entrenched throughout the Cold War, as the accepted view in the government was that "the excrescence of international communism and the constant presence of total war, hot or cold, has made the keeping of national secrets an absolute necessity."[30] Fear of domestic infiltration by communist sympathizers further contributed to the push for secrecy within the government.[31]

This created a problem in terms of access to information regarding the activities of the national security state. While those in government can use expanded classification powers to protect crucial information, they can also be used to limit transparency and prevent citizens, watchdog groups, and others in government from monitoring those in power. Indeed, numerous investigations have identified the tendency for government agencies to abuse the classification system to overclassify information that is not crucial for the nation's security.

In 1956 the Defense Department Committee on Classified Information, also known as the Coolidge Committee, concluded that "overclassification has reached serious proportions." Subsequent investigations of classified information over the following decades—the Wright Commission in 1957, the Moss Subcommittee in 1958, the Seitz Task Force in 1970, the Stillwell Commission in 1985, the Joint Security Commission in 1994, the Moynihan Commission in 1997, and the 9/11 Commission—made similar findings and recommendations to prevent the abuse of classification powers.[32] These recommendations were largely ignored. As Steven Aftergood, who directs the Project on Government Secrecy at the Federation of American Scientists, notes, "Over the past fifty years, generations of critics have risen to attack, bemoan, lampoon, and correct the excesses of government secrecy. Only rarely have they had a measurable and constructive impact."[33]

Institutionalized secrecy and overclassification creates significant space for political opportunism.[34] As one legal scholar commented, "the present security system [as of 1955] is susceptible to many abuses and that although such abuses are relatively infrequent, they do exist in substantial numbers."[35] Another noted that "a large amount of information concerning military affairs has been withheld by the military establishment since the end of World War II and continues to be withheld. Few in a position to know and assess the facts would deny that much of this withholding has either served no significant public purpose or the benefits derived are outbalanced by the public harm."[36]

The collapse of the Soviet Union did nothing to end the culture of secrecy, and confidentiality remains a defining feature of the U.S. national security state. This became evident in the wake of the September 11, 2001, attacks, when "the same objections to national security secrecy—relating to government accountability, transparency, and the rule of law—that were raised in the early Cold War era have been resurrected."[37] In the post-9/11 period, the secrecy enveloping the U.S. security state has manifested itself in numerous ways, including domestic and foreign surveillance, the use of drones for targeted killing, the use of torture, and the government's tendency to employ its state secrets privilege regarding its activities as part of the war on terror. The USA PATRIOT Act of 2001 and the National Defense Authorization Act of 2012 further reinforced secrecy by granting the U.S. government and military the ability to determine which sensitive information was subject to nondisclosure as part of the war on terror.[38]

The secrecy that permeates all aspects of the national security state exacerbates the information asymmetries that exist in ordinary democratic politics and results in even further deviations from the ideal model of the protective state presented at the beginning of this chapter.[39] This amplification occurs because mechanisms fostering transparency and the flow of information regarding government performance, which are already highly imperfect under normal democratic politics, are especially weak or altogether absent in the realm of national security. Secrecy, which is a defining feature of the U.S. national security state, empowers and incentivizes political actors to strategically control information flows, which limits the ability of outsiders to effectively monitor and punish politicians. A recent example will illustrate this logic.

An accurate and transparent accounting of U.S. troop deployments in various global locations is one important piece of information for voters and the legislature to monitor the members of the national security state and to make informed political decisions. Information regarding troop deployment, however, is purposefully obscured by the Department of Defense.[40] When the Department of Defense recently reported on global troop deployments, it listed the location of forty-four thousand deployed soldiers as "unknown."[41] Further, the White House has excluded troop deployment numbers for ongoing wars in Afghanistan, Iraq, and Syria when it reports to Congress on the status of the government's activities in these countries.[42] Note that this is total troop deployments and does not include any sensitive information about the allocation of those forces within specific countries or the specific military strategies being employed. By purposefully obscuring the number of troops abroad, the members of the U.S. government limit the ability of those outside the national security state to be informed and critically monitor state activities.

The broader implication of this example is that even *if* voters desire to be informed about foreign affairs and the operation of the national security state, they are severely limited because crucial information is simply not available for public consumption. There was no way for the discerning citizen to review the complete evidence regarding the possibility of weapons of mass destruction in Iraq in the run up to the U.S. government's invasion. Instead, citizens were solely reliant on the information that the Bush administration chose to reveal. Likewise, when the government disseminates information regarding potential terrorist threats, there is no way for citizens to verify the accuracy of these threats because the information underlying the claims is not publicly available.

The government's monopoly over national security information also allows it to neuter the media as a check on political misbehavior. This is done by limiting media access to information or to conflict zones through the issuance of "voluntary guidelines" to publishers, as during World War I, or by providing talking points to experts who work with media agencies. Members of the media face a strong incentive to avoid being overly critical of the national security state in order to maintain access to key policymakers. And as history demonstrates, members of the media have often been active participants in disseminating government's war-related propaganda.[43]

Summing Up

The significant information asymmetries that characterize the operations of the national security state in conjunction with the pathologies of ordinary democratic politics set the stage for the production and dissemination of government propaganda. Because those operating under the national security umbrella possess monopoly control over information, they can regulate the flow and content of public information. This monopoly control creates the opportunity for those in positions of power to disseminate biased, partial, or incomplete information through state-produced propaganda. Walter Lippmann, a reporter and political commentator, noted that in order to produce effective propaganda, "there must be some barrier between the public and the event. Access to the real environment must be limited, before anyone can create a pseudo-environment that he thinks wise or desirable."[44] He went on to argue that "military censorship is the simplest form of barrier" because of the state's centralized control of information.[45] Since the U.S. national security state is shrouded in secrecy, the information made public is difficult, if not impossible, for interested outsiders—ordinary voters or highly skilled experts outside the national security state—to verify at the time it is presented. This allows political insiders to produce and disseminate propaganda in pursuit of their ends irrespective of whether they align with those of the broader citizenry.

The messages contained in propaganda can gain traction in society if (1) they fall within the frame of behaviors deemed acceptable by recipients or succeed in shifting that frame, and (2) there are enough people who believe the credibility of the government and its message. Other, less credulous citizens may go along with the message as long as they have an incentive to coordinate with their fellow citizens to avoid negative social repercussions from deviating from what is viewed as socially acceptable beliefs and actions.[46] This is especially likely in matters of foreign affairs and war, which historically has a unifying effect in an American society grounded in patriotism.[47] Public deviations from the government narrative are, therefore, viewed as "unpatriotic" and are met with scorn. This incentivizes some who may actually disagree with their government's foreign policy to show support, at least outwardly. Under this scenario, propaganda can effectively coordinate citizens around supporting the militarism of government even if those actions are grounded in half-truths or outright deception that lead to undesirable policies.

THE MYTH OF "NOBLE DECEPTION"

One justification for propaganda is that it may be used by those in power to promote and protect the national interest in instances where ordinary people are either unable to access the truth or incapable of handling the realities of that truth to advance their interests. Journalist Irving Kristol captured the essence of this position when he noted that "there are different kinds of truths for different kinds of people. There are truths appropriate for children; truths that are appropriate for students; truths that are appropriate for educated adults; and truths that are appropriate for highly educated adults, and the notion that there should be one set of truths available to everyone is a modern democratic fallacy. It doesn't work."[48] Under this scenario, the "highly educated" political elite can strategically use propaganda in a noble and benevolent manner to nudge the public toward certain behaviors for their own good. This "noble deception" justification, while perhaps attractive in principle, is highly problematic in practice for three reasons.

First, there is no reason to believe that systematic incentives exist to consistently promote the noble outcome over time. In stark contrast to the noble deception scenario, members of the national security state have a strong incentive to protect their monopoly control over information because of the power it affords them in controlling policy and the benefits associated with that control, not out of benevolence. Empowering those in the security state to use propaganda for noble ends also empowers them to use it for ignoble ends. Given the pathologies in democratic politics discussed earlier, there is reason to expect that over time, the power to deceive, once normalized, will eventually be abused.

The noble deception scenario ultimately depends on good people consistently doing good things. If benevolent people possess control over the monopoly information of the security state, good things will happen. But what if benevolent people are not in control? As we introduce the possibility of narrow self-interest and malevolence into the equation, it becomes likely that the power necessary to nobly deceive will instead be used for opportunism. As Lord Acton famously warned, "power tends to corrupt and absolute power corrupts absolutely. Great men are almost always bad men."[49] The concern is that those who rise to positions of great political power often abuse that power in a variety of ways. Even *if* one can identify past cases where political leaders wielded power for noble causes, this does not mean that it will be the case in the future. When power is highly concentrated, the competition for control of that power tends to reward the unscrupulous challenger who is comfortable wielding power over others and doing what is necessary to secure the privilege of doing so.[50] This creates a strong incentive to use deceit in the pursuit of narrow self-interest. Once the precedent for deception is established, it is probable that it will be used for both benevolent *and* malevolent purposes.

The second reason that the noble deception justification is problematic is that it assumes that citizens are unable to process and act on truthful information. While this might be possible, there is no reason that this is necessarily the case. It might also be that citizens simply disagree with the goals of the elites. As John Mearsheimer writes, "whenever leaders cannot sell a policy to their public in a rational-legal manner, there is a good chance that the problem is with the policy, not the audience."[51] The risk is that noble deception will be used as cover for the elite to avoid the check of the citizenry under the guise that they are simply unable to grasp what is good for them. This has the effect of masking the true costs of military activities—both in terms of monetary costs and non-monetary costs, such as expansions in state power—since citizens are prevented from considering the reality of the situation.

Finally, the idea of noble deception is problematic because it neglects the nature of state propaganda and the implications for a free society. Propaganda is the result of secrecy and direct efforts to obfuscate reality. These conditions, whether intended for benevolent or malevolent purposes, create a culture in which the citizenry is viewed as an oppositional power that stands in the way of the political elite achieving their goals. Rather than seeking genuine consent, the political elite conceals and manipulates information so that potential opposition is neutered. Whether this deception is well intentioned or not does not change the fact that it reverses the relationship between citizens and state from one where the former is viewed as the driving force in politics to the reverse. Moreover, the use of propaganda normalizes purposeful deceit by the state in domestic life and incentivizes similar behavior in matters outside of foreign policy, further contributing to the expansion of state power relative to that possessed by citizens.

POST-9/11 PROPAGANDA

The subsequent chapters present cases of U.S. government propaganda in the post-9/11 period. Each case illustrates how members of the U.S. government have taken steps to convince the American public of certain threats and the government's need to act—both domestically and abroad—to protect citizens from imminent dangers. These propaganda efforts take place in the context of democratic politics discussed in this chapter. Each case illuminates some of the techniques and functions of propaganda discussed in the previous chapter. They appeal to authority and patriotism while creating "us versus them" distinctions. They do so in a simplified manner that downplays, misrepresents, or ignores realities that run counter to the message being communicated. In doing so, the cases discussed seek to coordinate citizens to provide support for and acquiescence to the activities of the government, all while fanning the flames of fear among the public in order to justify government action.

CHAPTER 3

Selling the Invasion of Iraq

On March 19, 2003, the United States and Great Britain invaded Iraq with support from several other nations, thus beginning one of the longest wars in U.S. history. The invasion, codenamed "Operation Iraqi Freedom," began with three weeks of traditional combat, including strikes against targets of "military importance" from U.S. bombers stationed in the Persian Gulf. On April 10, 2003, the Iraqi capital city of Baghdad fell to coalition forces, effectively ending the twenty-four-year rule of Iraqi president Saddam Hussein. On May 1, 2003, U.S. president George W. Bush declared that major combat operations in Iraq had concluded. Despite the defeat of Iraq's traditional military forces, however, the conflict was far from over. Almost immediately, coalition forces confronted a fierce insurgency from multiple groups, a reality that continued until the official U.S. troop withdrawal in 2011. In 2014, in the wake of the Syrian Civil War and the emergence of the Islamic State of Iraq and the Levant (ISIL), President Obama redeployed American troops to Iraq. As of late 2020, thousands of U.S. troops remain in Iraq, and dialogue between the Iraqi government and the U.S. government regarding future troop levels is ongoing.

Today many consider the Iraq War to be a mistake on the part of U.S. policymakers, while others consider the conflict a complete and utter failure. When asked, "In general, how would you say things are going for the U.S. in Iraq," nearly half of all U.S. respondents in a July 2010 Gallup poll responded with "moderately badly" or "very badly."[1] As of late 2007, some 20 percent of Americans believed that while the United States could win the war in Iraq, it would not. Another 37 percent stated the war was unwinnable.[2] That same year, 49 percent of people surveyed said the war with Iraq had made the United States *less* safe from terrorism, and another 10 percent thought the war had done nothing to improve U.S. safety.[3]

While contemporary support for past and present U.S. operations in Iraq may reflect serious skepticism on the part of the public, this was not always the case. For instance, when asked, "In general, how would you say things are going for the U.S. in Iraq" just after the beginning of the war in April 2003, 21 percent of respondents stated that things were going "very well" while another 64 percent responded "moderately well." Only two percent believed operations were going "very badly."[4] That same poll found that 58 percent of Americans believed the Iraqi invasion made the United States safer from terrorism, and some 71 percent of those surveyed favored the war in Iraq.[5]

The stark contrast in the opinions of the American public between the time of the invasion of Iraq and subsequent polls may be attributed in large part to the use of propaganda by U.S. officials to "sell" the Iraq War to the American public. Taking full advantage of the information asymmetries between government officials and the general public and the secretive nature of war and issues of national security, the Bush administration became nearly the sole source of pre-invasion media material. From September 2002 to February 2003, more than 90 percent of all stories on ABC, NBC, and CBS regarding a possible invasion came from the White House.[6] Government officials employed a variety of propaganda techniques—appealing to authority and patriotism, appealing to an "us versus them" mentality, and simple images and slogans—to frame the Iraqi conflict as a necessary and noble endeavor. These techniques worked to unify the populace around supporting the government's initial military intervention.

A BRIEF HISTORY OF U.S. INVOLVEMENT IN IRAQ

The 2003 invasion of Iraq was not the first time the U.S. government intervened in Iraqi affairs.[7] In order to appreciate the motives facing elected officials regarding the 2003 Iraq War, it is imperative to understand the historical relationship between the two countries and, particularly, past interventions in Iraq by the U.S. government.

While private corporations with interest in Iraq's oil reserves maintained a significant presence in the country since the early 1900s, U.S. government involvement in Iraq was largely limited. With the start of the

Cold War the U.S. government looked to influence the country's government, providing it with economic and military aid. Focused on preventing the spread of communism throughout the Middle East while maintaining its influence in the region, the U.S. government was integral in the creation of the Central Treaty Organization (CENTO), also known as the Middle East Treaty Organization (METO) or the Baghdad Pact. Founded in 1955, the pact was a defensive organization similar to the North Atlantic Treaty Organization (NATO) and tied together the countries of Great Britain, Iran, Iraq, Pakistan, and Turkey.[8] Optimism that Iraq would serve U.S. government interests quickly evaporated, however, when Iraqi military officers launched a successful coup d'état in 1958. Other civil conflicts followed throughout the next two decades.[9]

Despite these internal clashes, the Iraqi government took a seat on the world stage and adopted a neutral stance regarding the Cold War. Although Iraq engaged with the Soviet Union throughout this period, the U.S. government sought to maintain political ties and influence with the Iraqi government, providing some $48.2 million in military aid between 1954 and 1957.[10] A U.S.-government-backed coup in 1963 helped to put a relatively small political group—the Ba'ath Party—into power. According to *New York Times* journalist Roger Morris, the CIA provided lists of suspected communists and other political enemies to the officials of the new Iraqi government, who subsequently engaged in the systematic mass murder of their rivals.[11]

In 1967, a group of young Iraqi military officers, including a young Saddam Hussein, came to the United States for the explicit purposes of studying weapons. According to Neil Livingstone, a security and counterterrorism expert, "Saddam came here . . . and was taken to all our principal chemical weapons facilities—Aberdeen, Edgewood, Dougway and Ainnistown. And he went through the process of seeing the design of weapons—at least, seeing something about the design—the manufacture of weapons, and their actual use and deployment on a battlefield."[12] That same year, Iraq cut its diplomatic ties with the United States during the Six Days War and later nationalized many U.S. oil interests and collaborated with Soviet partners.[13] From this point through the late 1970s, the U.S. government equipped Kurdish rebel groups in efforts to weaken the Iraqi government.[14]

In 1979, Saddam Hussein seized power in Iraq. He left no room for resistance. In a videotaped meeting with hundreds of party officials shortly after gaining power, Hussein publicly announced the names of individuals who he believed had plotted against him. The accused were taken out of the room and executed.[15] Though highly publicized, these executions were only a small fraction of the people killed under Hussein's regime. The U.S. State Department estimates that Saddam had thousands of his political rivals murdered.[16]

The year 1980 marked the beginning of an eight-year war between Iraq and Iran resulting from territorial disputes between the two countries as well as Iran's Islamic Revolution. During this period, the Hussein regime was responsible for the disappearance of some five thousand Iraqi males, some as young as age ten. Thousands of Kurds (an ethnic group native to the mountainous region of western Asia known as Kurdistan) were expelled to Iran or executed.[17] Toward the end of the war in 1988, Saddam ordered what has been referred to as a genocide against Iraq's Kurdish and Shi'a Muslim populations, resulting in an estimated hundred thousand deaths.[18] According to Human Rights Watch, Iraqi forces began their extensive use of chemical weapons in 1983–1984. They estimate that twenty thousand people were killed with mustard gas and the nerve agents Sarin and Tabun.[19]

Although the U.S. government officially maintained a position of neutrality during the war, and despite consistent protests over Iraq's human rights record, the United States supported Hussein and the interests of Iraq in the conflict, fearful that Iran's staunch anti-American Islamist sentiments and the Islamic Revolution would spread throughout the Middle East. In 1981, the U.S. government announced an embargo on arms sales to Iran. The following year Iraq was removed from the list of states sponsoring terrorism. Between 1983 and 1987, the Reagan administration offered Iraq $2 billion in agricultural purchase credits. The sale of items with dual civilian and military uses—that is, ambulances, electronics, automobiles, and helicopters—was authorized.[20]

In 1984 the United States began to share intelligence with Iraq, including communication intercepts and satellite images. President Reagan issued National Security Decision Directive (NSDD) 114 in November of that year, stating that the United States should engage in "whatever measures may be necessary" to maintain Iraq's oil supply. "Because of the real and psychological impact of a curtailment in the flow of oil from the Persian Gulf on the international economic system," it reads, "we must assure our readiness to deal promptly with actions aimed at disrupting that traffic."[21] Another NSDD (139) issued in 1984 stated that U.S. officials would "prepare a plan to avert Iraqi collapse."[22] The United States helped to broker a ceasefire between the two countries in 1988 and maintained relations with Iraq despite high tensions over the Iran-Contra affair, in which members of the Reagan administration sold weapons to Iran despite the official embargo.

United States officials had hoped that the end of the Iran-Iraq War would bring peace and stability to the region along with continued good relations with Iraq. Such hopes were short lived. In 1990 Hussein's forces invaded the neighboring country of Kuwait. When he refused to withdraw his forces by the deadline imposed by the United Nations, U.S. forces, under the command of President George H. W. Bush, led a military campaign to drive the Iraqis out of Kuwait. After one hundred hours of combat, the war concluded. Hussein, however, remained in power. According to former deputy director of National Intelligence David Gompert and political scientists Hans Binnendijk and Bonny Lin, while the "United States would have preferred a regime change in Baghdad [following the Gulf War] . . . it settled for containment."[23] While President George H. W. Bush would authorize the CIA to engage in activity to overthrow Saddam, attempts during this period were ultimately unsuccessful.[24]

The U.S. government's policy toward Iraq in the following years remained one of containment. No-fly zones were enacted in northern and southern parts of Iraq with the goal of protecting Shi'a and Kurdish groups. The United Nations imposed economic sanctions, and Iraq was ordered to undertake a disarmament program. As part of this program, the regime was required to allow inspections of its facilities to ensure compliance. During his tenure in the White House, President Clinton ordered several air strikes on targets throughout Iraq. At one point in 1994, when Hussein sent troops to the Kuwaiti border, Clinton deployed some thirty-six thousand troops and one hundred aircraft to the area. He broadened the southern no-fly zone and ordered air strikes against targets in the newly prohibited territory.[25]

Conservatives pressured Clinton to pursue a more aggressive strategy in Iraq. Publishing an open letter to the President, eighteen prominent political figures, including individuals who would later be important in the 2003 invasion, such as Donald Rumsfeld and Paul Wolfowitz, called on the President not to contain the Iraqi leader but to overthrow him. They wrote,

We urge you to seize that opportunity [the State of the Union Address], and to enunciate a new strategy that would secure the interests of the U.S. . . . . That strategy should aim, above all, at the removal of Saddam Hussein's regime from power. . . . This will require a full complement of diplomatic, political, and military efforts. Although we are aware of the dangers and difficulties in implementing this policy, we believe the dangers of failing to do so are far greater. We believe the U.S. has the authority . . . to take the necessary steps, including military steps, to protect our vital interests in the Gulf. . . . We urge you to act decisively.[26]

Clinton did not pursue a military overthrow of the Iraqi regime but rather adopted other policies to destabilize the Iraqi government and oust Saddam Hussein. In October 1998, Clinton signed the Omnibus Consolidated and Emergency Supplemental Appropriations Act, making $8 million available "for assistance to the Iraqi democratic opposition."[27] Later that month he signed the Iraq Liberation Act into law, allowing for U.S. government support of radio and television organizations in Iraq and military assistance to rebel groups, among other items, for the express purpose of "establish[ing] a program to support a transition to democracy in Iraq."[28] Two months later, Hussein stopped allowing weapons inspectors into Iraq, resulting in four days of air strikes by U.S. forces. Between January and August of 1999, the United States struck four hundred targets in Iraq.

George W. Bush was elected president in 2000 and took the oath of office on January 20, 2001. While on the campaign trail, he had clearly discussed the "threat" imposed by Iraq and argued that this danger would "require firmness" on the part of the U.S government.[29] In other speeches, Bush also laid the groundwork to continue and expand military intervention abroad, painting the U.S. military as a force who would not only "protect our homeland" but one that would also spread U.S. ideals globally.

We must master the new technology of war—to extend our peaceful influence, not just across the world, but across the years. In the defense of our nation, a president must be a clear-eyed realist. There are limits to the smiles and scowls of diplomacy. Armies and missiles are not stopped by stiff notes of condemnation. They are held in check by strength and purpose and the promise of swift punishment. . . . American foreign policy must be more than the management of crisis. It must have a great and guiding goal: to turn this time of American influence into generations of democratic peace.[30]

It would not be long before events would present an opportunity to use military force against the Iraqi regime. The Bush administration would utilize the same sentiments and its exclusive ability to disseminate information to rally domestic popular support for the overthrow of Iraq's government following the September 11 attacks on U.S. soil.

INVADING IRAQ: PROPAGANDA
VERSUS THE KNOWN REALITIES

On the morning of September 11, 2001, nineteen men hijacked four California-bound commercial aircraft leaving from the northeastern United States. Two of the aircraft crashed into the North and South Towers of the World Trade Center in New York City. The third crashed into the Pentagon outside of Washington, DC, and the fourth plane crashed in a field southeast of Pittsburgh, Pennsylvania.

Vice President Dick Cheney and National Security Adviser Condoleezza Rice, along with several others, were taken to a safe bunker under the White House. From almost the moment the attacks occurred, government officials surmised that the terrorist group al-Qaeda and its leader Osama bin Laden were responsible for the attacks. In a 2001 interview, Rice stated that "everyone assumed it was al-Qaeda because the operation looked like al-Qaeda, quacked like al Qaeda, seemed like al-Qaeda."[31] The terror group, however, was not the exclusive focus of Bush administration officials. According to Sir Christopher Meyer, U.K. Ambassador to the United States from 1997 to 2003, in the hours following the attacks, Rice also stated that "one thing we need to look into is whether Iraq's had anything to do with this."[32]

The National Security Advisor was not the only one with eyes on Iraq. A note from the Department of Defense, written just hours after the attacks, mentioned the Iraqi dictator directly as a potential target for military action. The note reads, "Judge whether to hit SH [Saddam Hussein] at the same time. Not only UBL [Osama bin Laden]."[33] Top officials, including Secretary of Defense Donald Rumsfeld, gathered for another meeting later that night, where Iraq was again a topic of discussion. According to investigative journalist Bob Woodward, "Rumsfeld actually puts Iraq on the table and says, 'Part of our response maybe should be attacking Iraq. It's an opportunity.'"[34]

Administration officials would continue to focus on the Iraqi regime as a possible military target in the days and weeks following the terrorist attacks. In a meeting at Camp David in Maryland shortly after the attacks, Iraq was again discussed. John McLaughlin, deputy director of the CIA from 2000 to 2001, said of the meeting, "There was a discussion of Iraq and whether Iraq was behind this [the 9/11 attacks] and whether Iraq should be included in any targeting."[35] Speaking of the same meeting, Secretary of State Colin Powell stated, "Paul [Wolfowitz, Deputy Secretary of Defense] put a case forward that, ultimately, Iraq would have to be dealt with."[36]

Ultimately, the Bush administration would "deal with" Saddam Hussein with the March 2003 invasion. Many reasons have been offered as to the "genuine" motive behind the U.S. government's operations in Iraq. One frequent explanation is that the invasion and war were motivated by oil. While the U.S. government's motivations were multifaceted, there is evidence that U.S. officials were indisputably concerned about securing Iraq's petroleum production processes.

A 2001 report from the Baker Institute for Public Policy candidly recommended that officials "review policies toward Iraq with the aim to lowering anti-Americanism in the Middle East and elsewhere, and set the groundwork to eventually ease Iraqi oil-field investment restrictions." It continued, "Saddam Hussein has also demonstrated his willingness to threaten to use the oil weapon and to use his own export program to manipulate oil markets. . . . The United States should conduct an immediate policy review towards Iraq including military, energy, economic and political/diplomatic assessments."[37] Other explanations for the war argue that George W. Bush was largely interested in revenge against Saddam plotting to kill his father, former president George H. W. Bush.[38] Still, others contend that the war in Iraq began based on honorable humanitarian motives—a concern for the Iraqi people and the supposed threat of terrorism posed by the regime.

Identifying the "true" motives behind the invasion is not of paramount importance for our analysis. What *is* critical is that the Bush administration, possessing information that was unavailable to the American public, deliberately misrepresented or concealed knowledge for the purposes of gaining popular support for military invasion and regime change in Iraq. In what follows we focus on three of the areas frequently offered as justifications for war by the Bush administration: (1) Iraq's supposed connection to known terror groups, (2) the country's supposed weapons programs, and (3) the idea that numerous countries desired military action in Iraq. In each of these cases, we examine the disconnect between what was known by U.S. government officials and what was presented to the public. In each case, officials deliberately misrepresented the actual state of affairs to sway the public toward supporting invasion.

Saddam Hussein and al-Qaeda

One justification offered to the public for the Iraqi invasion was the supposed link between the Hussein regime and terrorism, particularly al-Qaeda and the 9/11 terror attacks. On November 7, 2002, President Bush stated that Saddam Hussein was "a threat because he is dealing with al Qaeda. . . . A true threat facing our country is that an al Qaeda-type network trained and armed by Saddam could attack America." In his State of the Union address in 2003, the president claimed that "evidence from intelligence sources, secret communications, and statements by people now in custody reveal that Saddam Hussein aids and protects terrorists, including members of al-Qaeda. Secretly, and without fingerprints, he could provide one of his hidden weapons to terrorists, or help them develop their own."[39]

Despite these claims, officials had in reality little to no evidence that a connection between Hussein and al-Qaeda actually existed. According to the United States House of Representatives Committee on Government Reform, the Bush administration, including President Bush, Vice President Cheney, Secretary Rumsfeld, Secretary Powell, and National Security Advisor Rice, "made 61 misleading statements about the strength of the Iraq-Al-Qaeda alliance in 52 public appearances."[40]

In separate interviews with *Meet the Press*, for example, Vice President Cheney referenced specific connections between Hussein and al-Qaeda, including a meeting between Mohammed Atta (one of the leaders of the 9/11 attacks) and Iraqi leaders in Prague just five months before the attacks. In 2001 Cheney stated that "it's been pretty well confirmed that he [Atta] did go to Prague and did meet with a senior official of the Iraqi Intelligence Service."[41] Later on, Cheney softened his claim, saying that "the Czechs alleged that Mohammed Atta, the lead attacker [of the 9/11 terror attacks], met in Prague with a senior Iraqi intelligence official . . . but we've never been able to develop anymore of that . . . in terms of confirming or discrediting it." However, even these caveats didn't reveal what the U.S. government knew to be fact.

The supposed connection between the Iraqi leader and al-Qaeda was tenuous from the start. According to Daniel Benjamin, who served on the National Security Council from 1994 to 1999 and as the State Department's coordinator for counterterrorism from 2009 to 2012, "Iraq and al Qaeda are not obvious allies. In fact, they are natural enemies."[42] He goes on to discuss that a major focal point of al-Qaeda's ideology is that secular Muslim leaders have "oppressed the believers and plunged Islam into a historic crisis" and that, "to contemporary jihadists, Saddam Hussein is another in a line of dangerous secularists, an enemy of the faithful."[43] Official documents likewise cast doubt on a Hussein–al-Qaeda link. The October 2002 National Intelligence Estimate (NIE) gave a "low confidence" rating as to "whether in desperation Saddam would share chemical or biological weapons with al Qaeda."[44]

Other reports from a variety of intelligence agencies cast serious doubt on the "nexus between Iraq and the al Qaeda terrorist network," though the White House did not disclose this information to the general public. Speaking of the CIA's efforts to link the Iraqi regime with al-Qaeda, Michael Scheuer, a former CIA analyst who led the intelligence gathering effort stated that, "[George] Tenet [the CIA Director], to his credit, has us go back 10 years in the agency's records and look and see what we knew about Iraq and al Qaeda. . . . And we went back 20 years. We examined 20,000 documents, probably something along the lines of 75,000 pages of information. And there was no connection between [al-Qaeda] and Saddam."[45]

While Vice President Cheney stated that officials were unable to "confirm or discredit" the supposed meeting between Mohammed Atta and Iraqi leaders before 9/11, both the FBI and CIA knew very early such a meeting never occurred. John McLaughlin, former director and deputy director of central intelligence, stated, "We went over that [supposed connection between Atta and Iraq] every which way from Sunday. I mean, we looked at every conceivable angle."[46] Former FBI director Robert Mueller would similarly discredit the idea: "We ran down literally hundreds of thousands of leads and checked every record we could get our hands on."[47] Soon, officials would learn that a meeting between Atta and an Iraqi official in Prague would have been impossible. Vincent Cannistraro, former director of intelligence for the National Security Council and chief of operations and analysis at the CIA's counterterrorism center, said of the supposed Atta meeting, "Very early on, both CIA and FBI knew it wasn't true because the FBI had Atta in Florida at the time."[48]

Even though no true connection could be made between al-Qaeda and Iraq, U.S. officials continued to report misleading information publicly to make the case for war. Speaking to the United Nations on Iraq, Secretary of State Colin Powell stated, "What I want to bring to your attention today is the potentially much more sinister nexus between Iraq and the al-Qaeda terrorist network. . . . Iraq today harbors a deadly terrorist network."[49] At a press conference on March 6, 2003, just days before the war began, President Bush "conflated 9/11 with the war in Iraq eight times."[50]

Propaganda statements from U.S. government officials had the desired effect. A series of polls conducted in 2003 by the Program on International

Policy Attitudes (PIPA) and Knowledge Networks (KN) found that while the U.S. Intelligence community had serious doubts regarding the Iraq–al-Qaeda connection, an overwhelming number of Americans believed the White House narrative. The PIPA/KN poll from January 2003 found that 68 percent of those polled "believed Iraq played an important role in September 11, with 13 percent even expressing the clearly mistaken belief that 'conclusive evidence' of such a link had been found."[51]

Another poll the following month offered respondents more choices but found a plurality of Americans had perceptions that did not comport with the known facts. Some 20 percent believed that "Iraq was directly involved in carrying out the September 11th attacks." However, another 36 percent responded, "Iraq gave substantial support to al Qaeda, but was not involved in the September 11th attacks," a position that PIPA notes is "still at odds with the dominant view of the intelligence community." Twenty-nine percent of those surveyed said there was some evidence of an Iraq–al-Qaeda connection and that "a few al Qaeda individuals visited Iraq or had contact with Iraqi officials." Only 7 percent of respondents said there was no connection between the two groups.[52] Other polls found that 32 and 37 percent of Americans, respectively, believed it was "very" or "somewhat likely" that Saddam Hussein was *personally* involved in the September 11th attacks.[53]

Other surveys found similar results—that many Americans believed officials had found hard evidence of a connection between Iraq and al-Qaeda. Polls in June, July, and September 2003 asked individuals, "Is it your impression that the US has or has not found clear evidence in Iraq that Saddam Hussein was working closely with the Al Qaeda terrorist organization?" In the successive polls, 52 percent, 49 percent, and 48 percent answered that the United States had found such evidence.[54]

Saddam Hussein and Weapons of Mass Destruction

In addition to the supposed link between Iraq, the 9/11 attacks, and terrorism, the justification for the invasion of Iraq largely hinged on Saddam Hussein's supposed possession and pursuit of "weapons of mass destruction," or WMDs. In the 2002 State of the Union address, President Bush left no room for doubt of Iraq's capabilities.

The Iraqi regime has plotted to develop anthrax and nerve gas and nuclear weapons for over a decade. . . . States like these [Iraq], and their terrorist allies, constitute an axis of evil, arming to threaten the peace of the world. By seeking weapons of mass destruction, these regimes pose a grave and growing danger.[55]

In other statements, the president made specific claims regarding Iraq's actions, saying, "Saddam Hussein recently sought significant quantities of uranium [for nuclear weapons] from Africa."[56] In March 2002, Vice President Cheney publicly stated that "we know the Iraqis have been engaged in such efforts [developing WMDs] over the years. We know they have biological and chemical weapons. . . . And we also have reason to believe they're pursuing the acquisition of nuclear weapons."[57] By September of that year, he had strengthened his position, saying that, "we do know, *with absolute certainty*, that he [Hussein] is using his procurement system to acquire the equipment he needs . . . to build a nuclear weapon."[58] Other White House officials, like Secretary Powell, said with regard to Iraq's WMD capabilities that "there is no doubt in our minds now that those vans [possible locations for mobile weapons laboratories] were designed for only one purpose, and that was to make biological weapons."[59]

The idea that the Iraqi regime either possessed or could build WMDs, including biological and chemical weapons or nuclear weapons, was not new. Following the conclusion of the Gulf War in 1991, the UN Security Council passed Resolution 687, which required the elimination of Iraq's WMDs. Under the terms of the resolution, Iraq offered a detailed accounting of its weapons inventory and programs and allowed for inspections by the United Nations Special Commission (UNSCOM). Over the coming months and years, Iraq would be less than cooperative with UN inspectors, stopping all UNSCOM inspections in the fall of 1998. Inspectors would return to Iraq in November of 2002 following the passage of UN Security Council Resolution 1441.[60]

According to the UN, Iraq *had* possessed chemical weapons as late as the early 1990s and had undeniably used them throughout the 1980s.[61] Despite the statements of President Bush, Vice President Cheney, and other officials, however, it was far from clear that Saddam Hussein still possessed chemical weapons or was actively seeking to develop WMDs.

Regarding Iraq's nuclear capabilities, for example, the intelligence community was deeply divided. The Bureau of Intelligence Research, for instance, found that the evidence did not "add up to a compelling case that Iraq is currently pursuing what INR [Institute for Nuclear Research] would consider to be an integrated and comprehensive approach to acquire nuclear weapons."[62] The International Atomic Energy Agency (IAEA) likewise found "no indication of resumed nuclear activities . . . nor any indication of nuclear-related prohibited activities."[63]

The supposed attempts by Iraq to procure uranium from Africa were often used by White House officials as clear evidence of Iraq's WMD program. However, there was no clear evidence that such a transaction ever occurred. The CIA sent Ambassador Joseph Wilson to investigate the claims and reported that it was "highly doubtful that any such transaction has ever taken place."[64] Moreover, the documents that purportedly showed that Iraqi officials were attempting to buy uranium from Africa were deemed "not authentic" after careful inspection by the United Nations.[65]

This was later acknowledged by the Bush administration, but officials pled ignorance. In July 2003, Condoleezza Rice stated, "If there were doubts about the underlying intelligence [with respect to the uranium] . . . those doubts were never communicated to the President, Vice President, or to me."[66] According to the House of Representatives Committee on Government Reform, however, "This statement [by Rice] is false because, as Ms. Rice's deputy Stephen Hadley subsequently acknowledged, the CIA sent Ms. Rice and Mr. Hadley memos in October of 2002 warning against the use of this information."[67]

In 2001 and 2002, shipments of aluminum tubes destined for Iraq were intercepted. These tubes were, like the uranium, treated as hard and clear evidence of Iraq's ambitions to develop WMDs. From the outset, however, the intelligence community debated the likely purposes of the tubes. While it was possible for the tubes to be used for nuclear centrifuges with modification, tubes of that specific size were most often used in conventional rockets. The Department of Energy (DOE) and the IAEA both doubted that the tubes were particularly suited for nuclear use. The DOE concluded, "the tubes probably are not part of the [nuclear] program."[68] The IAEA found that "there is no indication that Iraq has attempted to import aluminum tubes for use in centrifuge enrichment."[69] The State Department likewise expressed doubts regarding the use of the aluminum tubes as evidence of a nuclear program, stating that "the very large quantities being sought, the way the tubes were tested by the Iraqis, and the atypical lack of attention to operational security in the procurement efforts are among the factors . . . that lead the INR to conclude that the tubes are not intended for use in Iraq's nuclear weapon program."[70]

White House officials failed to publicly acknowledge or emphasize these doubts, however, instead arguing that the tubes were clear evidence of Iraq's nuclear ambitions. In September of 2002, Vice President Cheney stated that "[Saddam Hussein] now is trying, through his illicit procurement network, to acquire the equipment he needs to be able to enrich uranium to make the [nuclear] bombs . . . specifically aluminum tubes."[71] That same day, Secretary Rice stated that "we do know that there have been shipments [of aluminum tubes to Iraq that] are only really suited for nuclear weapons programs, centrifuge programs."[72]

The effect of these and similar repeated, coordinated public statements is evident in polls conducted during the period. When asked, "Do you think that Saddam Hussein does or does not have the capability to use chemical or biological weapons against targets in the US?," an overwhelming 79 percent of respondents answered that he "Does have [the] capability."[73] A poll by CNN/USA found that 95 percent of Americans felt that Iraq either already had (55 percent) or was trying to obtain (40 percent) WMDs. Another poll reported by The New York Times asked, "To the best of your knowledge, do you think Iraq currently possesses weapons of mass destruction, or doesn't it have those?" Eighty percent of respondents answered "yes," while only eleven percent answered "no."[74]

Moreover, respondents believed that the Iraqi regime could use these weapons against the United States. Of those who answered in the affirmative that Saddam Hussein possessed weapons, 62 percent believed that Iraq was "planning to use those weapons against the United States."[75] By June 2002, 86 percent of Americans polled thought that the development of WMDs by Iraq was a "critical" threat to the interests of the United States.[76]

The Coalition of the (Un)Willing

In the run-up to the war in Iraq, many Americans were concerned that the U.S. government would take unilateral action. Although many supported the removal of Saddam Hussein and believed that the regime was pursuing or possessed WMDs, was directly linked to known terror groups, or was a direct threat to the United States, polls indicated that Americans were leery of the idea of "going it alone." A report by the RAND Corporation on the public support of U.S. military operations, for instance, found that "Some polling—and even more commentary—seemed to suggest that the American public would not support a U.S. war in Iraq without a United Nations authorization."[77]

Indeed, there is evidence that most Americans wanted UN or other allied support before undertaking military operations. For example, a Gallup poll from September 2002 asked, "Do you think it is necessary for the Bush administration to get a resolution of support from the United Nations before it attacks Iraq, or not?" Some 68 percent of respondents said "yes, it is necessary," while 30 percent said "no."[78] Analysis from the same period described similar sentiments.

Public support for sending U.S. ground troops to Iraq is highly contingent on the role that U.S. allies and the United Nations play in sanctioning and participating in the invasion. If the United Nations sanctions the invasion, or if other countries join with the United States in sending troops, then public support could soar to nearly 80%. On the other hand, without these elements, a majority of Americans generally say the United States should not invade Iraq. Only 38% would favor an invasion if the United States has to do it alone, and 37% favor it if the United Nations were opposed.[79]

Many Americans were particularly concerned with the stance of the UN. In addition to the Gallup poll mentioned above, a PIPA/KN poll from September 2002 found that 68 percent of respondents agreed that if Iraq allowed for unrestricted UN inspections, the U.S. government should agree not to invade Iraq or remove Saddam Hussein and that military action should only be used as a "last resort."[80] Although Congress passed the Iraq Resolution (also known as the Authorization for Use of Military

Force against Iraq Resolution of 2002), the administration recognized it needed to promote the idea of allied support if domestic popular opinion were to remain favorable to the invasion.

It was within this context that Secretary of State Colin Powell spoke to the UN Security Council in February 2003. Reflecting on his address in an interview in 2016, Powell stated that, "You have to remember that at the time I gave the speech [to the UN], the president had already made the decision for military action. The dice had been tossed. That's what we were going to do. . . . The reason I went to the U.N. is because we needed now to put the case before the entire international community in a powerful way, and that's what I did that day."[81]

Despite the lack of UN endorsement or approval of the use of force against Iraq and (as will be discussed below) the fact that the U.S. faced vast international opposition, officials worked to cultivate the idea that the international community supported U.S. government actions. In fact this idea of international unity had been an official talking point well before the invasion. Speaking at a news conference with Czech president Václav Havel in Prague in 2002, President Bush made clear that any military action would be done with broad international support.

As to Iraq, it's very important for our nations, as well as all free nations, to work collectively to see that Saddam Hussein disarms. If the collective will of the world is strong, we can achieve disarmament peacefully. However, should he choose not to disarm, the United States will lead a coalition of the willing to disarm him. And at that point in time, all our nations—we will consult with our friends, and all nations will be able to choose whether or not they want to participate.[82]

The supposed support of the international community was a consistent talking point. In a press statement on March 18, 2003, State Department spokesman Richard Boucher stated that "there are 30 countries who have agreed to be part of the coalition of the immediate disarmament of Iraq." The following day, President Bush again mentioned the coalition, stating that "Every nation in this coalition has chosen to bear the duty and share the honor of serving our common defense."[83] Bush and other U.S. officials would frequently reference the collective action of "coalition" forces and even invoked the name of the UN in discussing U.S. operations. Following the start of the war, President Bush made a variety of statements to this effect. For example, he stated, "Our coalition enforced the demands of the U.N. Security Council in one of the swiftest and most humane military campaigns in history."[84] In another instance, he made a similar point, stating, "I have concluded, along with other coalition leaders, that only the use of armed forces will . . . restore international peace."[85]

These statements failed to reflect the true nature of the "coalition" or the state of global public opinion. The "coalition of the willing" was largely symbolic. Bush's statements conjuring images of multinational forces working in joint, legitimate offensive operations were at best wishful thinking. There were no requirements to be a part of the coalition. In fact, merely asking to be named to the coalition or nominally agreeing to the request was sufficient grounds for inclusion.

In the aforementioned press conference given by Richard Boucher, for example, he was asked, "Can you, in any way, describe the functions of the 30 countries listed as part of the coalition? The first question, of course, would be, are more than a handful contributing troops?" Boucher replied, "I'd have to say these are countries that we have gone to and said, 'Do you want to be listed [as a member of the coalition]?' and they have said, 'yes.'"[86] He went on to say that each country was assisting in their own ways but did not directly answer the question regarding combat troops.

In actuality, the United States and Great Britain (and to a smaller degree Australia and eventually Spain) were the only countries supplying substantial numbers of combat troops.[87] Countries like Japan had agreed to be a part of the coalition but would only participate in reconstruction efforts. Others agreed to offer intelligence or allow U.S. and British planes to fly over their airspace. Emma Brockes, a journalist, phoned various embassies of the countries in the coalition to ask about their level of support. Despite being on the coalition list, when asked how Panama would support United States and British operations, embassy personnel replied, "We aren't sending anyone to the Gulf." When asked whether Panama was offering the coalition moral support, the spokesman said, "Not really. No. Not really."[88]

Eritrea, a country with a GDP per capita of US$1,300 in 2016 and some 50 percent of its population living below the poverty line, was also a part of the coalition.[89] Brockes described the response to her call to the Eritrean embassy, in which she asked how the country intended to show its support. "There is a long, stunned pause," she says, "before the spokeswoman says: 'Can I call you back tomorrow morning?'"[90] Although eventually more than 40 countries would be listed as part of the coalition, private security firms would provide the war effort with nearly the same amount of combat forces as coalition nations (around twenty-five thousand troops).[91]

Global opinion polls indicated people in most countries strongly opposed the war. A January 2003 Gallup poll found that out of thirty-eight countries surveyed, none showed majority support for unilateral military action on the part of the United States. Another question asked, "If military action goes ahead against Iraq, do you think [survey country] should or should not support this action?" Of the thirty-eight countries polled, the majority in thirty-four of them said they would oppose their country's support of military action.[92] Polls from March 2004 of the "unwilling" countries found that between 68 and 88 percent of those surveyed were pleased with their country's decision to abstain from supporting the U.S. government's use of force in Iraq.[93]

CONCLUSION

The 2003 invasion of Iraq continues to be mired in controversy. While some 72 percent of Americans favored the war in March of 2003, this number fell to 36 percent by January 2007.[94] Many Americans now believe that government officials deliberately misled the public regarding the Iraq War and occupation. A February 2008 poll found that 53 percent of those surveyed believed "the Bush Administration deliberately misled the American public about whether Iraq has weapons of mass destruction."[95] A report by the Committee on Government Reform, released in 2004, concluded that the White House had used its advantageous position to deliberately sway public opinion to support the desired policy outcome. Highlighting the issues of secrecy and information asymmetry that enable the dissemination of government propaganda, the committee concluded that,

Because of the gravity of the subject and the President's unique access to classi-fied information, members of Congress and the public expect the President and his senior officials to take special care to be balanced and accurate in describing national security threats. It does not appear, however, that President Bush, Vice President Cheney, Secretary Rumsfeld, Secretary Powell, and National Security Advisor Rice met this standard in the case of Iraq. To the contrary, these five officials repeatedly made misleading statements about the threat posed by Iraq. In 125 separate appearances, they made 11 misleading statements about Iraq's nuclear activities, 84 misleading statements about Iraq's chemical and biologi-cal capabilities, and 61 misleading statements about Iraq's relationship with al Qaeda.[96]

The Bush administration's propaganda was integral in rallying popular support behind the U.S. invasion of Iraq. The start of the war, however, would not be the end of elected officials manipulating the flow of in-formation. As the next chapter makes clear, throughout the war White House officials utilized their control of information related to the war to their advantage.

CHAPTER 4

The Post-invasion Propaganda Pitch

While the Bush administration was able to secure significant support for the initial invasion of Iraq, that support did not last long. On May 1, 2003, two weeks after the fall of Baghdad, President Bush declared that the invasion had accomplished its mission. However, that was just the beginning of the U.S. government's occupation and the "rebuilding" of Iraq. The popular support displayed by the U.S. populace for the invasion soon dissipated. "From a high of 76% approval during the invasion itself, a majority disapproved of the president's handling of the war by September 2003—just four months after the United States declared an end to major combat operations."[1] To provide some context, "support for the war in Iraq dropped faster than support for Vietnam between 1965 and 1971."[2] The decline in popular support was driven by three factors—the U.S. public's demand for fast and successful nation-building, the absence of WMDs, and worries about U.S. casualties.[3] Bush administration officials knew that continuing the military occupation in Iraq required generating and maintaining popular support at home. The result was a massive domestic propaganda campaign aimed at reinvigorating support for the government's occupation.

THE IRAQ PROPAGANDA MACHINE: TALKING POINTS, EMBEDDING, AND "UNBIASED" EXPERTS

Scott McClellan, who served as White House press secretary from 2003 to 2006, was integral in painting the Iraq War in a positive light for the American public. Writing of his tenure on the White House communications staff, McClellan states that the goal of officials was to "win every news cycle."[4] "Our job," he wrote, "was all about keeping the focus on national security and specifically the war on terrorism, which would become the central theme of the president's re-election campaign. In this context, the war in Iraq was not only justifiable but essential." He continues, "it was a determined campaign to seize the media offensive and *shape or manipulate the narrative to our advantage.*"[5]

As discussed in the previous chapter, government officials had actively employed an intense domestic "sales pitch" before the Iraq War. The public repetition of false information regarding things like uranium from Africa, aluminum tubes for supposed centrifuge construction, and Saddam Hussein's pursuit of chemical and biological weapons were part of a larger coordinated effort by U.S. officials to garner support from the general public. While rallying the public's support for the initial invasion of Iraq was one thing, maintaining that support was another and required a massive undertaking by government officials.

From the outset of the war, the information offered to the public was dictated not by a desire to present citizens with accurate reports but rather to paint government activities in a positive light and to serve the interests of officials in continuing the occupation. For example, the White House Iraq Group (WHIG), established in the summer of 2002 by chief of staff Andrew Card, met weekly to "coordinate the marketing of the war to the public."[6] What information would be released and when it would be made available to the public was carefully calculated. Historian Susan Brewer, emphasizing how the White House utilized patriotism to sway other officials, notes that "the timetable [for releasing information] would not be based on events in the Persian Gulf but on the upcoming November Congressional elections; its activities would be aimed at pressuring politicians to back the president or risk charges of weakness and disloyalty."[7] WHIG also worked with other official organizations to ensure that the same messages were being sent throughout the United States and around the world. Although officially charged to combat the "untruths and lies" coming from the opposing side within a global context, the Coalition Information Center (CIC), formed by Bush advisor Karen Hughes in 2001, joined WHIG in coordinating and disseminating talking points.[8]

These unified talking points were not the only method of coordinating the media surrounding the war in Iraq. Administration officials offered various new pieces of pro-occupation information to particular news outlets who would subsequently relay these new "leads" or "facts" to the public. In later discussions, officials would cite the press pieces as the source of their information, although officials generated and provided materials to the news outlets in the first place.

That this technique had worked well before the invasion is illustrated by the now infamous aluminum tubes Iraq supposedly sought for use in its nuclear program. The *New York Times* ran the original story on the tubes in September 2002 after receiving information from government officials.[9] Speaking on this incident, Tom Rosenstiel, executive director of the American Press Institute and founder and former director of the Project for Excellence in Journalism, discussed the source of the *Times* story. "We now know that you had people on the vice president's staff talking to Judy Miller, who was one of the key reporters doing these stories for the *Times*, leaking that material to her or helping her with her stories."[10] The same day the story appeared in the popular paper, Vice President Cheney and Condoleezza Rice referenced the report on television. Speaking on *Meet the Press*, Cheney was careful to assert that the paper was the source of the information as an indication of independent credibility outside the administration. "There's a story in the *New York Times* this morning," he said, "and I want to attribute *The Times*."[11]

This pernicious feedback loop provided clear benefits to elected officials, who would cite trusted media sources as the origin of their information regarding the supposed realities of the Hussein regime. These government-manufactured feedback loops likewise created obvious problems for anyone seeking true information about the intelligence on Iraq. Simply put, even if someone was interested in investigating the origins of a particular claim, it would be an impossible task. The aluminum tubes were not the only case of officials offering data to journalists in such a scheme. "Those stories would appear [in the media]," said Tom Rosenstiel, "and then they [officials] would reference the very material that they'd given to her [media outlet reporters] and say, 'See, this is coming from the *New York Times*, not just us.'"[12] He continued, "It had an echo effect. It had an echo effect that the administration was conscious of and employed."[13]

Officials utilized other methods to influence the public's perception of the war and occupation. For example, the Pentagon undertook a policy of "embedding" reporters with troops. Officials selected some six hundred journalists and assigned them to military units.[14] Each journalist was intended to reach a different audience in an effort for officials to "dominate the information market."[15] In addition to sending journalists from major news networks and papers into the field, the Pentagon reached out to reporters from outlets like *Rolling Stone*, MTV, *Men's Health*, and *People*.[16] One frequent criticism of embedding as a journalistic method is that entrenched journalists can only offer a very limited perspective of a conflict. While a reporter away from the field may review information within a broader context, an embedded journalist reports from a "soda straw's-eye view," unable to provide any general context by virtue of their relatively narrow assignment.[17]

Another issue with using embedded reporters was that they were kept away from the front lines, thus further limiting their ability to accurately view and report from the war. Describing his research with the Project for Excellence in Journalism, Tom Rosenstiel said of embedding,

The embedded program gave hundreds of reporters a very limited perspective. . . . You could only see what a grunt, what one soldier would see. . . . The studies we did of the embedded program suggested that the dominant use [of the reporters] was to just go live; that you'd see one embedded reporter doing a kind of extemporaneous, off-the-cuff report, and then they'd go to another embedded reporter whenever they were in a place where they could transmit.

It was very frustrating for the American public, because they were just getting these disconnected snippets of information. It was very difficult to know what they added up to.

It was also very sanitized, because the reporters were kept at a safe distance. We monitored the first week of embedded coverage, which was the heaviest week [of fighting] of the war. You would see bombs and artillery and weapons fired, and you would see, occasionally, where they would strike. But you didn't see any video of the effect. . . . This stood in contrast, of course, to what people were seeing in the Middle East.[18]

In addition to these issues, the practice of embedding creates perverse incentives regarding objectivity. By embedding journalists in the field with active troops, field reporters face strong incentives to offer favorable reports toward those responsible for their physical safety and who control access to war-related information. Favorable reports are likely to be rewarded with information, stories, and visuals that make for good media, while unfavorable reporting is likely to be met with the opposite.

This point was articulated clearly by Seymour Hersh, a Pulitzer Prize–winning journalist known for, among many other stories, his exposés and reporting on the My Lai Massacre during the Vietnam War and the abuse of detainees at Abu Ghraib prison in Iraq. Speaking at the Global Investigative Journalism Conference, he stated, "embedding is the worst single thing to happen to journalism in the last decade and a half." He continued,

Ultimately, we are not partners of the government. And this is what happened too much after 9/11. Too many of the American reporters became jingoistic, they joined the team. We were embedded. We were embedded with military units. I'm very much against embedding, because that's not our job—to be embedded. Our job it to report on them with no obligations, none whatsoever. . . . When you are embedded with a military unit, the inevitable instinct is not to report everything you see, because you get to know them, they are protecting you.[19]

Despite some concerns and objections to the practice, many media outlets were quick to embrace embedding and the flood of reports their journalists could send from the field, eager to report stories that would capture television audiences during the never-ending news cycle on the occupation.

Other entanglements between government, media, and special interests further created a false sense of objectivity about U.S.-government activities in Iraq and elsewhere. "Military analysts" appeared as frequent guests on all kinds of media—including television, radio, and print—offering their supposedly objective opinions on the war. What was unknown to the public, and in some cases to the media outlets themselves, was that many of these "objective experts" had direct ties to military contractors and lobbyists—companies whose financial bottom lines were directly linked to U.S. military operations. These same individuals had been included in hundreds of private meetings with senior military leaders, including those with influence over government contracts and military budgets.[20]

Pulitzer Prize–winning investigative journalist David Barstow described the practice as "a kind of media Trojan horse—an instrument intended to shape [the war on] terrorism coverage from inside the major TV and radio networks."[21] Emails and other Pentagon documents referred to the analysts as "surrogates" or "message force multipliers," individuals who could be counted on to further official talking points "in the form of their own opinions."[22] Although the Pentagon and many of these analysts deny any sort of conflict of interest, there is evidence that officials knew such relationships would be questioned if exposed. Those who attended meetings with government officials were instructed not to "quote their briefers directly or otherwise describe their contacts with the Pentagon."[23]

According to Brent Krueger, an aide to the former public relations executive who oversaw the Pentagon's work with the military analysts, their strategy had the desired effect. "You could see that they were [using Pentagon] messaging." He continued, "You could see they were taking verbatim what the secretary was saying or what the technical specialists were saying. And they were saying it over and over and over. We were able to click on every single station and every one of our folks were up there delivering our message. You'd look at them and say, 'This is working.'"[24]

In addition to these "objective experts," other individuals connected to the administration were "pushing [the] message" set forth by the White House.[25] Press Secretary McClellan pointed out that some groups were particularly useful in spreading the White House narrative. "Republicans in Congress and allies in the media, such as conservative columnists and talk radio personalities, would be given comprehensive talking points aimed at helping them pivot to the message [of the White House] whenever they could. Daily talking points and regular briefings for members and staff would be provided, and rapid, same news cycle response to any attacks or negative press would be a top priority."[26]

Between creating unified talking points for officials, providing messaging and insider information to "unbiased experts," citing their own source material as objective journalism, and embedding reporters in the field, government officials sought to carefully control the information disseminated to the American public on the war in Iraq. This affected the nature of the information available to news consumers and influenced their perceptions of factors surrounding the government occupation.

A study of more than 3,300 survey responses found that some 80 percent of Americans tended to get their news from television and radio—particularly Fox News, CNN, NBC, ABC, CBS, and PBS-NPR, while 19 percent reported print materials as their primary news source.[27] When examining the "misperceptions" of the respondents, researchers found that 80 percent of Fox News viewers held at least one or more incorrect beliefs with regard to Iraq and WMDs, al Qaeda links, or foreign public opinion. This trend was consistent across other networks. Some 71 percent of CBS viewers surveyed, 61 percent of ABC viewers, 55 percent of NBC and CNN viewers had at least one misperception. Nearly half of those who received their news from print media had at least one or more misperceptions. The NPR/PBS audience had fewer individuals with incorrect insights about Iraq, though nearly a quarter still had at least one misperception.[28]

One may conclude that such findings are a result of failure on the part of viewers. Such a high rate of misperception on the part of the public may be attributed, for instance, to a lack of attention or to individuals who do not consume a significant amount of news. Evidence indicates, however, that this was not true of those who received most of their news from television. Instead of becoming better informed about the state of affairs in Iraq as one consumed more news, those who watched more coverage of the Iraq War were just as likely, or *more likely*, to have misperceptions than those who watched less.

It would seem natural to assume that misperceptions are due to a failure to pay attention to the news and that those who have greater exposure to news would have fewer misperceptions. This was indeed the case with those who primarily get their news from print media. However, for most media outlets, increased attention did not reduce the likelihood of misperceptions. Most strikingly, in the case of those who primarily watched Fox News, greater attention to news modestly *increases* the likelihood of misperceptions.[29]

While these propaganda tools were undeniably essential in advancing the agenda of the White House and rallying the support of the general public, they were not the only methods used by government officials. The Bush administration produced propaganda relying on patriotic appeals, ideas of international unity, and an "us versus them" mentality to cultivate support on the home front.

WITH US OR AGAINST US, LIBERATORS VERSUS DEATH SQUADS

During the buildup to and subsequent start of the Iraq War, the White House paid particular attention to convincing the U.S. public that military forces would be greeted as "liberators" who would bring peace, prosperity, and democracy to a people oppressed by malevolent, criminal leaders. Officials presented the proposed "regime change" as a well-planned, straightforward, and widely supported mission by Iraqis that would end quickly, cost little, and engender democratic change throughout the Middle East—an overall great deal for American taxpayers.

The idea that Iraqis would welcome U.S. forces and that the war would be quick and decisive was repeated in the public statements of administration officials. This sentiment is captured clearly in a speech delivered by Vice President Cheney to the Veterans of Foreign Wars (VFW) national convention in 2002.

Regime change in Iraq would bring about a number of benefits to the region. When the gravest of threats are eliminated, the freedom-loving people of the region will have a chance to promote the values that can bring lasting peace. As for the reaction of the Arab "street," [experts predict] that after liberation, the streets in Basra and Baghdad are "sure to erupt in joy the same way the throngs in Kabul greeted the Americans." Extremists in the region would take heart. . . . In other times the world saw how the United States defeated fierce enemies, then helped rebuild their countries. . . . Today in Afghanistan, the world is seeing that America acts not to conquer but to liberate. . . . We would act in the same spirit after a regime change in Iraq. With our help, a liberated Iraq can be a great nation once again.[30]

After the invasion began, administration officials were quick to spread messages to Americans of victory and positive reactions among the Iraqi people.

On April 9, 2003, a group of Iraqis attacked a statue of Saddam Hussein in Firdos Square in Baghdad. One man repeatedly hit the base of the statue with a hammer, but was unable to destroy the monument to the Iraqi leader. Marines eventually pulled down the statue after draping it with an American and then an Iraqi flag.[31] The toppling of the statue quickly became one of the most iconic images of the war. American media repeatedly showed crowds of Iraqis cheering and the statue falling over. In fact, Fox and CNN news showed the footage an average of once every six minutes in the day following the event.[32] Less than a month later, President Bush stood on the deck of the aircraft carrier the USS *Abraham Lincoln* in front of a giant banner that read "Mission Accomplished." Although he acknowledged there was still work to be done in Iraq, he assured the American people that major combat operations had concluded.

This could not have been further from reality. While some Iraqis were pleased that the U.S. military had managed to topple the Saddam regime, a fierce insurgency emerged almost immediately. While Rumsfeld described "the scenes of free Iraqis celebrating in the streets, riding American tanks" as "breathtaking," others pointed to major problems, namely the administration's naive plans for post-invasion Iraq.[33] Michael Gordon, the chief military correspondent for the *New York Times*, described officials' plans for what to do after major combat operations ended as the "ding dong the witch is dead school of regime change," referring to the 1939 film *The Wizard of Oz*. "You know, we go in, kill the wicked witch, the Munchkins jump up and they're grateful. And then we get in the hot air balloon, and we're out of there."[34]

Laith Kubba, an Iraqi opposition leader, described how Iraq descended into chaos. The behavior of the Iraqi people "was not normal. It's not a sign of liberated people. I think it's a sign of people who sense there is no authority. Iraqis are used to military coups. When they take place, they tune into their radios and they obey orders, and people know exactly how to respond to it. Instead, there was . . . no authority."[35] In April 2003, U.S. officials sent Iraqi exile Ahmad Chalabi back into Iraq with the expectation that he would quickly rally the support of the Iraqis and usher in a new government. This did not occur. Speaking of the Iraqi reception of Chalabi and his cohort, General James Conway said, "My overarching observation is that these folks [Chalabi and his supporters] were generally not well received. People were not responding to them like we had hoped. They were never significantly engaged."[36]

As opposed to the fall of Baghdad creating an environment of stability, crime was rampant. People took to looting and set fire to buildings. In the post-invasion chaos, any social services that may have worked to maintain law and order were absent. According to Michael Gordan, "the fires would have to burn themselves out because there was no fire department."[37] Ambassador Clayton McManaway painted an even bleaker picture. "There was no government. There were no police. The army was gone."[38]

While U.S. government officials continued to publicly report that regime change in Iraq was under control, well planned, and succeeding, this did not reflect the known realities. In fact, intelligence assessments from January 2003 warned officials that establishing a stable democracy in Iraq would not be an easy task. A report from the Senate Select Committee on Intelligence from 2007 stated a variety of major obstacles.

The Intelligence Community assessed prior to the war that establishing a stable democratic government in post-war Iraq would be a long, difficult and probably turbulent challenge. In January 2003, the Intelligence Community assessed that building "an Iraqi democracy would be a long, difficult and probably turbulent process, with potential for backsliding into Iraq's tradition of authoritarianism." . . . The Iraqi political culture did "not foster liberalism or democracy" and was "largely bereft of the social underpinnings that directly support development of broad-based participatory democracy."[39]

Others likewise had serious doubts about the plans to rebuild Iraq. Various government officials warned the White House that an insurgency was not only possible but likely, and that this would pose significant challenges to rebuilding Iraq.[40] Years of political turmoil and deep ethnic fractionalization further contributed to the problems. According to journalist Bob Woodward, Secretary Powell warned President Bush in summer 2002 about his military plans to Iraq.

You are going to be the proud owner of 25 million people. You will own all their hopes, aspirations and problems. . . . You need to understand that this is not going to be a walk in the woods. It's nice to say we can do this unilaterally, except you can't. . . . You need to understand not just a military timeline but other things that are going to be facing you.[41]

Privately, Powell and others would refer to the above sentiments as the "Pottery Barn rule"—you invade it, you break it, you buy it.

Surveys of Iraqis during the war found that, indeed, Iraq was broken. When asked about the most urgent issue facing Iraq, a 2004 poll found that nearly 60 percent of Iraqis were primarily concerned about security. The same survey found an astounding 92 percent of Iraqis viewed coalition forces as "occupiers." Only two percent identified them as "liberators." Some 40 percent said that U.S. and British forces should leave immediately.[42] More than half of those surveyed said they would feel "more safe" if the U.S. coalition left immediately.[43] When asked why they held their opinion regarding U.S. forces, the top two answers given were "CFs (coalition forces) are occupiers" and "they [coalition forces] have brought only death and destruction."[44]

Another 2004 survey asked respondents a variety of questions regarding conditions in the neighborhood or village in which they lived and in Iraq as a whole. The majority said that their security situation, the availability of jobs, the supply of electricity, the availability of clean water, access to medical care and other basic needs, the local schools, their family's protection from crime, freedom of movement, and the availability of fuel for cooking or driving were either "quite bad" or "very bad."[45] When asked about how much confidence they had in occupation forces, more than half of Iraqis said they had "none at all" while another 20 percent responded "not very much confidence."[46]

As the war continued, Iraqi opinions continued to sour, and these majorities grew. By 2007, 80 percent of those surveyed said the availability of jobs was "quite bad" or "very bad." Ninety-three percent had unfavorable views of their access to electricity and 75 percent said they did not have good access to clean drinking water.[47] Nearly 90 percent believed that the security situation in Iraq had become worse or remained the same in the past six months.[48] Some 85 percent of those surveyed said they had "not very much confidence" or "no confidence at all" in coalition forces.[49]

Other surveys of predominantly Muslim countries found overwhelming opposition to the war as well. In summer 2002, six of the eight groups surveyed said they opposed a U.S. war with Iraq, with between 56 and 85 percent expressing their disapproval. By May 2003, these majorities ranged from 67 to 97 percent of those surveyed.[50]

Despite these drastic results and known problems with the plans to rebuild Iraq, a significant portion of the American public seemed to believe the narrative told by U.S.-government officials, a story opposite from the underlying realities. A poll from August/September of 2003 asked Americans whether they thought "a majority of people in the Islamic world favor or oppose US-led efforts to fight terrorism." Some 48 percent responded that the Islamic world favored U.S. policy, while 46 percent responded, correctly, that opinions were unfavorable toward U.S. government policies.[51] While the majority correctly believed that the Islamic world thought U.S. policies would destabilize the Middle East, more than a third of those surveyed thought "a majority of people in the Islamic world think U.S. policies make the Middle East more stable."[52]

In addition to downplaying or denying internal disputes about the ease with which Iraq could be rebuilt, the seriousness of the insurgency, and true global opinion, U.S.-government officials were careful to paint their actions in the best light possible while demonizing any and all resistance. Discussing how officials and media were careful to adopt framing that "sanitized American actions and dehumanized the enemy," Susan Brewer notes the language used in discussing U.S. operations— "Americans 'cleaned up,' 'mopped up pockets of resistance,' launched 'surgical strikes,' hit 'targets of opportunity,' or 'drained the swamp' of 'enemy thugs,' 'death squads,' and 'terrorists.'"[53]

Nowhere is this sanitization of U.S.-government actions more apparent than in the handling of the Abu Ghraib prison scandal. In 2004, CBS News and the *New Yorker* published shocking reports and photos regarding the treatment of prisoners at Abu Ghraib prison in Iraq. In one photo, a naked Iraqi man cowers before two German shepherds restrained by smiling American soldiers. Other photos depict prisoners naked on the ground with dog collars attached to leashes around their necks. Still, other photos show soldiers smiling next to an inmate's dead body, a variety of images of sexual assault, and other forms of humiliation.[54]

The photos caused an outcry both within the United States and globally. In response, the Bush administration assured the public that the abuse was the result of a few "bad apples," low-ranking military personnel who failed to follow orders.[55] In reality, however, U.S. forces enacted a clear and systematic program of torture in Iraq (and elsewhere) in violation of international treaties and protocols on human rights. In 2014, the Senate Committee on Intelligence released 525 pages of its report on the use of torture in the war on terror, detailing tortures such as "rectal feeding," sleep deprivation, stress positions, waterboarding, and threats of rape, murder, and other physical violence against detainees' children and mothers.[56]

Domestically, the Bush administration and its supporters fostered public animosity against those who questioned or objected to the war, the actions of members of the military, or the larger war on terror. Statements questioning U.S. military activity were quickly equated to an affront to U.S. military personnel and deemed "un-American." One such example involves a public exchange between Senate Minority Leader Trent Lott (R-MS) and Senate Majority Leader Tom Daschle (D-SD). After the fighting had begun in Iraq, Daschle and other members of Congress publicly asked that President Bush and his administration clarify plans for the next part of the conflict because of doubts about the operations' long-term success. In response, Senator Lott fumed, "How dare Senator Daschle criticize President Bush while we are fighting our war on terrorism, especially when we have troops in the field? He should not be trying to divide the country while we are united."[57]

Perhaps nowhere are the "us versus them" and "with us or against us" mentalities more on display than the sentiments displayed by members of the U.S. government and media toward France after the French government declined to support U.S. policy. Susan Brewer discusses how officials utilized the lack of French support to rally U.S. citizens around the conflict and the military, noting that

The issue of Iraq was pushed aside as officials and supporters of the war unleashed anger at France, America's oldest and least loved ally. . . . Rumsfeld dismissed France and Germany as "old Europe," while Fox commentators expressed outrage that in contrast to the United States' moral approach to foreign policy, France based its on crass economic self-interest. . . . French fries became freedom fries and French toast became freedom toast. On Capitol Hill, House cafeteria workers put red, white, and blue freedom stickers on packets of French dressing. People . . . poured French champagne into the street. . . . Bumper stickers promised, "First Iraq, then France." Dismissing "Euroweenies" and "EU-nuchs," pro-war Americans proclaimed their toughness.[58]

While the American public was aware that some U.S. allies and others were opposed to the U.S. war in Iraq, polls indicate that many Americans were misled by official discussions of the "coalition of the willing." One poll conducted shortly after the war began in March 2003 asked respondents, "How [do] all of the people in the world feel about the U.S. going to war with Iraq?" Thirty-one percent stated mistakenly that most people supported the United States' military actions. Another 31 percent expressed the still-incorrect perception that views on the war were "evenly balanced."[59] The same question was asked again in separate polls in June–September of that year, but opinions changed little. Between 30 and 33 percent believed that the international community's opinions were "evenly balanced," while 24–27 percent believed that most favored the war.[60]

By putting forward a message of national and international unity toward regime change in Iraq, officials reinforced the notion of patriotic duty and an "us versus them" dynamic when it came to the war. These efforts worked to develop and maintain support for U.S. foreign policy after the conflict began while masking the underlying realities of both support for the intervention and its likelihood of success.

CONCLUSION

Today, many consider the war in Iraq to be, at best, a mistake. Some find fault with the initial decision to invade, while others take issue with the subsequent policies adopted by the U.S. government. A 2016 survey found that more than 50 percent of Americans think "the United States made a mistake sending troops to Iraq."[61] President Trump has stated multiple times, on record, that the Bush administration lied about WMDs and other intelligence to sell the war to the public.[62] Despite the fact that no WMDs were ever found in Iraq, no links were ever uncovered between Saddam Hussein and al-Qaeda, and stories about a nuclear program proved to be unfounded, the stories offered to the American public by U.S. officials have had a lasting effect. In 2011 some 38 percent of Americans believed that the U.S. government had found "clear evidence" that Hussein was working closely with al-Qaeda. Another 15 percent believed that Iraq was *directly* involved in carrying out the 9/11 attacks.[63] As recently as 2015, four out of ten Americans, and more than half of Republicans, believed that the U.S. government found WMDs in Iraq.[64]

United States government officials were able to sell the continued occupation of Iraq by framing and disseminating select information to the American public. This propaganda, which was intentionally designed to present a biased picture, was distributed through public statements and repeatedly aired by the media, reaching hundreds of millions of people. We now know that much of this information did not comport with the underlying realities. Government officials were aware of this disconnect and intentionally framed information to shape public perception in support of their goals.

The monopoly on war-related information possessed by a small group within the U.S. government allowed officials to develop a narrative that served their interests during the pre-invasion period (as discussed in the previous chapter) and after the invasion began. Following the commencement of the war, without immediate evidence to support what officials had sold to the public as justification for the conflict, and in the face of military casualties, the Bush administration used its control of information to yet again mislead the American public.

Government officials purposefully excluded details and facts that would have called into question the feasibility and desirability of the occupation. Interested citizens and watchdog groups were unable to access and consider crucial information that would have allowed them to weigh the true costs and risks of intervening in Iraq. Given the fiscal implications of war and, more importantly, the fact that human lives were (and continue to be) at stake, being able to consider information, which was readily available, is of the utmost importance to checking government power. The result of the U.S. government's Iraq propaganda campaign continues to be felt to this day as the United States remains entrenched in Iraq.

While certainly one of the most long-lasting and obvious illustrations of post-9/11 propaganda in the United States, the selling of the invasion of Iraq and the war itself are not the only examples of officials utilizing their monopoly on information to garner support for their policies. United States government propaganda associated with the war on terror permeates America through sports, air travel, and popular entertainment. In the following chapters, we explore how propaganda has become a normalized part of American life and the perverse effects it poses for individual freedom and democracy.

CHAPTER 5

Paid Patriotism
Propaganda Takes the Field

In January 2014 two teams from the National Hockey League (NHL), the Minnesota Wild and the Colorado Avalanche, met for a regular season game at the Xcel Energy Center in St. Paul, Minnesota. The contest began with a "ceremonial puck drop" in which an honored guest drops a hockey puck at center ice to mark the end of pre-game activities and the start of the official game. In a video of the ceremony, the announcer directs the attention of fans to the center of the arena.[1]

Wild fans, tonight we are paying tribute to the trusted men and women who serve us each and every day with the Minnesota National Guard. Right now, please direct your attention high above the scoreboard and welcome Sgt. First Class Richard Babineau as he rappels down from the arena catwalk for tonight's ceremonial puck drop. SFC Babineau has been serving in the Army for over 24 years!

Fans cheered wildly as Babineau, clad in camouflage, hung upside down from the ceiling and quickly descended toward the ice. Flipping to his feet, he removed his helmet and exchanged it for a puck held by another guardsman waiting on the ice. Stepping between the team captains, Babineau removed one of his gloves and posed for pictures before dropping the puck on the ice. The feat has been called one of the "greatest ceremonial puck drops of all time."[2]

This is certainly not the only instance where a national sports league like the NHL has prioritized honoring the military. In fact, nearly *every* U.S. sporting event, both at the professional and college levels, contains some sort of effort to honor or recognize the military, its members, or a branch of the U.S. Armed Forces. From the singing of the national anthem and "God Bless America" by various military-affiliated groups to full-field flag displays, surprise homecomings of deployed troops, and on-field enlistment ceremonies, the military is highly integrated into American sports.

While the announcer at the Wild game was sure to point out SCF Babineau's military credentials and the team's tribute to members of the military, fans were unaware of one critical detail—that the Minnesota Army National Guard (MNARNG) had paid the Wild for the stunt. It was far from the only instance. In fact, the Department of Defense (DOD) paid the Minnesota Wild some $570,000 between 2012 and 2015 for not only the "opportunity for a MNARNG soldier [to] rappel from the catwalk to deliver the game puck" but also for an on-ice "soldier appreciation ceremony" and recognition of a "MNARNG soldier of the game" and flag bearer on the center scoreboard at every Wild home game in 2012, 2013, and 2015.[3] Five other NHL teams received similar contracts totaling more than $1 million over a four-year period.[4]

This dollar figure pales in comparison to the amount received by the teams of the National Football League (NFL). Between 2012 and 2015, more than half (18) of the NFL's 32 teams received at least $6 million of taxpayer funds from the DOD to host a variety of "patriotic displays." Once exposed, the contracts received intense scrutiny from the public as well as lawmakers. A report from the offices of the late Senator John McCain (R-AZ) and Senator Jeffry Flake (R-AZ) provided the details of some of these contracts, prompting an apology and an "external audit" of the partnership between the DOD and NFL. In a letter to McCain and Flake, NFL Commissioner Roger Goodell offered to repay more than $700,000 that "may have been mistakenly applied to [military] appreciation activities."[5]

While the report and stories surrounding the controversy have been dubbed "paid patriotism," such a moniker fails to capture the true nature of these activities. These displays are propaganda by another name. The effects of these programs may be observed throughout the history of sports in the United States and following 9/11 and the start of the war on terror. By paying major sports teams and other enterprises to engage in seemingly voluntary displays of patriotism and by working to link ideas of patriotism and "Americanism" with sports, the DOD and other government officials sought to deliberately and systematically shape the perceptions, beliefs, and behaviors of sports spectators. In particular, the use of propaganda in sports in the post-9/11 period sought to reinforce and extend a general culture of militarism while garnering support for U.S. military operations overseas.

While the recent controversy regarding paid patriotism has renewed interest in how the military interacts with some of the nation's leading sports franchises, the relationship between the Armed Forces and sports dates back more than a century. In order to appreciate the contemporary usage of sports as a propaganda tool, it is important to understand this historical context. Sports have historically served multiple, sometimes overlapping functions as state propaganda tools to shape the thoughts, ideas, and actions of both enlisted military personnel and the broader public. We first explore how officials historically used sports to normalize militarism and shape public opinion on U.S. military policy through the cultivation of a shared "American" identity. We discuss these elements within their appropriate historical contexts before returning to specific post-9/11 cases.

Going back to at least World War I, sports provided a clear bridge between foreign policy and the American public. Baseball, for instance, long known as "America's favorite pastime," was a relatively easy way for government officials to reach a large number of Americans.[6] So popular was the sport that by 1869, a mere thirty years after the game's invention, the first professional team in the United States took the field. By 1876, the National League was established.[7]

When the U.S. entered World War I in April 1917, such iconic stadiums as Fenway Park had opened to the public.[8] It is at this juncture we observe a clear connection between war, sports, and influencing public perception. The choice of players to either continue their athletic pursuits or join the war effort was frequently displayed in a manner that praised those fighting and disparaged those who stayed behind. Highlighting the connection between "citizen and soldier," many major and minor league players ultimately joined the armed forces during the conflict. Those who did received praise from the military and general public, while those who abstained from the conflict saw their patriotism questioned. *Stars and*

Stripes made the following statement regarding those players who chose to fight and those who chose to remain Stateside, stating, "[those men] who are today throwing grenades instead of baseballs, who are wielding bayonets instead of bats, will be adjudged the men who played the game 'for the good of baseball.'"[9] To offer another example of the infusion of patriotism into baseball during the war, consider that it was not until 1918 that the "Star-Spangled Banner" was heard at a professional game—a full eighty years after the game was invented and forty years following the creation of the National League.[10]

It is also at this time that clear connections developed between the military and a variety of private organizations throughout America. Looking to send equipment to overseas troops for entertainment and as a means of maintaining physical fitness, the military contracted with sporting goods manufacturers to supply different products. Recognizing the opportunity to "take advantage of the situation by tying their products into the patriotism growing out of the war effort," companies placed advertisements showing American doughboys using their equipment and boasted about being awarded government contracts to supply sports equipment to members of the military.[11] It wasn't just those firms making balls, bats, and mitts that looked to bolster the sports-patriotism connection. Organizations like the YMCA, the Knights of Columbus, and others also sought to provide troops with equipment and publicly link their organization with the war effort. Per the military's request, the YMCA became an integral part of creating athletics programs on behalf of the government, a partnership the association proudly displayed.[12]

As part of the military buildup before the U.S. government's entry into World War II, political leaders and the military confronted a divided population. While many were keen to join the fight against fascism in Europe, others were entirely uninterested in engaging in another European conflict with such fresh memories of the Great War.[13] The buildup of the military, particularly the expansion of existing military bases and the creation of new ones, raised concerns within many communities regarding how a sudden influx of young male soldiers would affect their communities. Looking to bridge the gap between the new and expanding military bases and the general public throughout the country, the military looked to sports as a means of cultivating patriotism as well as normalizing interactions between members of the military and civilians.

According to historian Wanda Ellen Wakefield, "the military's sports program served as a mechanism for relieving civilian concerns about the soldiers in their midst."[14] Men and women living in communities surrounding military bases were invited to attend athletic contests on base while soldiers were encouraged to attend civilian contests.[15] At least in some instances, these methods appear to have had the intended effect. At Bowman Field, a base in Louisville, Kentucky, an anonymous civilian donated a trophy to the winning team of an intersquad baseball tournament. The civilian was said to be "interested in the morale of the men stationed at Bowman Field."[16] When the field's softball diamond was destroyed because of construction, a neighboring park opened its facilities to host the base's contests. The University of Louisville and a number of local high schools reduced their admission prices in an effort to encourage the attendance of enlisted servicemen.[17]

Perhaps the clearest illustration of the use of sports to sway public opinion and normalize conflict comes in the years following World War II. The Smith-Mundt Act, passed in 1948, prohibited the creation and dissemination of formal government-produced propaganda (e.g., posters) domestically, leaving officials to seek out alternative means of influencing the minds of the public. In addition, ever more complicated geopolitical issues (e.g., the rise of permanent, global war in the form of the Cold War) made sports an attractive means of communicating political agendas. Writing on the use of sports in politics in the 1960s, political scientist Richard Lipsky argued that "the increasing complexity of American society functioned to hinder effective communications between highly-specialized sub-groups of people, each having its own unique language. . . . Sport language and metaphor, then, was said to fill this linguistic gap . . . presumably supplanting an otherwise uninteresting and uncompelling political discourse."[18]

As the Cold War firmly gripped both political officials and the American public, sports were used extensively as a means to put U.S. government activities in a common language, cultivate support for American policies, and promote a common "American" identity. Sports—particularly on the international stage—provided an opportunity for government officials to establish a clear "us versus them" mentality among the population through the creation of clear "in groups" and "out groups." Political scientist Michael Shapiro captures this idea clearly: "The depth of the social penetration of sports discourse," he notes, "relates two opposed aspects of the social body: those processes that produce consensus and solidarity and those that produce or reinforce cleavage and difference."[19] Writing on this effect, anthropologist and ethnologist Claude Lévi-Strauss noted that games "have a *disjunctive* effect: they end in the establishment of a difference between individual players or teams where originally there was no indication of inequality. And at the end of the game they are distinguished into winners and losers."[20]

The Olympic contests during this period offer numerous examples of this dynamic. While engaged in "friendly" athletic competition, the games were often used as a way to establish superiority between the two superpowers, a mechanism through which the U.S. populace could be unified behind a common team while simultaneously painting the Soviet Union (USSR) as the "other." Writing on the issue of propaganda, the Olympics, and U.S. foreign policy, American studies expert Allen Guttmann noted that, "from [the Olympic Games in] Helsinki in 1952 to Montreal in 1976, there was a widely held perception that the games were a continuation of politics by other means."[21]

To offer but one example from the period, the U.S. government was the first to "weaponize" the Olympics during the Cold War. After the Soviet Union invaded Afghanistan in late 1979, the Carter Administration faced few viable options. According to Guttmann,

Diplomatic protests are useless. Economic reprisals bear political costs. The Soviet Union can veto [U.N.] Security Council resolutions. An Olympic boycott is obviously a weak and ineffectual weapon, but it was attractively available and relatively inexpensive in political as well as economic terms. . . . He [Carter] indicated the possibility of an Olympic boycott on 4 January and announced his ultimatum on the twentieth: Soviet withdrawal or American boycott.[22]

The House of Representatives voted to support the boycott in late January by a vote of 386–12. The Senate also affirmed the policy 88–4. Although the U.S. Olympic Committee (USOC) initially opposed the measure, they quickly backed down after the White House "threatened to not only cut off federal support for Olympic sports but also tax the USOC on its other sources of income."[23] In April, the USOC voted 1604–797 *in favor* of the boycott, arguing that the decision had ultimately been a matter of national security.[24]

Backing the boycott quickly became a hot political issue. Support for the measure came to be seen as patriotic, as supporting the "greater good" and the broader U.S. cause in the Cold War. Opposition came to represent dissent from U.S. policies related to the nation's security. Ultimately, American public opinion was overwhelmingly supportive of the administration, with some 73 percent of survey respondents supporting the boycott.[25] Some sixty-two countries joined the boycott—creating a clear distinction between allies of the United States and allies of the USSR.[26]

Other examples from the Olympics abound. Consider, for instance, the Winter Olympics of 1980. With the Soviet invasion of Afghanistan, the Iranian Revolution, and the concurrent Iranian hostage crisis, the matchup between the United States and Soviet hockey teams was seen as an extension of Cold War competition between the two superpowers. When the young, relatively inexperienced American team beat the USSR— which had won four consecutive gold medals in hockey—the players, the public, and elected officials were stunned.[27] The "Miracle on Ice," as it came to be known, continues to be a source of patriotic fervor. Writing of the "miracle" in 2018, nearly forty years later, journalist and former congressional political aide Brent Budowsky stated, "Let's remember that moment in Lake Placid [New York] when Americans stood together, and American patriotism lit the skies. Let's remember the history of the 20th century when we consider how to respond to the Russian challenge to American democracy today."[28]

The Olympic contests are not the only example of the use of sports to rally support for U.S. foreign policy during the Cold War. The use of "sports-speak" and sports metaphor as a way to justify and discuss policies became a popular and often utilized tactic of many government officials. Communications scholars have long recognized the ability of sports metaphors to both describe events outside of sports and to *shape* the broader public's understanding and framing of political issues. Analyzing the use of sports rhetoric in the American presidency, Michael Hester finds that

The ability of sports symbolism to be both politically useful while appearing to be apolitical would explain how sports has become so influential as a rhetorical resource. Sports language is both easy for the public to comprehend and a subject they find interesting. The values emanating from the sports can supplement the ideological arguments of both conservatives and liberals, and politicians of various stripes in between. . . . Sports have an "in-between" quality, able to serve the interests of the dominant ideology without being overtly associated with it.[29]

Along similar lines, Richard Lipsky articulates how both the political right and the political left have used, and continue to use, sports to advance their goals and to influence public framing. "By using sports symbolism in political discourse," he argues, "the politician or commentator tends to transpose sports' ideologically unproblematic nature onto politics. This has the effect of underscoring the organization (instrumental) imperatives at the expense of articulating substantive goals." He continues, "It promotes an interest in who is 'winning' or 'losing' without looking at the reasons why one side should win and the other side should lose."[30]

As an illustration, the Nixon administration frequently adopted sports language in articulating and defending policies regarding the war in Vietnam. Discussing the intensified bombing campaign in Vietnam, Defense Secretary Mel Laird referred to the South Vietnamese allies as a "sort of expansion ball-club. . . . The South Vietnamese will not win every battle or encounter, but they will do a very credible job."[31] In perhaps the clearest illustration of the intensive use of sports language by the Nixon "team," the new offensive strategy in Vietnam was given the name "Operation Linebacker." Nixon himself was given the codename of "Quarterback."[32] Discussing the use of sports metaphor during the Nixon years, political theorist Ike Balbus noted that

This corruption of the discourse of politics by the discourse of sports alerts us to a possibly profound transformation in the way in which governmental activ-

ity in America is defined and understood: to envelop politics with the symbolism of sports is to transfer the meanings which we attribute to the latter to the
former. Thus the political ascendency of the sports metaphor may well signal
the increasing importance of sports as a legitimating mechanism of the American state.[33]

The use of sports to describe military conflict was also prominent throughout the first Gulf War. Speaking about the strategy used in the conflict,
General Norman Schwarzkopf stated that "once we had taken out his [the
enemy's] eyes, we did what could best be described as the 'Hail Mary'
play in football."[34] Lance Corporal Scott Cornell stated in an interview
that "it [confronting the Iraqi army in Kuwait] will be like the Super Bowl
to end Super Bowls."[35]

Officials involved in subsequent conflicts used sports metaphors as
well. In 1998, during his State of the Union address, President Clinton
likened U.S. operations in Bosnia to a football game. "This is like being
ahead in the fourth quarter," he said. "Now is not the time to walk off
the field and forfeit the victory."[36]

By adopting the language of sport to describe military action and
other policies, political leaders like Nixon, Schwarzkopf, Clinton, and
others were attempting to convey particular messages and shape public
attitudes regarding foreign policy. In doing so, they were only the latest to
appreciate that sports "is indeed a prominent institution through which
ideology is communicated and politics is engaged and enacted."[37] To this
day, sports continue to be used as part of the war on terror as a means to
both disseminate partial and sometimes false information to the public
and foster militaristic attitudes.

SPORTS PROPAGANDA IN POST-9/11 AMERICA

From World War I onward, members of the U.S. government have utilized the language of sports, and the culture surrounding sporting events,
to shape the attitudes, beliefs, and actions of U.S. citizens, particularly as
they relate to the military, while fostering a general culture of militarism
and nationalism. Speaking to this link, sociologist Alan Bairner states that
"sports is frequently the vehicle for the expression of nationalist sentiment

to the extent that politicians are too willing to harness it."[38] In what follows, we explore this connection between sports and propaganda in the
post-9/11 period. We begin by returning to the controversy that opened
this chapter—"paid patriotism." We explore how officials utilized various sports leagues—particularly the NFL—to cultivate and maintain
support for U.S. military and foreign policies. We then examine a striking and specific example of propaganda relating to football and the war
in Iraq by analyzing the reporting and subsequent scandal surrounding
the enlistment, deployment, and death of former NFL player and Army
Ranger Pat Tillman.

The NFL, Propaganda, and Nationalism

The United States is a country of sports spectators. Since the year 2000,
an average of six in ten Americans describe themselves as sports fans.[39]
While individuals from upper-income households are more likely to say
they like sports, general enjoyment of athletic contests spans a number of
divides. According to data from 2015, 58 percent of whites and 62 percent
of nonwhites described themselves as sports fans. Various age demograph-
ics between eighteen and sixty-five and over reported their sports fandom
with similar frequency. Individuals from all parts of the United States and
across *all* education levels likewise report being sports fans at similar rates.
Particularly relevant to our analysis, sports cross the political divide. The
same study found that 59 percent of those who identified as "conservative" were self-reported sports fans. For "liberals," that number was 58
percent. Of those who reported their political affiliation, 64 percent of
Republicans and 60 percent of Democrats stated they were sports fans.[40]

   While the use of sports as a propaganda tool in the post-9/11 period
is widespread, we focus our analysis on professional American football
for two reasons. First, the greatest controversy surrounding the aforementioned "paid patriotism" centered on the interplay between the DOD and
the NFL. While other sports outfits received funding, the lion's share of
taxpayer dollars went to the NFL. Second, of the sports played throughout the United States, professional football is by far the most popular.
Some 37 percent of Americans surveyed by Gallup in 2017 indicated
that football is their favorite sport to watch.[41] To put this in perspective,

basketball came in a distant second with 11 percent, followed by baseball and soccer at 9 and 7 percent, respectively.[42]

Just as sports fandom, in general, crosses a variety of gender, educational, and other socioeconomic divides, so, too, does football. For perspective, a 2011 poll from Adweek/Harris found that nearly two thirds of U.S. adults watch NFL football. Accounting for gender, the poll found some 55 percent of American women and 73 percent of American men tune in to NFL games.[43] Over a quarter of U.S. adults report they spend between six and ten hours a week watching game coverage during the NFL season, while 13 percent report spending more than 11 hours per week watching.[44] Nineteen of the twenty most watched U.S. television broadcasts of all time are Super Bowl broadcasts. The 2018 Super Bowl, for instance, drew an average of 111.3 million viewers—more than a third of the U.S. population.[45] Total revenue from broadcasting, ticket sales, and the purchase of official NFL merchandise is staggering. In 2001 the NFL reported some $4.28 billion in revenue. By 2008, that number had climbed to $7.57 billion. In 2016, the NFL reported $13.16 billion in revenue.[46]

Given its popularity among Americans, it should come as no surprise that U.S. government officials focused a great deal of effort and resources on cultivating and coordinating public attitudes regarding U.S. policy decisions through the use of football and the NFL. With such a large segment of the U.S. population attending or tuning into games, the NFL presents officials with a ready-made means of reaching citizens with information related to U.S. foreign policy and the military, allowing for the cultivation of shared expectations among the populace.

Writing on sports in the aftermath of the 9/11 attacks, Shaun Scott argued that "in the campaign for America's hearts and minds . . . baseball only won the battle. Football has won the . . . war. . . . Football has been more than a sport these last 15 years; it's been the medium to relay America's military response to the trauma of terrorism."[47] Other scholars echo Scott's analysis, suggesting that football has become the "root metaphor of American political discourse."[48] Just as the YMCA, Knights of Columbus, and other organizations sought to highlight their connections to the armed forces during the World Wars, the NFL actively boasts of its close connections with the military today. The NFL's website states that "the National Football League and its players have answered America's call during times of crisis and military conflicts." It further discusses the organization's past "support for America's fighting forces in Vietnam," and their enduring relationships with the United Service Organizations (USO) and the Wounded Warrior Project.[49]

The first Sunday after the 9/11 attacks on the Pentagon and World Trade Center, the NFL canceled its games. Describing the first games after the attacks, former NFL commissioner Paul Tagliabue referred to the contest in which the Kansas City Chiefs hosted the New York Giants: "You didn't know when the teams took the field if it would be a somber cloud of tragedy over the entire situation or whether there would be this vocal support for the people of New York."[50] As the Giants took the field, the stadium erupted in loud support for the opposing team. Chiefs fans hung banners reading "KC loves NY."[51] Sportswriter Bill Reiter said of the warm reaction, "People cried. Players knew this moment was different. And the NFL, perhaps by waiting, had given its fans enough time to turn a football game in the heartland into so much more."[52]

"So much more" would soon follow. Over the coming years, NFL games would become awash in patriotic fervor. National Guard units singing the national anthem, full-field flag displays, surprise homecomings, and soldier recognitions at *every* home game for some franchises would become the norm. Military appreciation nights, salutes to "hometown heroes," and on-field enlistment ceremonies would likewise look to link Americans' obsession with football to the increasingly militarized U.S. foreign policy. Football became synonymous with patriotism and support for "the country."

The patriotic pomp and circumstance surrounding the resumption of NFL gameplay on September 24, 2001, demonstrates the ability of sports to unify people around a shared national identity. The NFL purchased a million miniature American flags, which were distributed to all fans entering stadiums. Full-field flag ceremonies were conducted at several games, and each end zone was decorated with red, white, and blue bunting. All hats worn by coaches and players were affixed with American flag details. Special pre-game ceremonies were arranged for every game, including the distribution of pamphlets to every fan with the words to the national anthem as well as "God Bless America" and "America the Beautiful."[53]

When the time came for the Super Bowl a few months later, Fox Sports worked with the NFL to change the format for the game to focus on the terror attacks, American patriotism, and the war on terror. Sports anchor James Brown opened the broadcast by stating, "We are united more than ever as we fight the war on terror." Following a commercial break, Brown returned to the screen and spoke of the Declaration of Independence before showing a reading of the document by past and present NFL players.

Following another sponsor break, the Boston Pops began a musical performance while former presidents Ford, Carter, Bush, and Clinton, as well as former first lady Nancy Reagan, read words from Abraham Lincoln while images from the World Trade Center site and patriotic scenes showed on the screen.[54] A video of players from both Super Bowl teams reading the words of former presidents, concluding with the words of former President John F. Kennedy, "ask not what your country can do for you—ask what you can do for your country," was shown.[55] Following the singing of the national anthem, during which "the flag raising ceremonies from Iwo Jima and the Trade Center were again re-enacted side-by-side," former president George H. W. Bush, described as a "World War II hero," emerged onto the field for the ceremonial coin toss.[56]

While such extreme patriotic displays could be attributed to the recent attacks, such a characterization would ignore the long history of the NFL partnering with U.S. government officials to promote patriotism. This intimate, though perhaps not commonly understood, connection between football and foreign policy, particularly war and general politics, has been studied in detail and recognized by scholars, government officials, and the NFL alike. Speaking about the upcoming Super Bowl at a news conference in January 1991, Paul Tagliabue, for example, stated that "we've [the NFL and the Super Bowl] become the winter version of the Fourth of July celebration," implying that the game had become just as much about patriotism as leisurely entertainment.[57]

Communications scholar Michael Real argues that football (particularly the Super Bowl) serves the same function as other mythical rituals. "In the classical manner of mythical beliefs and ritual activities, the Super

Bowl is a communal celebration of and indoctrination into specific socially dominant emotions, life styles, and values. . . . Rather than mere diversionary entertainment, it can be seen to function as a 'propaganda' vehicle strengthening and developing the larger social structure."[58]

The use of military language in football following the 9/11 attacks was, and continues to be, prevalent. Writing just weeks after the attacks, journalist Scott Stossel noted that "after September 11 it wasn't long before martial terminology returned to the airwaves: There was once again talk of blitzes and bombs, of aerial assaults and ground attacks." He continued, "There was talk of heroes and warriors, of duty and sacrifice, of trying to penetrate deep into enemy territory. I refer, of course, to the language of football."[59] During a broadcast on the second day of the Iraq War in 2003, Vietnam veteran David Christian compared the U.S. "professional" army to Iraqi resistance, associating the latter with a high school football team.

The use of this language has clear links to one of the three functions of propaganda. By framing discussions of football in terms of war and vice versa, the two activities are effectively equalized in terms of importance and complexity. By comparing the U.S. military and Iraqi resistance to football teams, for instance, the conflict in Iraq and the complexities surrounding the insurgency were reduced to the simplicity of a game. As opposed to appreciating the fierce (and ongoing) opposition to the U.S. occupation, Iraqi fighting forces were portrayed as fumbling adolescents. War is transformed into the sort of entertainment Americans consume on a regular basis.

Another important function of sports-speak, sports metaphor, and patriotic images during this period was that they served to cultivate a common identity and expectations among the larger population. The use of sports propaganda has been remarkably effective in the creation of clear "in groups" and "out groups," reducing the overwhelming intricacies of international and domestic issues into something seemingly simple and generating shared expectations of self and others.

To give but one example, while interviewing former Beatle Paul Mc-Cartney before his performance at the Super Bowl in 2002, former NFL wide receiver turned sports broadcaster Cris Collinsworth made it a point to question McCartney's (a British citizen) allegiance to the United States—"You weren't born in America . . . but you are proud to be here, *right?*"[60] The implications were clear. Failure to express pride in being in the United States was a one-way ticket to the "out group"—those "against us." Writing on this issue, a team of communications scholars notes that

Sports metaphors . . . risk equating good citizenship with good fanship. If good fans wear their team's colors and root for their favorite players in good times and bad, and despite any questionable decision making, then the language of sport in politics may also position citizens to acquiesce to the decisions of their elected leaders, whether or not these decisions are the best interests of the people. . . . [Using sports language in these contexts] may end up limiting, or even eliminating, the open discussions of policy that are essential in a free society.[61]

Nowhere is the creation of shared expectations regarding support for the military and patriotism more apparent than in observing the relationship between the NFL and the U.S. government in the post-9/11 period. Writing on the ties between the Bush administration and football, Samantha King, a scholar of cultural studies and sociology, states, "events such as the Super Bowl are only the most visible expressions of the variety of ways in which sport has been harnessed to the Bush administration's agenda both at home and abroad." She continues, "A variety of sporting events . . . have become key vehicles for reproducing and channeling military and nationalist identifications . . . since 2001. . . . The NFL incorporate[s] Bush administration policy into their business strategy with the aim of enhancing brand identification and capital accumulation."[62]

Take, for example, the launch of the NFL's 2003 season. In May of that year, Tagliabue met at the Pentagon with General Richard B. Myers, chairman of the Joint Chiefs of Staff, to pitch a plan for a kickoff event in Washington, DC, and discuss the NFL's support of the troops in Iraq and Afghanistan. While the Pentagon (which is forbidden to engage in commercial enterprise) did not officially endorse the NFL or its sponsors, the DOD did incorporate the events into its own project—"Operation Tribute to Freedom," heavily promoting the event on its website. The operation, according to the DOD, was intended to "thank servicemen and women, strengthen the tie between citizens and military, and recognize that the war on terror is not over yet."[63]

In September, the NFL (partnering with Pepsi), under the auspices of the DOD's Tribute to Freedom program, hosted their Kickoff Live event on the National Mall in Washington, DC. The week of activities began with a meeting in the Oval Office with NFL executives, President Bush, Vice President Cheney, Secretary of State Colin Powell, and National Security Advisor Condoleezza Rice. The NFL officials presented President Bush with an inscribed football.[64] The week ended with the event on the National Mall. It was the first time in history that a private company had been permitted to take over most of the space between the Washington Monument and the Capitol grounds.

The three-hundred-thousand-person crowd included some twenty-five thousand members of the military and their families "shipped in for the event by the Department of Defense with the promise of a free t-shirt and prime concert viewing."[65] "The purpose of this 'new tradition,'" writes Samantha King, "was to 'celebrate the resilient and indomitable spirit of America' through a focus on the veterans of the Global War on Terror."[66] Indeed, the presence of military members was carefully managed. Writing on the event, journalist David Montgomery commented, "This week the Mall is going to be the physical incarnation of that powerful place in the American psyche where sports and war . . . intersect."[67]

While military members attending the event were not required to wear their uniforms, the Pentagon strongly encouraged military personnel to wear their short-sleeve, open collar uniforms "to make a good impression on tv."[68] NFL spokesperson Brian McCarthy stated that the push for placing military members in uniforms was "for visual effect."[69] Discussing the event, John Collins, former NFL senior vice president of marketing and entertainment, stated, "We also have an opportunity to inspire the mood of the country. . . . It's an inspiring celebration of American values." Addressing the issue of linking NFL events with the ongoing war, he responded, "I guess you could cynically look at it and say, well, the NFL is exploiting [the war]. . . . We look at it as an opportunity to celebrate and thank everyday heroes who protect and support our American values. . . . At the NFL we do two things pretty well. . . . We bring people together . . . [and] we do a pretty good job of wrapping ourselves in the American flag."[70] It was these two strengths that served as the foundation for the paid patriotism relationship between the NFL and DOD.

Activities associated with paid patriotism sought to create common knowledge and shared expectations among sports spectators that being "American" correlated with supporting the war on terror and the military. To do otherwise placed dissenters in an "out group," labeled as "un-American," "unpatriotic," and so on. Legal scholar Peter Gabel describes the social pressures created by the use of patriotic displays at sporting events during this period.

The crowd of some 50,000 was instructed to stand and remove our hats for the Star Spangled Banner. . . . The National Anthem was accompanied by the unfurling of a gigantic American flag. . . . As an opponent of the war in Iraq and coercive patriotism, my son never wants to stand for the Anthem, and I've had to go through verbal contortions to persuade him that in spite of our common feelings about this matter, he should still stand in order to not appear to show contempt for others around us or at least to avoid being punched in the mouth, but that we could do so without standing at attention or putting our hats over our hearts, as is the custom of true believers.

At a higher level we had participated in a ritual that had reaffirmed our national unity. The point is even more telling when you consider that since the game was in Los Angeles, and even factoring in . . . more than half that crowd likely voted for [John] Kerry, opposed the war, and felt confusedly pulled along by some iconic larger "We" that overpowered and more-than-half-silenced them. The point here is that sports . . . [are] an important public activity saturated with moral meaning that plays a role in shaping the popular consciousness.[71]

Sports journalist Howard Bryant echoes similar sentiments.

The atmospheres of the games [after 9/11] are no longer politically neutral but decidedly, often uncomfortably, nationalistic. The [patriotic displays] are no longer spontaneous reactions to a specific event, but fixtures.

For a dozen years, public support [for U.S. policies]—at least at a surface level—has been forced upon anyone who chooses to buy a ticket to a sporting event or watch on television. The indirect message goes unmentioned: codifying these elements into the sports experience is forcing the fan to tacitly endorse them. . . . The selling [of patriotism in sports and elsewhere] comes with the same subtle, customary intimidation that permeated the aftermath of 9/11: anyone who disagrees with this trend is immediately branded as unpatriotic.[72]

In each of these cases, even if the individuals involved did not fully believe the underlying messages being offered, the desire to conform, cooperate, and avoid conflict with fellow fans incentivized them to act as though they agreed with the underlying idea, thus creating and reinforcing the common knowledge that everyone believed and supported the war effort.

It is important to note that the full extent of the partnership between the DOD and NFL is unknown. According to the report by Senators McCain and Flake, the "DOD still cannot fully account for the nature and extent of paid patriotism activities. In fact, more than a third of the contracts highlighted in this report were not included in the DOD's list. . . . Our offices discovered the additional contracts through our own investigative work."[73] Further, the report from McCain and Flake, acknowledged as incomplete, covers only the period from 2012 to 2015, leaving over a decade of contracts and activities unaccounted for. What is known, however, is that the DOD paid at least $6 million to NFL teams for such activities between 2012 and 2015.[74] All the while, taxpayers, game attendees, and viewers were completely unaware that these patriotic displays were bought and paid for by the U.S. government as a form of propaganda.

Propaganda and the Pat Tillman Scandal

In December 2019, former Arizona Cardinals cornerback, Army Specialist Jimmy Legree offered an interview to a local CBS affiliate in Arizona. In the article that followed, journalist Briana Whitney reported that Legree was inspired to join the army by the life and career of another former Cardinal—Pat Tillman. "It was Tillman's passion for the game and his love of country that helped encourage him to join," she wrote.[75] Whitney quotes Jeremy Staat, a former marine who played with Tillman at Arizona State University. "It really makes me excited to see there are still individuals ready to serve and put their own life on the line for this country. . . . Here we are, you know, 15 plus years after Pat's death, and he's still motivating and inspiring people to go in and serve and be the best that they can be."[76] The Army shared the story on its Facebook page with the caption, "#MotivationMonday From field goals to training exercises, this former NFL Arizona Cardinals cornerback trains with a new team, the #USArmy."[77]

This is but one example of the military using the "patriotism" of Pat Tillman as a means of recruitment and garnering support for military actions. Pat Tillman was a former NFL player and army ranger who was killed by friendly fire in Afghanistan. From the moment of his enlistment, the military attempted to use Tillman and his connection to the NFL as a propaganda tool. Upon his death, officials deliberately withheld and concealed information about the specifics of his death and continue to use his military tenure, death, and connection to major league sports as a propaganda tool—one intended to boost recruitment and garner support for U.S. foreign policy.

In 1998, the Arizona Cardinals drafted Tillman, who quickly gained the respect and admiration of his fellow players and coaches.[78] In May 2002, Pat, along with his brother Kevin (who was under contract to play professional baseball with the Cleveland Indians), decided to enlist in the Army with the goal of joining the elite army rangers. His enlistment, for which he gave up a $3.6 million contract with the Cardinals, made news and immediately caught the attention of top Pentagon and elected officials. Senator John McCain bluntly stated that Tillman would be beneficial from a recruiting perspective. He said, "I don't think there will be any doubts about his capabilities as a soldier but also as a recruiting tool. He'll motivate other young Americans to serve as well."[79]

While Tillman was in basic training, Defense Secretary Donald Rumsfeld sent a memo to Secretary of the Army Tom White containing a newspaper article about Pat. "Here is an article on a fellow who is apparently joining the [Army] Rangers," read the memo. "We might want to keep an eye on him."[80] This memo was followed up days later with a personal note from Rumsfeld to Tillman in which the Secretary praised his enlistment as "proud and patriotic."[81] Rumsfeld's senior assistant, General Bantz Craddock, stated he could not recall another time the defense secretary wrote a personal note to commend an individual soldier.[82] Just a month later, Tillman would receive yet another correspondence from military leaders, as Major General John Vines, Commander of the 82nd Airborne Division, wrote to Pat and Kevin and urged them to join his division as opposed to the rangers.[83]

The interest in Tillman on the part of senior military leaders was obvious. Here was a professional athlete giving up his individual success for the sake of the greater good of "the nation." Unfortunately for the military, Tillman would have none of it. He took care to distance himself from his football celebrity and sought to prove himself on his own merits as a soldier. He detested the idea of being used as a poster boy for the military, telling a friend at one point, "I don't want them to parade me through the streets."[84] As he was deployed to Iraq and later Afghanistan, his journals expressed frustration and disappointment with the U.S. government's conflicts overseas.[85] He refused to give interviews to the media.[86] Writing on the Tillman case, author Jon Krakauer notes how "the [Bush] administration had tried to make Tillman an inspirational emblem for the Global War on Terror when he was alive, but he had rebuffed those efforts."[87] While he may have been able to prevent his situation from becoming fodder for the war effort during his life, however, his death provided officials with the opportunity to cultivate and disseminate a narrative that would serve the agenda of top officials—a narrative that was knowingly and patently false.

On April 22, 2004, Pat Tillman was killed in Afghanistan near the Pakistani border. It quickly became clear that Tillman's death was not what it first seemed. As opposed to being killed in a firefight with enemy combatants, Tillman was killed by his fellow rangers in an instance of "friendly fire." When Staff Sergeant Matthew Weeks, who was positioned just up the hill from where Tillman was shot, and others arrived on the scene, they were alerted to exactly what happened. According to later testimony from Weeks, Ranger Bryan O'Neal, "in a state of hysteria," drenched in Tillman's blood, and covered in pieces of bone and brain, shouted at them—"It was our guys who did it! . . . They fucking killed him! We were waving our arms! How did they not know we're here?"[88]

Immediately, word of the fratricide went up the chain of command. While some of the rangers, including Pat's brother Kevin, were under the impression Pat had died at the hands of enemy forces, the truth was well known in other parts of the unit and by top officials in short order.[89] In order to better understand the timeline of events and place individuals within the military hierarchy, a summary of the chain of command, from Commander in Chief George W. Bush down to Pat Tillman, is below. Ranks listed correspond to the individual's role at the time of Tillman's death.[90]

- President and Commander in Chief George W. Bush
- Secretary of Defense Donald Rumsfeld
- General John Abizaid, Commander, U.S. Central Command (CENTCOM)
- General Bryan Brown, U.S. Special Operations Command (USSOC)
- Brigadier General Stanley McChrystal, Commander, Joint Special Operations Command (JSOC)
- Colonel James Nixon, Commander, Seventy-Fifth Ranger Regiment
- Lieutenant Colonel Jeffrey Bailey, Commander, Second Ranger Battalion
- Major David Hodne, Cross-functional Team Commander, Second Ranger Battalion
- Captain William Saunders, Commander, Alpha Company
- Captain Kirby Dennis, Executive Officer, Alpha Company
- First Lieutenant David Uthlaut, Platoon Leader, Second Platoon
- Sergeant First Class Eric Godec, Platoon Sergeant, Second Platoon
- Staff Sergeant Matt Weeks, Squad Leader, Third Squad
- Specialist First Class Patrick Tillman, Acting Team Leader

By the end of the day on April 22, both Captain William Saunders and Major David Hodne knew that Tillman had most probably been killed by friendly fire.[91] Around 8:30 a.m. on April 23, Lieutenant Colonel Jeffrey Bailey arrived on scene and, upon meeting with relevant personnel, concurred with fratricide as the likely cause of death. Bailey testified under oath that he phoned Colonel James Nixon in the afternoon of April 23, stating, "I'm sure it's a fratricide, sir, but I think I owe you the details. Let me do this investigation [into the death] and I'll give it to you as quickly as I can."[92]

That same day, Nixon delivered the strong suspicions of fratricide in person to then Brigadier General Stanley McChrystal. McChrystal subsequently informed General Bryan Brown. While Donald Rumsfeld would later testify that he could not recall when he learned of suspicions of fratricide, it is unlikely such information would have been withheld once it reached Brown. Writing on the topic, journalist Jon Krakauer cites the words of a civilian DOD employee who interacted frequently with the defense secretary. "There is absolutely no way that Tillman's fratricide would have been withheld from Rumsfeld" states the source. "You cannot overstate the fear that military people had of Rumsfeld. They would never withhold bad news from him. Never. To have it appear in the news and surprise him, that's the worst thing that could happen. Something like that, damn right he would have been told."[93]

Even if Rumsfeld was not informed on April 23, it is almost certain he knew by April 28. On that day, McChrystal, in anticipation of the president speaking at the White House Correspondents' Dinner (discussed further below), sent a high-importance "Personal For" or "P4" memo to General Abizaid, General Brown, and Lieutenant General Kensinger, commander of the U.S. Army Special Operations Command. He wrote,

It is anticipated that a 15–6 investigation [a specific type of investigation in which a commander appoints an officer to investigate misconduct, property loss, accidents, etc. The investigator reports back to the commander with suggested recommendations] nearing completion will find that it is highly possible that Corporal Tillman was killed by friendly fire. This potential finding is exacerbated by the unconfirmed but suspected reports that POTUS [President of the United States] and the Secretary of the Army might include comments [about Tillman in their remarks]. . . . I felt it was essential that you received this information as soon as we detected it in order to preclude any unknowing statements by our country's leaders which might cause public embarrassment if the circumstances of Corporal Tillman's death become public.[94]

Although military officials were quick to learn of Tillman's cause of death and quick to pass word up the chain of command, the narrative offered to the Tillman family and the public was far from the truth. Although Tillman's wife Marie was informed of his death on April 22, she was never told that his death was under investigation (a direct violation of protocol). Pat's brother Kevin, who had been present on the mission in which Pat was killed but who was separated from him at the time of the incident, was purposefully kept in the dark about his brother's cause of death.

On April 26, Pat Tillman's body arrived at Dover Air Force Base in Delaware, accompanied by his brother Kevin—who was still unaware of the fratricide. Dr. Craig Mallak performed Pat's autopsy and was immediately alarmed. The body had arrived naked, and his clothing was nowhere to be found. This was yet another direct violation of policy. Deceased soldiers were to be sent to Dover with their uniforms, helmets, body armor, and so forth, for examination, as these things were considered to be evidence.[95] What Mallak didn't know was that within hours of Pat's death, on April 23, Sergeant James Valdez was ordered to burn Tillman's personal effects. He testified that he was ordered to "burn what was in the bag for security purposes. . . . He [the captain] relayed he wanted me alone to burn what was in the bag to prevent security violations, leaks, and rumors."[96]

Mallak was not informed about the suspicions of friendly fire—another breech of protocol—but quickly became suspicious when examining the body. "The gunshot wounds to the forehead were atypical in nature, and . . . the initial story we received didn't—the medical evidence did not match up with the scenario as described [the death being the result of enemy fire]."[97] Mallak and his colleague refused to sign the autopsy examination report and requested that the army Criminal Investigation Division (CID) investigate the death. The CID is responsible for examining crimes of military law within the army. Writes Krakauer, "Because fratricide is considered negligent homicide under military law, Army regulations obligated McChrystal, Nixon, and Bailey to notify the CID if fratricide was even expected . . . which would in turn compel the CID to launch an independent criminal investigation."[98]

When the CID sent a special agent to inquire further as the result of Mallak's suspicions, Nixon's legal counsel, Major Charles Kirchmaier, was sent to discuss the issue. He gave explicit instructions not to disclose any information from the 15–6 investigation to the investigator. After the CID, thrown off by Kirchmaier's deception, concluded there was nothing to warrant further investigation, Kirchmaier received an email from Lieutenant Colonel Norman Allen—McChrystal's legal advisor—offering him commendation for "keeping the CID at bay."[99]

Within hours of Tillman's death, paperwork was already in the works to award Tillman the Silver Star—the military's third highest honor—awarded for valor and gallantry against an enemy of the United States. McChrystal signed off on the papers despite being shown the preliminary findings of the 15–6 investigation. None of the documents provided to support the Silver Star nomination mentioned anything about the possibility of fratricide. One of the witness statements, provided by Private O'Neal was, by his testimony, so altered after its writing that he refused to sign it. When investigated, the supposed provider of the second witness statement, Sergeant Mel Ward, stated he didn't remember writing a recommendation at all. "It was unsigned," he said, "which is a big red flag for me, because in the Army you can't submit anything without signing it. . . . It [the statement] didn't sound like my words. . . . It sounded really hokey . . . like something I'd never have written."[100] Nevertheless, Tillman was awarded the Silver Star on April 30 and posthumously promoted to the rank of corporal, the same day McChrystal sent the aforementioned P4 memo.

Why the military and other officials chose to conceal and deceive the Tillman family and the general public is still up for debate. Without a doubt, the circumstances surrounding Tillman's fratricide would have been remarkably embarrassing for the army. However, there is evidence that both the army and other top officials sought to use the false narrative of Tillman's death to promote the policies of the Bush administration regarding the war on terror and to garner support for the president's re-election campaign.

By April 23, the U.S. news media learned of and began reporting on Tillman's death. Officials were quick to realize the attention the story received. An internal "Weekend Media Assessment" created and distributed by the army chief of staff's Office of Public Affairs on April 25 found that reports on Tillman had generated the most media interest in the army "since the end of active combat last year."[101] The report also stated that "the Ranger Tillman story had been extremely positive on all accounts."[102] A report by the Committee on Oversight and Government

Reform states that emails reviewed from this period show that the coverage of Tillman's death was discussed by public affairs officials in the Office of the Secretary of Defense, Army, and Joint Chiefs of Staff on April 23. These meetings potentially included a "front office" morning meeting led by Larry Di Rita, Rumsfeld's public affairs chief.[103]

In subsequent investigations about what would eventually become the scandal surrounding Tillman's death, McChrystal would testify that there was no deliberate cover-up only to tip his hand moments later to the reality facing the administration at the time of Tillman's death. "As you remember, Senator, we were still in combat when we were doing all of that. . . . We were in the first battle of Fallujah at the time, so we were making mistakes."[104] The administration was still recovering from the firestorm surrounding Private Jessica Lynch, in which the Pentagon had perpetuated the false narrative that she had heroically fought back against her captors after she'd been taken captive following an ambush of her convoy in Iraq. Just weeks earlier in Fallujah, four American security contractors were killed, burned, and dragged through the streets of the city by insurgents before their charred remains were hung from a bridge over the Euphrates river.[105]

A week before Tillman was killed by his fellow Rangers, Donald Rumsfeld was notified that 60 Minutes II was going to air a broadcast about the torture of detainees by U.S. forces at Abu Ghraib prison (coincidentally, the broadcast would air on April 28, 2004, the same day McChrystal sent over the final paperwork for Tillman's Silver Star). The now infamous images, also published by the New Yorker, show detainees cowering before dogs with smiling U.S. soldiers, naked detainees with dog collars and leashes around their necks, soldiers posing next to dead bodies, as well as a variety of other images of sexual assault and humiliation.[106] The domestic and international outrage over the torture was severe and swift.

All the while, President Bush was in the midst of his re-election campaign. With near 50 percent approval ratings, the NFL star turned army ranger provided a much welcome distraction from compounding scandals and bad news abroad. "A narrative about Tillman was invented to distract the American public," writes Krakauer. "The fact that Tillman had been cut down by his Ranger buddies rather than by the Taliban was potentially problematic for the White House, although there were ways to keep that information from entering the public domain."[107] Shortly after Tillman's death, White House spokesman Taylor Gross made sure to highlight both Pat's military service and football career, stating, "Pat Tillman was an inspiration on and off the football field, as with all who have made the ultimate sacrifice in the war on terror."[108]

The information in the P4 memo that McChrystal sent to other top military officials would indeed reach White House officials and prevent the president from making any direct references to Pat Tillman's cause of death in his remarks at the White House Correspondents' Dinner. In his remarks, President Bush again praised Tillman for sacrificing his NFL career to join the Army.[109] On May 3, a memorial service for Tillman drew some two thousand people to the San Jose Municipal Rose Garden. Lieutenant General Kensinger personally attended, and while he knew of the fratricide, he did not tell Tillman's family.

The only reason the truth surrounding Tillman's death came to light was that too many people knew the actual details. A full month after Tillman's death, weeks after the memorial service, and weeks after the final 15–6 report confirmed what had been known since April 23—that Pat had been killed by his fellow rangers—Lieutenant Colonel Bailey stated that he called Colonel Nixon. "We're back, and I cannot separate these guys. I mean, you've got 600 Rangers. Everybody knows the story [about the actual cause of death]. This is going to get out."[110] Pat's brother Kevin was notified on May 24 about his brother's death and immediately called his sister-in-law Marie, Pat's wife. The decision to disclose this information to Kevin came as an unwelcome surprise to the White House, especially Rumsfeld, who "wanted to come up with a plan for containing the damage before the news was released to the media."[111]

In an effort at damage control, the story was not made public until five days later, on Saturday, May 29. This happened to be the start of the Memorial Day weekend "when few reporters would be at their desks and not many Americans would be paying attention to the news."[112] When the official announcement did finally come, it was stated that

Tillman *probably* died as the result of friendly fire—despite the fact that fratricide had been suspected from the very beginning and already confirmed by the 15–6 report.

Perhaps the best summation of the deceit surrounding Pat Tillman's death is provided in testimony offered by his brother Kevin.

Revealing that Pat's death was a fratricide would have been yet another political disaster during a month already swollen with political disasters. . . . So the facts needed to be suppressed. An alternative narrative needed to be constructed. . . . Over a month after Pat's death, when it became clear that it would no longer be possible to pull off this deception, a few of the facts were parceled out to the public and to the family. General Kensinger was ordered to tell the American public . . . that Pat died of fratricide, but with a calculated and nefarious twist.

There *was* specific fault [in Pat's death], and there was nothing probable about the facts. . . . After the truth about Pat's death was partially revealed, Pat was no longer of use as a sales asset, and became strictly the Army's problem. . . . The handling of the situation after the firefight was described as a compilation of "missteps, inaccuracies, and errors in judgment which created the perception of concealment.". . . . Writing a Silver Star award before a single eye-witness account is taken is not a misstep. Falsifying soldier witness statements for a Silver Star is not a misstep. These are intentional falsehoods that meet the legal definition of fraud. Delivering false information at a nationally televised memorial service is not an error in judgment. Discarding an investigation that does not fit a preordained conclusion is not an error in judgment. These are deliberate acts of deceit. This is not the perception of concealment. This *is* concealment.[113]

Tillman's military and NFL careers and death continue to be used as propaganda by public officials. In September 2017, President Donald Trump shared a photo of Pat Tillman on Twitter with the caption "He fought 4our country/freedom."[114] He was making a comparison between Tillman and contemporary NFL players protesting by kneeling during the national anthem. Marie Tillman, Pat's widow, pushed back against the use of Pat's image and time in the military, stating "Pat's service . . . should never be politicized."[115] Yet it continues to be as one of many examples of state-produced propaganda in support of the government's militaristic foreign policy.

CONCLUSION

The links between sports and U.S. foreign policy are deeply ingrained. By utilizing sports' seemingly neutral space, government officials on both sides of the political aisle are effectively able to bolster support for their policies. Sports in the post-9/11 period, particularly American football, have been used as a means to frame and transmit information and to create shared expectations around foreign policy in the name of patriotism. Beginning in the immediate aftermath of the terror attacks in 2001 and continuing to today, football not only normalizes conflict in the minds of the American public but also works to frame and transmit information about U.S. actions, particularly as they relate to militarism, both domestically and abroad.

The links between patriotism and the NFL continue to make news. The aforementioned social media post by President Trump, in which he praised Pat Tillman's military career, was a direct response to controversy surrounding NFL players kneeling during the national anthem to protest the treatment of black Americans in the criminal justice system.[116] The president would go on to call for a boycott of the NFL for its lack of respect for America and supposed unpatriotic displays by some of its players. "If a player wants the privilege of making millions of dollars in the NFL, or other leagues, he or she should not be allowed to disrespect our Great American Flag (or Country) and should stand for the National Anthem. If not, YOU'RE FIRED. Find something else to do!"[117]

Writing about this controversy and the NFL response, sports commentator Charles Pierce points directly to the long-established use of sports as a tool for elected officials.

There's a reason why the NFL was uniquely vulnerable to the emotional riptides currently roiling the country's politics. The league enjoyed a free ride on glib patriotic display for more than 60 years, and now the bill is coming due. . . . [The NFL could regain its independence from this patriotic fervor by] demonstrating to its players that the NFL is committed to the values of the country as deeply as it is to the forms and pageantry that get draped over those values. But that would require the league to re-evaluate everything about how it perceives itself. . . . I believe that the NFL would do this about as much as I believe that champagne will fall from the sky like rain.[118]

If history is any indication, the use of sports as a propaganda tool is likely to remain as American as apple pie.

CHAPTER 6

Flying the Propagandized Skies

"Remember how it felt to feel safe? Make it a personal challenge. Be smart, be vigilant." These were the words written on an official poster, displayed at airports, from the Transportation Security Administration (TSA). Accompanying the text is a picture of a young girl standing with her hand over her heart, looking intensely upward at the U.S. flag. On the side of the poster are two additional photos, each containing a pair of children draped in the American flag. In one photo, the children are smiling. In the other, the children look pensive and concerned. The official seal of the TSA is displayed prominently at the top of the poster.[1]

The message of the poster is clear. First, Americans taking to the skies in the post-9/11 world are less safe than they were before the attacks. Flying is cause for concern, and passengers must remain on constant alert. Second, the TSA is an essential agency, present to protect the flying public and to ensure that those who take to the skies feel safe.

The reality is that the American public is no better off, in terms of reduced risk, for the actions of the TSA. Security experts often refer to TSA programs as "security theater"—measures taken to make individuals feel safer without actually enhancing safety.[2] As we will discuss, empirical evidence provides strong support for this characterization. The messaging around air travel and TSA "security" provide yet another example of post-9/11 government propaganda. By overinflating the threat to U.S. commercial air passengers and overstating the effectiveness of the agency, government officials aimed to transmit and frame a particular message surrounding air travel—that it is dangerous, that it is fraught with potential terror threats, and that a vast expansion in government is necessary to contain the threat. By disseminating propaganda about air travel and the TSA, officials have effectively normalized and expanded their reach while garnering support for the broader war on terror. The TSA, and the larger Department of Homeland Security (DHS) of which it is a part, has

invested significant effort and resources in creating a culture of fear surrounding the use of air transportation. In doing so ,they have successfully
increased their budgets, personnel numbers, and the scope of their power.
The secrecy surrounding many of the actions of the agency and their programs limits or altogether eliminates the ability of the public, officials, or
other groups to analyze and critically assess the agency and its activities.

Unlike the tactics employed surrounding the war in Iraq, propaganda
surrounding the TSA has not been used to foster support for a particular conflict but instead to cultivate broader support for the overly broad
"war on terror" by providing inaccurate, false, or biased information
about faceless terror threats and the efficacy of the government's response
to these threats. The primary outcome of this propaganda has been the
generation of fear within the American populace, enabling the expansion
of the scale and scope of government.

A BRIEF HISTORY OF AIRPORT
SECURITY 1958–2001

Before turning to our discussion of post-9/11 air travel, it is helpful to place
the creation and expansion of the TSA, as well as the historical safety of
flight, in the appropriate context. Many know that the Wright brothers
were the first to take flight on the beaches near Kitty Hawk, North Carolina, in 1903. Commercial air travel soon followed. On January 1, 1914, an
aircraft escorted the first paying passenger across the bay between Tampa
and St. Petersburg, Florida.[3] In 1928, what is now Newark International
Airport opened, and by 1939 the airport saw more than 481,000 passengers annually—an extraordinary number for the period.[4]

The World Wars sparked rapid development in the realm of aviation,
prompting many to make the switch from other means of transportation
to air. By 1956 more people traveled between cities by air than by train.
By 1958 transatlantic air travel surpassed transport by ocean liners, and
the Boeing 707 made its first commercial flight from New York to Paris.[5]

In the early decades of air travel, only the wealthy could afford to
fly—primarily for business. This began to change with improvements
in technology and large-scale industry deregulation. Prices for air travel began to fall dramatically in the 1970s.[6] As a result, more and more

U.S. adults availed themselves of air travel. In 1970, for example, only 21 percent of U.S. adults had flown the previous year, while just under half had *ever* set foot on a plane. By 2015, nearly half of all U.S. adults had made a trip by plane in the previous year, and 81 percent had flown at least once in their lives.[7] As opposed to traveling mostly for business, nearly 70 percent of contemporary commercial flights are for "personal leisure" or "personal non-leisure purposes."[8]

According to data from the Bureau of Transportation Statistics (BTS), passenger enplanements (boarding an aircraft) in the United States reached an all-time high in 2017 of more than 849 billion.[9] With so many Americans flying in post-9/11 America, many assume the TSA's security measures to be standard and necessary responses to threats against passengers. While the TSA is a relatively new agency, airport security is not a recent phenomenon. It may be surprising to learn, however, that government was practically uninvolved in commercial aviation security for some thirty years after the opening of airports like Newark in 1928.

It was not until 1958, in fact, that President Eisenhower signed the Federal Aviation Act into law, creating the Federal Aviation Agency (FAA). In 1961, the first aerial hijacking of a U.S. aircraft occurred when Florida resident Antulio Ramirez Ortiz used a steak knife to coerce a National Airlines pilot to divert a flight to Havana in an attempt to warn Cuban president Fidel Castro of a supposed assassination attempt.[10] As a result of the incident, the U.S. government began placing armed guards on commercial airlines when requested by the FBI or airlines.[11] That same year, President Kennedy signed an amendment to the Federal Aviation Act, making it a crime to hijack an airplane, interfere with a flight crew, or bring weapons aboard an airliner. In response, FAA safety inspectors began to train for operations aboard U.S. aircraft.[12]

In 1966, the Federal Aviation Agency changed its name to the Federal Aviation Administration (FAA) and became responsible for civil aviation safety.[13] After a string of hijackings in 1972, the FAA created the Explosives Detection Canine Team Program and required that passengers and carry-on baggage be screened either by hand or metal detector.[14] In 1972, hijackers threatened to fly Southern Airways flight 49 into a nuclear reactor after having the plane diverted to multiple states, Toronto, and Cuba.

After this incident, the FAA required all passengers and their carry-on bags to be screened at security checkpoints overseen by the airlines and privately contracted security personnel.[15] Congress passed the Air Transportation Security Act in 1974, requiring metal detector and X-ray screening at all U.S. airports. Despite legal challenges on Fourth Amendment grounds, the searches were deemed legal as long as the screening was universal and only used to search for weapons and explosives.[16] In 1988, Pan Am Flight 103 was destroyed by a bomb as it made a typical route from Frankfurt, Germany, to Detroit, Michigan. All 259 people aboard were killed. Following what became known as the Lockerbie bombing, the FAA required that all checked luggage, in addition to carry-on bags, be screened for explosives.[17]

Even with these various procedures in place, security protocols through 2001 appear lax relative to the post-9/11 era. For example, passengers could carry blades up to four inches long aboard a plane along with baseball bats, box cutters, knitting needles, and scissors.[18] Family and friends could greet or see off a traveler at their gate as opposed to having to separate at the security checkpoint before the gates.[19] Passengers could take bottles of water and other liquids in their carry-on luggage and use any lock of their choosing on their checked baggage. Outside of airport terminals things were different too. Those coming to retrieve passengers could wait at the airport curbside.

At the time of the terror attacks in September 2001, the FAA was required by federal law to "protect passengers and property on aircraft operating in air transportation or intra-state air transportation against an act of criminal violence or aircraft piracy."[20] The Civil Aviation Security System in place at the time of the 9/11 attacks consisted of seven distinct "layers" of defense—intelligence, prescreening, airport access control, passenger checkpoint screening, passenger checked baggage screening, cargo screening, and onboard security.[21]

On the morning of September 11, 2001, nineteen militants associated with al-Qaeda carried out the deadliest terror attack in the United States in its history. Groups of attackers boarded four domestic U.S. aircraft at three airports on the East Coast of the United States (Boston, MA, Washington, DC, and Newark, NJ). Soon after takeoff, the hijackers took control of the planes, possibly stabbing members of the flight crews with box cutters. At 8:46 a.m., American Airlines flight 11 was flown into the north tower of the World Trade Center in New York City. Seventeen minutes later, United Airlines flight 175 was piloted into the south tower of the World Trade Center.

A third aircraft, American Airlines flight 77, leaving from Dulles International Airport in Virginia, crashed into the Pentagon just outside of Washington, DC, at 9:37 a.m. The fourth plane, United Airlines flight 93, crashed in a field in Pennsylvania. Passengers, told of the other attacks via cell phone, attempted to thwart the hijacking.[22] At 9:59 a.m., the south tower of the World Trade Center collapsed, followed by the north tower 29 minutes later. Other buildings suffered serious damage and collapsed because of compromised structural integrity. The subsequent fires at the site of the World Trade Center burned for more than three months.

The attack resulted in substantial civilian losses. Some 2,750 people died in New York City, including more than four hundred first responders who had gone to the scene as a part of rescue efforts. Outside of Washington, DC, 184 were killed as a result of the attack on the Pentagon. The 40 people aboard United Flight 93 also died.[23]

As a result of the attacks on September 11, 2001, security procedures at U.S. airports were dramatically altered. The attack, according to officials, illustrated a glaring weakness in U.S. security. In the years that followed, TSA officials and other policymakers would point to the attacks and other threats as the impetus behind expanding government reach not only into flight but into a variety of forms of travel.

While undeniably tragic, the attacks on the World Trade Center and Pentagon represent *extreme* outliers when it comes to terrorism in the United States. In actuality, Americans—including those taking to the skies—have been, and continue to be, remarkably safe. Despite these known statistical realities, government officials continually misrepresent the threat of terrorism to the American public.

THE REALITIES OF THE "TERROR THREAT"

While the government's rhetoric surrounding the risk of terrorism in commercial air travel is that of a clear and imminent danger, the actual threat posed by terrorism is much smaller than officials publicly admit. While the war on terror moved the issue to center stage, concerns over terrorism are not new, and the topic has been studied for decades. In fact, a large body of literature on terrorism—including airplane hijacking—dates back to the mid-1970s.[24] Writing in 1976, for example, the political scientist Chalmers Johnson wrote of a state department conference in which participants discussed and addressed concerns regarding terrorism in the United States. Among other things, Johnson noted that one of the participants explicitly discussed the small risk posed by terrorism. "Loss of life [from terrorism seems] relatively minor compared to the three quarters of a million people who lost their lives in all forms of civil strife during the 1960s," Johnson wrote of the discussion, "or in light of the city of Chicago's annual murder rate of nearly one thousand per annum."[25]

In more contemporary writing on the risks, costs, and efficacy of counterterrorism policy, political scientist and national security expert John Mueller and civil engineer Mark Stewart have examined the overall risk posed by terrorism in detail. Analyzing the period between 1968 and 2006, they found a yearly *worldwide* probability of being killed in a terror attack to be about 1 in 14 million—some 420 deaths per year.[26] In other work, Mueller and Stewart find that if another 9/11 attack were to happen every three months for the next five years, the chances of an American being killed in an attack would come to approximately 0.02 percent.[27] The lifetime probability of being murdered in an act of international terrorism—for any one person on the planet—is 1 in 80,000 and even less for a U.S. citizen. For perspective, this is the same probability as being killed by an asteroid or comet.[28] More Americans are killed every year from parachuting accidents than by jihadist-inspired terrorists. In fact, more Americans are killed by lightning strikes, drowning in bathtubs, and choking.[29] More people in the United States are killed by dog bites than by terrorists.[30]

Between 1975 and 2000, terror attacks on U.S. soil were responsible for 322 deaths. Between 2001 and 2017, 3,246 people were killed by acts of terror in the United States.[31] It would be incorrect to assume from these numbers that terrorism is a greater threat, however. Though tragic, the 9/11 attacks represent an outlier when it comes to terror fatalities and heavily skews many statistical analyses of the true threat posed by terrorism. When the September 11 attacks are excluded from multiyear analyses, the period before 2001 and the period after 2001 are practically indistinguishable with respect to the risk posed by terrorism.[32] When examining the number of deaths related to terrorism in the United States in 2001—the deadliest year on record—more individuals died from diarrheal diseases, drowning, and nutritional deficiencies. Terrorism accounted for 0.31 percent of all deaths that year.[33] As a particularly rare type of terrorism, the risk of being killed or injured in a terror attack involving air travel is necessarily smaller than the general risk of terrorism. This was true before 9/11 and remains true today.

As highlighted earlier, air travel has expanded exponentially since the early 1970s. In 2015, more than half of all U.S. adults had flown in the previous year, and some 81 percent had flown at least once in their lives. Between 1970 and 2017, U.S. commercial air carried more than 24 billion passengers.[34] Despite this remarkable increase in air travel, the number of hijackings and terror incidents involving airplanes or airports has not increased. In fact, there is no clear pattern to the number of attacks other than to say that they occur rarely—*very* rarely.

Utilizing data from the Global Terrorism Database (GTD) on the number of "terror incidents" in the United States between 1970 and 2017, fifty-seven may be classified as targeting an airport, aircraft, or airline. This includes unsuccessful attacks, attacks that occurred at airline offices (not necessarily located at an airport), ambiguous cases (where the incident may or may not have actually been an act of terror), cases where the perpetrator group remains unknown, cases where fatalities and casualties are unknown, and cases (fifteen) where the intended target was not the United States or its citizens but a foreign entity.[35] Restricted to hijackings, the number of incidents falls to fourteen (including the 9/11 hijackings). The year 2001 saw the highest number of hijackings (four)—all related to the 9/11 attacks. No hijackings were recorded in thirty-eight of forty-seven years for which data is available. At the time of 9/11, there hadn't been a hijacking on a commercial U.S. flight in sixteen years.

Taking all incidents involving airplanes, airports, or airlines into account, a total of 3,028 deaths occurred over a period of forty-seven years according to the GTD. If 9/11 is excluded as an outlier, the number of fatalities resulting from terror incidents involving airplanes, aircraft, or airlines falls to twenty-seven—an average of 0.57 fatalities per year. If the 9/11 fatalities are included, this number increases to 64.42 fatalities per year. (While this may sound substantial, consider that, in 2017 alone, some 17,284 people in the United States were murdered—an average of 47.35 people *per day*.[36]) As opposed to being carried out by jihadists, only six of these attacks are attributable to jihadists or "jihadi-inspired" groups. According to the GTD data, black (e.g., the Black Panthers and the Black Liberation Army) and Jewish (e.g., the Jewish Defense League [JDL]) groups carried out more aviation-related attacks (and attacks overall) than Islamic groups over the period, as did anti-Castro groups.

Numerous scholars have highlighted that the risk of another 9/11-style attack is remarkably remote. This is not because of any efforts by the TSA or officials, but because terrorists have lost the element of surprise with respect to suicide hijackings and terrorism aboard aircraft. The overall attitude of passengers has changed as well. Recall that one of the hijacked aircraft on 9/11—United 93—crashed in a field in Pennsylvania and failed to strike its intended target. This is because passengers, notified of the other hijackings via cell phone, thwarted the plans of the hijackers and tried to regain control of the plane.

Roger Roots, a sociologist, writes that because "of the future impossibility of replicating the blind-sided, unprepared human cargo of September 11, suicide terrorist attacks using commercial airliners are unlikely to succeed again. Any future attempts to take over an airliner probably will be met by intense physical resistance from both passengers and crew."[37] Aviation security expert Brian Jenkins shares similar sentiments: "today," he said, "the assumption by passengers—if they feel threatened by hijacking—is not one of compliance."[38] The cases of the "underwear bomber" and the "shoe bomber," discussed in more detail below, illustrate that this is indeed the case.

THE DISCONNECT BETWEEN RISK
PORTRAYALS AND REALITY

Despite these remarkably low risks, popular rhetoric emanating from U.S. government sources suggests that terrorism presents a greater threat today than it did before the 9/11 attacks and that air travel is particularly dangerous. Although President George W. Bush made the war on terror a top priority of his administration, his successors have done little to quell fears of terrorism or calm public fears as they relate to flying. This matters because the public's fear of terrorism is, at least partially, endogenous to the government's rhetoric and actions. By overstating the risk of terrorism, the government contributes to the negative psychological effects of potential terrorist acts. Government officials then use this fear, which they help to create and perpetuate, to justify their actions to combat the threat of terrorism. Propaganda plays a central role in this process.

Examples of propaganda with respect to threat inflation and the supposed solutions offered by the TSA abound. Officials within and outside of the TSA have worked diligently to present the agency as both necessary and effective despite the known statistical realities related to the risks to flying (and terrorism in general). The agency has withheld information regarding its policies and their efficacy from both the general public and lawmakers, making it difficult if not impossible for citizens and legislators to effectively monitor and assess the agency. Since its inception, the TSA and other officials have consistently inflated the true risk of terrorism and have presented specific instances of "terror activity" in a manner that is at best hyperbolic and alarmist and at worst intentionally deceptive.

President Bush signed the Aviation and Transportation Security Act into law on November 19, 2001, marking the official creation of the TSA. Though originally part of the Department of Transportation, the agency became part of the Department of Homeland Security upon its creation in 2003.[39] The TSA spent $1.3 billion in 2002 and $4.8 billion in 2003 on security measures.[40] The enacted budget for FY 2018 was more than $7.4 billion.[41] The TSA requested a budget of $7.79 billion for FY 2020.[42] As of late 2019, the TSA maintains security at some four hundred airports, employs more than forty-three thousand transportation security officers

(TSOs), and boasts that nearly 50 percent of TSA officers have five or more years of experience as "counterterrorism professionals." The agency screens more than 750 million passengers every year.[43]

From its inception, officials portrayed the TSA itself (and the federalization of air travel as a whole) as *the* solution to the threat of terrorism in aviation. Flying was, and continues to be, framed by officials as a risky activity, an arena in which terrorists are bound to strike. These sentiments are reflected clearly in the statements of President George W. Bush in the moments just before signing the Aviation and Transportation Security Act in 2001.

Today, we take permanent and aggressive steps to improve the security of our airways. . . . The law I will sign should give all Americans greater confidence when they fly. . . . Congress worked closely with my administration to develop a bipartisan conclusion that will help protect American air travelers. . . . We have our political differences, but we're united to defend our country, and we're united to protect our people. For our airways, there is one supreme priority: security. Since September the 11th, the federal government has taken action to raise safety standards. . . . For the first time, airport security will become a direct federal responsibility, overseen by [a] new undersecretary of transportation for security. Additional funds will be provided for federal air marshals, and a new team of federal security managers, supervisors, law enforcement officers and screeners will ensure all passengers and carry-on bags are inspected thoroughly and effectively. The new security force will be well trained, made up of U.S. citizens. And if any of its members do not perform, the new undersecretary will have full authority to discipline or remove them. Security comes first. The federal government will set high standards, and we will enforce them.[44]

The use of similar rhetoric continues. Speaking before members of Congress in 2017, for example, former TSA administrator Huban Gowadia stated that "[The TSA] faces a persistent and evolving threat from terrorist groups around the world, exacerbated by homegrown violent extremists."[45] Administrator David Pekoske, in his agency's budget request for 2019, boasted that since the inception of the TSA, no successful terror attacks have occurred in the United States.

Since September 11, 2001, there have been no successful attacks on the U.S. aviation system. Our motto, "not on my watch," speaks to our commitment to defeat terrorist attempts to attack our transportation systems. Every day we are reminded anew that we face ambitious adversaries who are watching us, studying our vulnerabilities and working hard to develop new attack strategies to replace those that have failed. . . . Since 9/11 we have taken bold and unprecedented steps to ensure the security of aviation.[46]

The TSA works to cultivate a clear and powerful presence at airports utilizing a variety of propaganda techniques. Perhaps the most obvious of these is the "appeal to authority." Although they are not official law enforcement agents, TSA agents, uniformed with official government patches and badges, man checkpoints throughout the country. From the moment they arrive at the airport, ubiquitous announcements instruct passengers to keep their bags within their possession at all times to prevent the introduction of articles "without their knowledge." This is despite the fact that there have been no reports of a bomb or other nefarious articles being slipped into a passenger's carry-on bag. Passengers are repeatedly encouraged to be on the lookout for suspicious behavior. "It is important to remain vigilant and recognize when a threat may be present," the TSA website says of the now common (and trademarked) DHS slogan—"See Something, Say Something."[47] The ever-present TSA personnel and announcements reinforce and perpetuate the overinflated terror threat to passengers, suggesting that the threat of terror is not only real but omnipresent. Citizens, therefore, must remain ever vigilant in order to maintain their own safety as well as the safety of others. Terrorists are hiding in plain sight and around every corner.

Owing to the nature of bureaucratic growth (discussed in chap. 2), the TSA has expanded its operations beyond airports and now operates in some capacity in freight rail, highway security, mass transit and passenger rail, maritime security, and pipeline security. Just as the TSA's presence and actions continuously remind passengers of supposed security threats at airports, so, too, does the agency—with its partners—work to bring awareness of potential threats like "rail sabotage" by providing posters and brochures, offering training courses and "pocket counterterrorism guides" aimed at "identifying security vulnerabilities" and "reducing threats" aboard school buses, in trucking, and highway infrastructure. The TSA works with the U.S. Coast Guard to provide training courses in crowd control, screening procedures, and maritime terrorism, and it provides training and brochures on pipeline security.[48]

The TSA also promotes its brand and activities through social media. The agency has operated a blog since 2008 and an Instagram account since 2013 with one million followers as of 2020. The account posts photos of everything from explosives detection canines to bug collections, coffee mugs shaped like grenades, bowling balls, and pecan pies brought through security checkpoints. The account also boasts about the number of weapons confiscated at checkpoints—mostly guns and knives. As opposed to being wielded by terrorists with malicious intent, most of the weapons confiscated were taken from passengers who neglected to remove the items from their carry-on luggage.

Criticisms of the TSA have been met with swift rebuttals, and officials are quick to point to the seriousness of the threat to the traveling public. Writing in 2010, former TSA administrator Jeff Sural, for instance, argued that those criticizing TSA pat downs and body scanners (discussed in detail below) were behaving as "adolescents" and that such "immaturity [on the part of those criticizing the TSA] is fitting for the sophomoric event that triggered the visceral outrage."[49] He further stated that the TSA security protocols at checkpoints are "justified in the context of our unfortunate reality . . . [that] bad people persist in trying to kill Americans en masse and in a way that captures global attention."[50] Sural went on to argue that "reasonable passengers don't put up much of a fuss about complying with safety and security requests. . . . A little extra scrutiny at the checkpoint is a small price to pay to keep our larger society uninhibited."[51] This type of grandiloquent language, utilized frequently by officials associated with the TSA and DHS to discuss the threats posed by potential terrorists to air travel, is at the foundation of post-9/11 propaganda that overemphasizes ever-present threats to American safety and the central role of government as *the* solution while dismissing concerns about concomitant losses of liberty due to expansions in state power.

SPECIFIC INCIDENTS—OFFICIAL
STATEMENTS VS. REALITIES

While the general disconnect between the stated threat of terrorism and the true threat is of interest, it is also useful to examine the few specific cases of terrorism (realized or unsuccessful) involving aviation that have taken place since 9/11. These cases highlight in greater detail the separation between the official representation of the TSA and counterterrorism policy and known realities regarding the incidents themselves.

Looking at post-9/11 terror plots (through 2018), John Mueller has detailed and cataloged 127 cases—both domestically and abroad—in which individual Islamic extremists and extremist groups have sought to target or actually have targeted the United States. While such a number may sound alarming, consider that this number includes those cases where "an Islamic extremist conspiracy or connection . . . *might* eventually develop into a plot to commit violence against the United States."[52] It likewise includes plots that were disrupted, "but not by infiltrating a police operative into the plot" (this accounts for 21 percent, or 27 of the 127 cases).[53] Furthermore, his quantification of terror plots also includes schemes that are "essentially created or facilitated in a major way by the authorities by infiltrating a police operative into the plot."[54] (Sixty-nine cases or 54 percent of all listed plots over the period fall into this category.) Of the cases in which Islamic terrorists actually committed (or attempted to commit) acts of violence, only ten led to fatalities, with the total number of deaths amounting to one hundred over a ten-year period.[55]

Of the 127 cases Mueller identifies, seven involve aviation in some capacity. A brief overview of these instances is presented in Table 1.

These cases each provided fodder for government-produced propaganda surrounding the TSA and air travel. Regardless of the true nature of the threat, the narrative offered by officials was one intended to cultivate fear among the populace and to instill the idea that government would provide protection against an ever-present terror threat. Some of these cases resulted in immediate action on the part of officials, including the TSA, and the implementation of additional security measures. Others did

TABLE 1 Islamic terror aviation incidents in the United States,
October 2001–2018

Year	Perpetrator/group	Successful?	Location of (intended) attack	Summary
2001	Richard Reid	No (attempted execution)	Flight from Paris to Miami, Florida	Attempted to detonate explosives in his shoes while aboard passenger aircraft
2002	Zachary Zaerr	Yes	Los Angeles International Airport, California	Shot and killed two individuals and wounded three more at the El Al ticket counter
2006	Twenty-four British citizens arrested. Ahmed Abdullah Ali, Assad Sarwar, Tanvir Hussain, Ibrahim Savant, Arafat Khanm, Waheed Zaman, Umar Islam, Mohammed Gulzar all tried	No (no attempted execution)	Various cities in the United States and Canada	Conspiracy to blow up transatlantic flights with chemical bombs
2007	Russell Defreitas, Abdul Kadir, Kareem Ibrahim, and Abdel Nur	No (no attempted execution)	John F. Kennedy International Airport (JFK) (intended target), New York	Conspiracy to blow up fuel pipelines supplying JFK
2009	Umar Farouk Abdulmutallab	No (attempted execution)	Detroit, Michigan	Attempted to detonate explosives sewn into his underwear aboard passenger aircraft
2010	Al-Qaeda in the Arab Peninsula (AQAP) (claimed responsibility), Hassan al-Asiri	No (attempted execution)	Chicago, Illinois	Plastic explosives concealed in computer printers shipped out of Yemen. Both planes carrying concealed explosives intercepted.
2013	Terry Lee Loewen	No (no attempted execution)	Wichita Airport	Plotted to blow up planes at Wichita Airport

Source: Table created by the authors with the data provided by Mueller (2019).

not. In the cases where new procedures were adopted, we discuss their efficacy to the extent data is available.

We exclude two of the cases from the discussion that follows. We omit the case of Zachary Zaerr at the Los Angeles International Airport for two reasons. First, evidence indicates that "his anger was only aimed at Israel and their relations with their neighboring countries" and not at the United States.[56] Second, although authorities eventually classified the shooting as a terror attack—it was originally categorized as a hate crime—controversy remains as to whether or not Zaerr's actions meet the official definition of *terrorism*.[57] We also exclude the case of parcel bombs on cargo planes in 2010. This plot, though involving planes, did not explicitly involve commercial aircraft. The parcels in question were not placed aboard, nor were they ever a threat to, commercial planes. Civilians aboard commercial planes or in U.S. airports were not the intended casualties. We examine the remaining five cases in turn, discussing briefly the events that took place, the official response, and the realities of the threat.

Richard Reid, The "Shoe Bomber" (2001)

A few months after 9/11, British citizen Richard Reid boarded an American Airlines flight from Paris to Miami. In flight, he attempted to ignite explosives packed into his shoes. He hoped that his actions would cause the public to "lose confidence in airline security and stop traveling . . . [and] hurt the American economy."[58] As he attempted to ignite his shoes, passengers and flight crew quickly subdued Reid and two doctors aboard injected him with sedatives. The flight was diverted to Boston and no one was injured. Reid was subsequently sentenced to life in prison for attempting to use a weapon of mass destruction aboard an aircraft. He received an additional fifty-year sentence for other charges related to the incident and was fined $2 million.[59]

The disconnect between official statements and the reality of the attempted bombing was immediate. Officials stated that Reid's explosive device was "highly unstable" and "powerful enough to have blown a hole in the plane."[60] Both characterizations of Reid's plot, however, are tenuous at best. As opposed to using a "highly unstable" material, Reid attempted to use pentaerythritol tetranitrate (PETN) in his bomb plot. Officials point out that PETN is difficult to detect as it is nonmetallic and will not appear on an X-ray. The compound, however, would be difficult (as illustrated by both Reid as well as the case of the "underwear bomber" discussed below) to use as a bomb on one's person. This is because PETN as a compound is relatively stable and difficult to ignite with a naked flame. In order to reliably detonate PETN, one needs a blasting cap—most likely made from metal. A metal blasting cap, of course, would be easily detected by existing security measures—namely metal detectors.

The assertion that Reid's bomb would have brought down the plane is questionable. Although government tests utilizing fifty grams of PETN (the amount carried by Reid) illustrated that such an explosion *could* blow a hole in the side of a plane, it is far from a certain outcome. Mueller, for instance, notes that "explosions do not necessarily breach the fuselage, and airplanes with breached fuselages may still be able to land safely. . . . A similar bomb [to Reid's] with 100 grams of [PETN] . . . detonated in 2009 in the presence of [the bomber's] intended victim . . . killed the bomber but only slightly wounded his target a few feet away."[61]

The immediate response by officials was to "enhance security" by implementing screening of passengers' shoes. In 2006, the TSA mandated that all shoes must be removed and scanned in the name of combatting future attacks.[62] Despite the supposed enhanced security provided by such measures, the TSA has to date provided *no* evidence that the measure of screening shoes enhances safety. Security expert Bruce Schneier points out that the TSA's shoe-removal policy is practically useless. "It's like saying, last time the terrorists wore red shirts, so now we're going to ban red shirts. Focusing on specific threats like shoe bombs . . . simply induces the bad guys to detonate something else. You end up spending a lot on the screening and you haven't reduced the total threat."[63]

Nearly two decades later, similar language is still used in discussing Reid's attempted attack, and the event is utilized as a justification for removing shoes at airports. In a display at Raleigh-Durham International Airport in 2017, TSA explosives expert Tony Aguilera showed a reporter a shoe rigged with fake plastic explosives. "Like Richard Reid, all that's necessary to get this [explosive] to function is to take a lighter and light the fuse."[64] The TSA and other officials continue to use the incident to reinforce the narrative that flying is dangerous and as an opportunity to expand security measures without having to provide any data related to the policy's usefulness. The effectiveness of these messages is observable even today. In the aforementioned television report from 2017, journalist Julie Wilson noted, "They [passengers] don't mind being barefoot in public as long as it's in the name of safety." "Happy to comply and happy to be safe when we're traveling," said one passenger in the story. "It's a pain. But if it keeps us safe, I'm willing to do it," says another passenger interviewed in the segment.[65] The problem is, of course, that there is no evidence the TSA's policy actually enhances safety or reduces the risk of terrorism.

Transatlantic Bombing Plot (2006)

In 2006, twenty-four British citizens were arrested in a plot to blow up transatlantic flights with liquid chemical bombs smuggled in beverage containers.[66] Targeting five U.S. cities, the number of casualties, had the plotters been successful, may have rivaled or possibly surpassed 9/11.[67] Of the twenty-four arrested, only eight were ultimately tried and convicted on various charges.[68]

Officials reacted strongly to the foiled plot. Speaking the day after the arrests in the United Kingdom, U.S. Department of Homeland Security secretary Michael Chertoff's comments reinforced the sentiment that the government is *the* solution to the imminent and ever-present threat of terrorism.

This plot appears to have been well planned and well advanced, with a significant number of operatives. . . . We believe that the arrests in Britain have significantly disrupted this major threat. But we cannot assume that the threat has been completely thwarted. . . . There is currently no indication of any plotting within the United States; nevertheless, as a precaution, the federal government is taking immediate steps to increase security measures with respect to aviation. . . . In light of the nature of the liquid explosive devices which were designed by the plotters, we are temporarily banning all liquids in carry-ons in aircraft cabins. That means no liquids or gels will be allowed in carry-on baggage. Any liquids or gels have to be checked as part of baggage to go into the hold. . . . Additionally, the Transportation Security Administration will be implementing a series of additional security measures, some of them visible and some of them not visible, to ensure the security of the traveling public and the nation's transportation system. TSA is immediately implementing these changes to airport screening, including the prohibition against liquids and gels of any kind in carry-on baggage. . . . We recognize these measures are going to be inconvenient. But they are proportionate to the very real threat to the lives of innocent people that was posed by this plot. And what is important here is that we are taking every prudent step to thwart new tactics of terror. Today, air traffic is safe. And air traffic will remain safe precisely because of the measures we are adopting today.[69]

Attorney General Alberto Gonzales echoed these sentiments while reinforcing the idea that government agencies must withhold information from the public for their own safety and security. He said, "We want to be very, very careful . . . about saying too much [to the public] that might, in any way, jeopardize [the investigation]. . . . Since 9/11, the threat reporting has consistently shown that there is a vicious and determined enemy that is intent on harming American lives. Every day is September 12th for those of us tasked with protecting America."[70] From this perspective a faceless and nameless enemy poses a constant and ubiquitous threat, but the government is unable to offer specifics in the name of "protecting America."

The reality, however, was much different from the official narrative. While researchers have noted that officials at the time may have been alarmed by intelligence that those involved had been experimenting with explosives, making martyrdom tapes, and may have had a connection to al-Qaeda, authorities "also knew that air tickets had not been purchased, that some members did not have passports, and that there had not been a "dry run" by the conspirators. They also knew that they [the authorities] were capable of preventing the plotters from getting anywhere near an airplane."[71]

Writing on the incident, John Mueller counters the narrative offered by Chertoff and others that the plot was remarkably sophisticated and well advanced. "This widely-held proposition [that the plot nearly succeeded] is simply preposterous." Noting a variety of disconnects between officials' statements and the realities known at the time the plot was shut down by authorities, Mueller states,

It is not clear that . . . the conspirators had anything like sufficient materials or effective bombs. . . . Bomb-making was in the hands of a 28 year old dropout who is described by analyst Bruce Hoffman as "a loser with little ambition and few prospects.". . . . In addition, the plot required two terrorist bombers per plane. . . . The "inner circle" of the plot contained only three people. . . . As this suggests, there was nothing imminent about the plot.

He continues,

The notion that none of the bombs, created by a "loser," would [fail to work properly] is, to say at least questionable, as is the notion that all of the ama- teurs . . . would be successful in detonating them. . . . There is also the almost impossible problem of simultaneity. If one bomb were to go off in an airliner restroom . . . all other airlines aloft and on the ground would likely be immedi- ately alerted. . . . This would render replications nearly impossible.[72]

Just as officials utilized the "shoe bomber" plot to immediately expand security programs, this incident likewise led to further expansions of TSA activities at security checkpoints. As noted in Chertoff's statement following the arrests, the TSA placed an immediate ban on liquids in carry-on luggage, as the plotters had sought to shepherd liquid explosives in beverage containers. As of this writing, the liquid ban largely remains in effect.[73] Passengers are only allowed a quart-sized bag containing liq- uids, gels, and aerosols. Containers are limited to 3.4 ounces (100 mL) or less per container.[74]

Just as the TSA has produced no evidence that requiring passengers to remove their shoes has provided any enhanced security, they have likewise failed to offer *any* data on the supposed benefit of banning liq- uids for reducing the risk of terrorism. Counterintuitively, the TSA's liq- uid ban may actually be counterproductive to increasing security. After implementing the ban on liquids, airports observed a 20 percent increase in checked luggage. This meant more volume for baggage screeners and a greater likelihood that bags may not have been properly screened for ex- plosives or other dangerous articles.[75] Despite these possible unintended consequences and the general lack of evidence that liquid bans or restrictions improve safety, the TSA continues to emphasize the importance of these measures for maintaining safety and national security.

JFK Airport Plot (2007)

In 2007, a group of Guyanese conspirators led by former cargo handler Russell Defreitas sought to blow up fuel pipelines serving John F. Kennedy International Airport (JFK). An FBI informant infiltrated the group, which lead to the arrest and subsequent conviction of those involved.

As in the case of the transatlantic plot the year before, the depiction of the attack has "been viewed in many cases to be alarmist."[76] Speaking at a press conference, U.S. attorney Roslynn Mauskopf referred to the scheme as "one of the most chilling plots imaginable" and said that "the devastation that would be caused had this plot succeeded is just unthinkable."[77] Senator Arlen Specter (D-PA) said the conspiracy "had the potential to be another 9/11."[78] Former assistant attorney general for national security Kenneth Wainstein noted that "The defendants sought to combine an insider's knowledge of JFK airport with the assistance of Islamic radicals . . . to produce an attack they boasted would be so devastating to the airport that 'even the Twin Towers can't touch it.'"[79]

Despite the sensationalist depiction by officials, the idea that the group posed an actual threat is highly questionable.[80] At the time of their arrests, none of the conspirators had weapons in their possession, and they lacked any true practical knowledge of how to carry out their proposed attack.[81] Contrary to Wainstein's claim that a larger group assisted the plotters, the men had *no* connection to organized terrorism.

Far from "chilling," the plot was simply unfeasible—a point made by multiple security experts. Writing on the plot, Mueller notes the plan's "daffy infeasibility" and points out that those involved had no practical knowledge of their target. He further discusses the conspirators' "apparent incomprehension about its [the plot's] essential absurdity."[82] As opposed to "another 9/11," those involved had expressly intended to avoid casualties and, as a result, stated they should carry out the attack on Christmas Eve or in the early morning, when few people would be in the area.[83] Had they somehow managed to attack the fuel tanks, experts noted that the pipelines would not have exploded. Safety features built into the fuel system would have contained any fire and prevented it from spreading. An industry spokesperson, speaking soon after the incident, put it succinctly, "To say that the pipeline would blow up is just not possible."[84]

While the plot did not generate any additional (publicized) security measures, it did contribute to generating fear among the public. "Led by the government," writes one commentator, "would-be terrorists seem to be imagined, created, poked, and prodded into convictions that can be sold to rationalize the public's continued fear. . . . Never mind that the majority of these so-called homegrown terrorists turn out to be idiots . . . who would have no means to attack the United States, let alone in spectacular fashion. . . . The continued insistence by the government . . . that terrorism poses an existential threat to the United States generates unnecessary alarm."[85]

Umar Farouk Abdulmutallab, the "Underwear Bomber" (2009)

On Christmas Day, 2009, twenty-three-year-old Umar Farouk Abdulmutallab boarded a flight from Amsterdam, Netherlands, to Detroit, Michigan. As the flight approached its destination, Abdulmutallab attempted to ignite explosives sewn into his underwear. Nearby passengers quickly noticed the fire. One passenger tackled him while the flight crew extinguished the flames. He was taken into custody upon arrival and subsequently charged, tried, and convicted on multiple counts. He is currently serving a life sentence in a U.S. prison.[86] Unlike the other incidents mentioned here, there is strong evidence that the attacker was directly connected to a larger terror group, namely al-Qaeda in the Arabian Peninsula (AQAP). Abdulmutallab was known to authorities, who failed to revoke his visa, before the incident.[87] His father had alerted U.S. officials to his son's ties to Islamic extremist groups before the attack.[88]

The authorities' immediate reaction to the plot was different from the other cases. Neither President Obama nor Vice President Joe Biden spoke about the incident in the days immediately following. Homeland Security Secretary Janet Napolitano initially praised aviation security, saying that "the system worked. Once the incident occurred the system worked."[89]

After swift backlash to her comments, given that Abdulmutallab had boarded the aircraft and attempted to ignite the explosives, she shifted course the following day, saying she had been "taken out of context" and that "no one is happy or satisfied [with how the system worked]."[90]

Like the "shoe bomber" several years earlier, Abdulmutallab's explosive of choice was PETN. He faced similar difficulties in its attempted use. Despite reports that Abdulmutallab could have "blown a hole" in the plane, this remains open for debate.[91] A test conducted by the BBC and a UN explosives expert, for example, found that successful detonation would not have breached the fuselage but would probably have killed Abdulmutallab and the person sitting next to him.[92] Regardless of whether or not a successful detonation would have brought down the plane, the incident prompted swift action on the part of the Obama administration and the DHS. Calling it a "race against time," President Obama ordered a "surge" of federal air marshals to be placed on commercial aircraft by February 1, 2010.[93] The TSA also pushed forward with the implementation of full-body scanners at airports. Both of these elements are worth discussing in more detail. At the time of their implementation (and currently), the narrative surrounding the air marshal and body scanner programs was categorically at odds with existing data.

President Obama touted the "surge" in air marshals as one of several "concrete steps" to enhance aviation security.[94] Despite these statements, clear evidence existed at the time that the Federal Air Marshal Service (FAMS) was ineffective. In 2008, John Mueller and Mark Stewart conducted an extensive cost-benefit analysis of aviation security measures and found that FAMS failed, and failed *miserably*, when using the government's own standards for success. While the regulatory goal of "cost per life saved" is $1–$10 million per life saved, the FAMS costs $180 million per life saved. And this assumes, unrealistically, the best-case scenario in which marshals are always successful in stopping terrorist attacks.[95]

In discussing the program, terrorism expert David Schanzer notes that in order for an air marshal to prevent an attack—say a bombing—on a plane, he or she must (1) determine that an attempted detonation is occurring, (2) ascertain the location of the bomber, (3) move to the bomber's location from his or her seat, (4) discern who is a terrorist and who is an innocent passenger, and then (5) act to disarm or kill the terrorist(s) in question. This must all occur in a matter of seconds within the cramped confines of an airplane.[96]

These issues were not unnoticed by some officials. At the same time President Obama called for an increase in the FAMS budget, members of Congress sought to investigate the program, with some stating pointedly, "They [FAMS] haven't done anything," and "we need to get a ready broom and sweep."[97] These calls have fallen on deaf ears. Reporting in 2017, some eight years after the surge took place, the Government Accountability Office (GAO) wrote that the TSA *admitted* they didn't have any evidence on the program's efficacy. The report states, "TSA officials explained that it is very difficult to empirically measure the effectiveness of [FAMS,] and the program has no efforts underway to collect such data."[98]

In addition to being highly criticized for being, as put by John Duncan (R-TN), "a total waste of money," other concerns about the program have also been raised.[99] Highlighting how secrecy has worked to obscure or prevent oversight by elected officials, citizens, and the media, journalist Michael Grabell worked for years to obtain data regarding misconduct, in the FAMS program. He eventually uncovered dozens of instances where marshals had been arrested for a variety of crimes, including human trafficking, drug smuggling, sexual abuse of minor children, prostitution, and fraud.[100] Some 250 air marshals have been fired for misconduct while another four hundred resigned in the face of being investigated. He recorded more than nine hundred suspensions (amounting to 4,600 lost workdays).[101] Grabell notes how the secrecy surrounding the FAMS program allowed the TSA to shield itself from criticism.

When the TSA finally responded to my seven-year-old request, it included its own analysis of the data along with an unsolicited statement. . . . The statement also said the agency saw a "significant reduction" in misconduct cases in 2015 as a result of its initiatives. But notably, the agency only provided data through February 2012, even though in my last email exchange with the office . . . I requested the entire database. This has become standard practice for many agencies. By delaying FOIA [Freedom of Information Act] requests for years, the TSA gets to claim the data it releases is old news. (The agency made the same claim back in 2008, which—because of the data we received recently—we now know isn't true.)[102]

In addition to evidence of marshals' malfeasance, the FAMS has come under fire for actively spying on innocent civilians as part of its Quiet Skies program. Under Quiet Skies, federal air marshals track unknowing citizens as they make their way through airports. Any citizen entering the United States after traveling internationally is automatically assessed for actions that would allow them to be surveyed under this program— though the exact criteria for being added to the watch list are unclear. Once added, however, marshals watch to see if a citizen is "abnormally aware," displays "excess fidgeting," has a "cold penetrating stare," or sleeps while aboard their flight—all apparent potential signs of danger. Passengers may remain on the Quiet Skies watch list for up to ninety days and are never informed of this fact.[103]

Once news broke about the program, a public backlash ensued, prompting the TSA to defend the program. The agency's website states that unflattering portrayals of the program are "inaccurate" and that Quiet Skies is an "important program" that has "defused dozens of situations that had the potential to escalate, placing the aircraft, crew, and passengers in further danger." They further claim, "These rules have strict oversight by the Department of Homeland Security, including the privacy, civil rights and liberties, and general counsel offices."[104]

No publicly available information about the program, however, has shown it to be effective. David Schanzer describes the "notion that would-be terrorists exhibit a set of uniform behaviors" as "discredited."[105] Of the approximately five thousand passengers monitored under the program, none have posed a serious terror threat or merited additional scrutiny.[106] When asked to further elaborate on the program's effectiveness, the TSA—appealing to "security"—stated that releasing such information would "make passengers less safe."[107] In 2017, Representative Jody Hice (R-GA) sought to introduce legislation that would require the FAMS to provide detailed information on their programs. Without this information, he wrote, oversight agencies are "not able to effectively conduct oversight."[108]

Perhaps no other aspect of the TSA's expanded security checkpoint procedures has come under more intensive scrutiny than the use of Advanced Imaging Technology (AIT) or "body scanners"—equipment that continues to be extensively utilized by the TSA in screening. While metal detectors have been in use at airports for decades, they have the obvious limitation of being unable to detect nonmetallic objects. After the attempts by the "shoe bomber" and the "underwear bomber," the TSA pressed forward with the implementation of two distinct types of body scanners to detect a greater range of potential threats. The first of these, called a millimeter-wave scanner, utilizes radio waves to search for "anomalies" on a person's body. The second type, "backscatter" X-ray scanners, utilize X-rays to examine passengers' bodies.[109]

U.S. officials were quick to publicly advocate the need for these scanners, pointing again to the threat posed by terrorists on commercial aircraft. Unlike the other policies and programs mentioned above, however, the implementation of scanners in airports received intense and immediate criticism—particularly with respect to privacy. Despite these concerns, the TSA rolled out the scanners in airports across the country all the while downplaying or dismissing privacy concerns completely. Speaking about the scanners, former TSA chief John Pistole said, "the reason we are doing these types of pat-downs and using the advanced imagery technology is trying to take the latest intelligence and how we know al Qaeda and affiliates want to hurt us."[110] Officials also argued that the scanners were (and are) the most effective means to detect hidden weapons—particularly those utilized by the "shoe" and "underwear bomber."

This is captured clearly in the statements of TSA spokesman Nicholas Kimball in 2010 when he stated, "the bottom line is that we are now able to detect all types of the most dangerous weapons—nonmetallic explosive devices."[111] Referring specifically to the Christmas Day bomber and his use of PETN, former homeland security secretary Michael Chertoff said the use of AIT, had it "been deployed . . . would pick up this kind of device."[112] Officials boasted of the machines' capabilities. Speaking less than a year after the failed Christmas Day bombing, TSA spokesman Greg Soule said, "This year alone, the use of advanced imaging technology has led to the detection of over 130 prohibited, illegal, or dangerous items," though he offered no context as to whether any of these were linked to attempted acts of terror.[113]

Whether these machines are actually effective, however, is far from clear. The TSA routinely fails to apprehend bomb-making materials and other hazardous items during inspections of passengers. In 2017, the DHS ran undercover tests of multiple airport security checkpoints and reported a remarkable failure rate. When asked by ABC News whether the failure rate was 80 percent (as had been reported), they were told such an estimate was "in the ballpark."[114] During similar tests in 2017, teams with the DHS were able to smuggle banned materials through TSA checkpoints in 67 of the 70 drills conducted.[115]

There are other issues with the capabilities of the scanners. Body scanners are unable to see inside an individual's body (though backscatter scanners can penetrate skin), making them unable to detect objects hidden inside body cavities. Just months after the attempted Christmas Day attack, a GAO report raised questions regarding the machines' efficacy—even in their ability to prevent the precise type of attack that spawned their increased use. The report states that "it is unclear whether the [body scanners] would have detected the weapon used in the December 2009 incident."[116]

Once again illustrating the use of secrecy in matters of "security" to prevent public scrutiny, the Obama administration denied a request made by Iowa Senator Chuck Grassley to release a GAO report on the efficacy of the scanners, stating that the results of GAO tests were "classified." The unclassified summary of the report states that after evaluating the TSA's use of AIT, liquid screening, and TSO performance, "we identified vulnerabilities in the screening process . . . at the eight domestic airports where we conducted testing. . . . The number of tests conducted, the names of the airports tested, and the quantitative and qualitative results of our testing are classified."[117] Speaking on the report and the administration's unwillingness to release the results, Grassley (R-IA) said, "Keeping the results secret will accomplish one thing . . . it will ensure the public has no idea how effective our airport screening strategy is."[118]

Soon after the body scanners began being utilized at more airports, a coalition of twenty-four privacy organizations, including the Electronic

Privacy Information Center (EPIC) and the American Civil Liberties Union (ACLU), began to challenge their use. In a letter to homeland security secretary Janet Napolitano, the coalition pointed out that "your agency will be capturing the naked photographs of millions of American air travelers suspected of no wrongdoing."[119] Officials quickly dismissed such concerns and criticized those concerned for passengers' privacy. "I do think privacy groups have some explaining to do" for pushing back against the TSA's use of body scanners, said Stewart Baker, a former homeland security official.[120]

When a "national opt-out day" was organized in November 2010 (the event encouraged passengers to opt for a full-body pat down as opposed to being scanned), then TSA administrator John Pistole referred to such an action as "irresponsible" and worked to place individuals into clear "in groups" and "out groups." Those who acquiesced to the scanners were helping to combat and defeat terrorism while those who objected were actively undermining public safety. He pointed to the machines' purported efficacy and the attempted bombing the year before. "It is irresponsible for a group to suggest travelers opt out of the very screening that could prevent an attack using non-metallic explosives. . . . I understand the serious threats our nation faces and the security measures we must implement to thwart potential attacks. This technology . . . is vital to aviation security and a critical measure to thwart potential terrorist attacks."[121]

Officials were keen to point out that images of passengers would not be stored and that anonymity would be protected. Before the expanded use of the scanners, a TSA press release in 2008 stated that "passenger privacy is ensured through the anonymity of the image. . . . The image won't be stored, transmitted or printed, and deleted immediately once viewed. In fact, the machines have zero storage capability."[122] Despite these and other assurances, it was quickly revealed that the machines *did* in fact have storage capabilities. As of 2010, a known thirty-five thousand images were stored in a courthouse in Florida.[123] Owing again to the lack of information made available to citizens, media, and other officials, it is unknown whether these images are still being stored, whether additional images were warehoused, and, if so, when and where.

Despite legal challenges for the government to release the images for scrutiny, a judge ruled that officials could withhold the images in the name of national security. According to court documents, releasing the images would expose "TSA's processes, routines, vulnerabilities . . . and the limitations on TSA's capabilities."[124] The TSA further argued that the images were stored solely for "training purposes." Writing on the issue, journalist Chris Mellor summarized the implications as follows. "So that leaves us with full body scanners that can capture strip search scanned images of people . . . and export them. . . . That leaves privacy campaigners salivating at the mouth with the possibilities of abuse, and the TSA with much egg on its face for issuing misleading statements."[125]

Issues of privacy are often dismissed in the name of security from terrorist threats. But this neglects the fact that there are multiple margins of security. Threats from terrorism are one margin on which safety can be compromised. But personal violations against individuals by government are another threat to personal safety. This became evident when the TSA discontinued the use of backscatter X-ray machines in 2015 and shifted to millimeter-wave technology.[126] As mentioned earlier, this technology detects anomalies on an individual's body. While seemingly less intrusive than the detailed images produced by backscatter technology, privacy advocates have questioned their use. In an amicus brief filed in 2016, the Competitive Enterprise Institute documented that "anomalies" that could cause a scanner to alarm included things like multiple layers of clothes, excess body fat, and sweat."[127] Passengers with cysts or hernias may also be flagged.[128] They argue that, as a result of these inefficiencies, "for many Americans, pat-downs are in effect a primary form of screening," as their bodies will seem an "anomaly" to the technology.[129]

The brief further describes a variety of abuses and injuries that occurred (and continue to occur) as a direct result of the scanners and the pat downs they spawn. Female, male, and transgender passengers have all reported sexual harassment. The brief likewise outlines a number of cases in which the security procedures of the TSA—particularly the use of pat downs triggered as a result of "anomalies" on scanners—have led to the humiliation of seniors and the disabled and possibly compromised the health and safety of passengers. In 2011, for example, retired special education teacher Thomas Sawyer went to the Detroit Metropolitan Airport to catch a flight to Orlando. Sawyer, a survivor of bladder cancer, was wearing a urostomy bag—a device that collects urine from an opening in his abdomen. Speaking of the bag, he said, "I have to wear special clothes and in order to mount the bag I have to seal a wafer to my stomach and then attach the bag. If the seal is broken, the urine can leak all over my body and clothes." When Sawyer went through the TSA's security scanner, the device alerted TSA agents to something unusual and he was selected for additional screening. In the course of a subsequent pat down, TSA agents broke the seal on his medical device and "urine started dribbling down my shirt and my leg and into my pants."[130] Less than a year later, Sawyer would suffer a similar humiliation at the same airport when screeners again broke the seal on his urostomy bag, once again leaving him covered in urine.[131]

Other cases are plentiful. Breast cancer survivor and flight attendant Cathy Bossi was forced to remove her prosthetic breast at the behest of a TSA agent in Charlotte Douglas International Airport. She'd undergone surgery as a result of her cancer.[132] When three-year-old Mandy Simmons was reluctant to relinquish her stuffed teddy bear to be scanned in 2008, she was flagged for additional screening. In a video taken of the incident, the child can be seen sobbing and screaming at agents to "stop touching me!"[133] A California mother was awarded a $75,000 settlement after TSA agents in Arizona detained her for carrying breast milk for her seven-month-old son despite the fact she had printed the TSA rules on the matter (passengers are allowed to carry larger quantities of breast milk) and had them in her bag.[134]

In addition to the utter mortification experienced by individuals with prosthetic breasts, colostomy bags, and other medical devices, the TSA scanners have proven to be dangerous to some individuals. In another incident, diabetic teenager Savannah Berry was forced to go through a body scanner despite carrying a letter from her physician saying she could not be scanned for medical reasons. After being scanned, she quickly noticed her $10,000 insulin pump, on which she relies to maintain appropriate blood sugar levels, was not working properly. She in turn called her mother who, in consulting with the manufacturer, said the scanner could damage the pump's software, causing it to malfunction.[135] In response to questions from the *Huffington Post* about the incident, the TSA seemed to place blame on the passenger, saying, "Signage posted at security checkpoints informs passengers that advanced imaging technology screening is optional for all passengers, including those traveling with medical devices."[136] Speaking of the incident, a staff attorney for the American Diabetes Association stated cases like Berry's "aren't isolated incidences."[137]

The specific people involved in these and similar situations probably do not feel more secure because of TSA procedures, at least not in their person. Even *if* they are safer from the threat of terrorism—a questionable assumption given the data available—the price they pay in terms of reduced security on other margins lowers the overall benefit of TSA security operations. Security is not limited to one arena. Attempts to enhance security on some margins (e.g., the threat of potential terrorist acts) may reduce security on other margins (e.g., reductions in security over one's personal privacy and health). This trade-off is even more relevant when one appreciates that the benefit of TSA procedures involves *potential* security from *potential* terrorists, while the costs in terms of reduced security in one's person are actual and concrete regardless of whether those dual potentialities are realized.

Wichita Airport Plot (2013)

The final case involves Terry Lee Loewen, an avionic technician at the Wichita Airport. As in the other cases, there is a clear disconnect between the nature of the threat as portrayed by officials and the reality of the planned attack. While the plot involved an airport, this was not the result of careful calculation on Loewen's part. Instead, the airport appears to have been a target of convenience.[138]

At age fifty-three, Loewen converted to Islam and later began to frequent radical websites.[139] On one site he connected with an FBI investigator, pretending to be a fellow radical Muslim. Over the course of several months, Loewen and the FBI investigator (and later a second investigator) would plot to blow up planes parked at the airport terminal with the intention of inflicting economic and psychological damage.

As he and one of the FBI employees drove to the airport to carry out the attack—utilizing a car bomb he had assisted one of the undercover agents in constructing with inert materials—Loewen was arrested and charged with several counts, including attempting to use a weapon of mass destruction. In exchange for a plea of "guilty" Loewen was sentenced to twenty years in prison, lifetime supervised release, and a mandatory special assessment of $100.[140]

Unlike some of the other cases, this incident does not appear to have spawned any known additions to checkpoint screening, as the plot did not involve posing as a passenger. This is not to imply, however, that officials failed to use the Loewen plot as a means of reinforcing the official narrative regarding the imminent terror threat. Officials treated the incident as "an outright terrorist attack" and sought to highlight the supposed threat posed not only by terror groups, but also "lone-wolf terrorists" (individuals who devise and perpetuate terror attacks alone and without any connection to a formal terror group).[141] Assistant attorney general John Carlin, for example, said that Loewen "utilized his privileged airport access to attempt a terrorist attack in Wichita."[142] Speaking on the issue of lone-wolf terrorism after the incident, special agent in charge Michael Kaste stated that Loewen and other lone wolves pose "a very serious threat to our nation's security."[143]

The problem with this narrative is twofold. As mentioned earlier, the threat from terrorism as a whole is incredibly small. The threat from lone-wolf terrorism is even less. A report from the FBI, for example, examined fifty-two cases of lone-offender terror attacks between 1972 and 2015. These offenders engaged in thirty-three acts of terrorism over the forty-three-year period, killing 258 and injuring 982.[144] Although Loewen identified as a Muslim and officials raised concerns about Islamic extremists, only nine of the twenty-six lone offenders who identified as religious claimed to be Muslim, and only 13 percent were Middle Eastern—the vast majority (65 percent) were white.[145] Second, the official narrative that Loewen acted as lone-wolf terrorist was patently false. Though Kaste referred to Loewen explicitly as a "lone wolf," he had substantial help from the two aforementioned FBI agents and, therefore, fails to meet the definition of a lone-wolf terrorist.

Despite this pointed language and the portrayal of Loewen as a dangerous lone wolf, there's a serious question as to whether he would have been capable of conducting any sort of attack without the assistance of the two undercover FBI agents. His lawyers, in fact, argued that the FBI's actions were equivalent to entrapment, though the judge dismissed a motion to throw out the case on such grounds.[146] Like the transatlantic terror plot uncovered in 2006, there was *no* possibility that Loewen's attack would have succeeded, as the FBI was carefully tracking him and working with him throughout his planning.

CONCLUSION

Citizens' fear of some external threat—whether real or perceived—sets the stage for state actors to expand their power over citizens.[147] As a result, governments may actively work to nurture and exploit fear among the broader population in order to serve their own narrow interests. The creation and expansion of the TSA in response to the 9/11 terror attacks is a prime example of this dynamic. From 9/11 onward, officials have used their privileged position and monopoly control over information to inflate the true threat posed by terrorism overall and the threat posed to passengers as they travel by air. By overstating the nature of the threat posed by a handful of terror plots and through the continued withholding of information regarding the efficacy of their programs, the TSA, DHS, and other agencies have effectively utilized a variety of propaganda to cultivate fear and, ultimately, support for their operations.

As the cases above illustrate, safety from terrorism is but one margin on which individuals may be made safer (even if the relative risk is already very small). In taking steps to provide this security, however, government makes people less secure on other margins (e.g., health and privacy of person and information). Through the control of information and the continued expansion of a number of questionable safety programs, officials *may* reduce the perceived threat of terrorism but probably decrease safety for some people on other margins.

The trade-off between margins of security is rarely, if ever, considered. Instead, government agencies narrowly focus on procedures that purport to stop the supposed existential threat from terrorists while dismissing, if not outright ignoring, the costs in terms of reduced security on other margins. Without the ability to obtain or critically assess the programs implemented and maintained by the TSA and other agencies, citizens are unable to determine whether these trade-offs are ones that they find beneficial or desirable.

CHAPTER 7

Propaganda Goes to Hollywood

In 2002, Lion Rock Productions and Metro Goldwyn Mayer (MGM) released the film *Windtalkers*. Directed and produced by John Woo and starring Academy Award–winning actor Nicolas Cage, the film follows U.S. Marine corporal Joseph Enders as he returns to active duty after surviving a battle in the Solomon Islands against the Imperial Japanese Army. Enders's new assignment is to protect Private Ben Yahzee, a Navajo code talker. Sergeant Pete "Ox" Henderson receives a similar order to protect code talker Private Charlie Whitehorse. The Navajo men, along with others, use their language as an effective means of coding sensitive messages and protecting their contents from the Japanese. This code, according to the military, must be protected at all costs. As a result, Enders and Henderson are ordered to kill Privates Yahzee and Whitehorse if their capture appears imminent.

The story, while a work of fiction, does relate to actual people and events. During World War II, the Marine Corps selected twenty-nine Navajo men to serve as the Navajo code talkers. Using their unwritten language, the men created a code that assigned Navajo words to certain phrases and particular military tactics. According to the CIA, the code talkers could translate, transmit, and retranslate messages in mere minutes. During the invasion of Iwo Jima, the code talkers sent more than eight hundred messages—without an error. Their skills were used in "every major operation involving the Marines in the Pacific theater."[1]

The original screenplay for *Windtalkers* includes a scene in which a Marine called "the Dentist" sneaks across a battlefield full of dead Japanese soldiers. In the scene, the audience sees "the Dentist, bent over a dead Japanese soldier, doing what he does, relieving the dead of the gold in their mouth. The Dentist twists his bayonet, struggles to get the gold nugget out of the corpse's teeth."[2] As detailed by journalist David Robb, this is one of several scenes in *Windtalkers* that was included in the

140

original script but never made it into the film. The scene was jettisoned at the behest of the Department of Defense (DOD).

"This [the scene] has to go," read a memo from Captain Matt Morgan, head of the Marine Corps' film liaison office, to Phil Strub, the DOD's Hollywood liaison. "The [defiling of corpses] is un-Marine. . . . I recommend these characters be looting the dead for intelligence or military souvenirs—swords, knives, field glasses. Looting is still not cool, but more realistic and less brutal."[3] Morgan sent a memo to Terence Chang, director John Woo's production partner, stating that the DOD was unhappy with the character and his conduct. In the next version of the script, not only had the scene in question been removed, but the entire character of the Dentist was removed. Other scenes were also removed at the request of the DOD. In another original scene, Enders commits a war crime when he kills an injured Japanese soldier while he is attempting to surrender by burning him alive with a flamethrower. Morgan wrote another memo to Strub and another memo to Chang. The scene was cut.

The DOD also instructed that the film should downplay a critical aspect of the story—that Enders and Henderson were to kill the code talkers in the event they were likely to be captured. Officials at the Pentagon claimed that such an order had never been given in the true story of the World War II code talkers. A memo from Congress issued in 2000, however, stated explicitly that "this Code was so successful that some Code Talkers were guarded by fellow Marines *whose role was to kill them in case of imminent capture*."[4] "In the end," writes Robb of the debate over the orders to kill the code talkers and the portrayal of this order in the film, "producers [of the film] who had originally brought the project to MGM, had to reluctantly agree to tone down that angle if they wanted to get the military's assistance."[5]

Windtalkers is only one of numerous major motion pictures altered to fit the narrative and preferences of the DOD. Indeed, officials within the Pentagon, the Central Intelligence Agency (CIA), and the National Security Agency (NSA) exert incredible influence over film production. In addition to successfully pushing to change scripts, scrub characters, and alter plot lines, the agencies are also successful at preventing films deemed "too critical" of the military and the U.S. government from being created in the first place. Analyzing thousands of documents received through the Freedom of Information Act, researchers Matthew Alford and Tom Secker found that the U.S. government has worked behind the scenes on more than eight hundred major motion pictures and over one thousand television titles.[6]

This dynamic between the DOD and film studios is undeniable propaganda. By exerting control over characters, plot, and production, government officials are able to frame messages related to activities involving the U.S. government in a positive light and are able to effectively censor would-be detractors. Film and television provide an effective means of transmitting the desired materials to the American public. So pervasive is the influence of the government in film that any discussion of propaganda in the United States, whether historical or contemporary, would be incomplete without an examination of the role of film and the industry that produces mass entertainment. Film is particularly interesting, as it has been used to garner support for particular conflicts *and* utilized as a means of cultivating militarism and a broader "American" identity. In this way, we observe many parallels between film and the propaganda utilized in promoting the Iraq War, as well as similarities between film and the more generalized propaganda discussed in earlier chapters in the context of professional sports and the TSA.

A BRIEF HISTORY OF U.S. PROPAGANDA IN FILM 1915–1989

The relationship between the DOD and Hollywood has a long history. Todd Breasseale, a retired army officer and liaison to Hollywood, discussed the long-standing relationship between the two groups, noting that "the Army's been there since Hollywood was first built from the Los Angeles canyons and desert."[7]

One of the earliest examples of the entanglement between Hollywood and the military dates back to before World War I and one of the country's most controversial films ever produced—*The Birth of a Nation* (1915). Originally called *The Clansmen* after the Thomas Dixon Jr. book of the same title, the silent, three-hour epic follows the U.S. Civil War and the subsequent Reconstruction period. It portrays black men as sexually violent toward white women and the Ku Klux Klan (KKK) as a heroic fighting force. Directed by D. W. Griffith, a personal friend of President Woodrow Wilson, the film was only completed with assistance from army engineers and artillery from West Point.[8]

Though *Birth of a Nation* may have been the first film to receive assistance from the U.S. military, it would not be the last, nor would it be long before filmmakers sought assistance from the U.S. Armed Forces on a routine basis. In fact, by the time Griffith turned to the military again in 1924 for assistance with his film *America*, the relationship between the film industry and the military was well established. Secretary of War John Weeks approved Griffith's request for the use of one thousand cavalrymen to recreate a battle scene from the American Revolutionary War.[9]

In 1927, former World War I fighter pilot William Wellman directed Paramount Production's *Wings*. In making the film, Wellman utilized military facilities in Texas as well as "hundreds of Army pilots, troops, and technical advisors."[10] The film went on to win the first Academy Award for Best Picture and is remembered for its flying sequences.[11]

Assistance for films like *America*, *Wings*, and numerous others was made possible by President Wilson's Executive Order 2594. Signed on April 13, 1917, the order established the Committee on Public Information (CPI) with the goal of shaping public opinion in support of the war. The committee's activities influenced a wide range of American media, including film. From its inception until its repeal following the conclusion of World War I, the CPI reviewed thousands of films. William Bradley, head of the National Association of the Motion Picture Industry at the time, stated pointedly why the government sought to use film and the motion picture industry as a means of transmitting propaganda. "The motion picture," he said, "can be the most wonderful system for spreading national propaganda at little or no cost."[12] And supply propaganda they did.

Discussing the role that Hollywood played in broadcasting the government's message domestically and abroad, George Creel, head of the CPI, wrote in 1920 that "motion pictures played a great part . . . ranking as a major activity."[13] He went on to emphasize how film provided a means of coordinating disparate groups around the government's central message—that American involvement in the war was desirable and good. "To millions unable to read," Creel wrote, "to literate millions unreached by newspaper or magazine, to city audiences and village crowds, the screen carried the story of America, flashing the power of our army and navy, showing our natural resources, our industrial processes, our war spirit, and our national life."[14]

Discussing the work of the committee, Creel made clear the relationship with film studios, noting that production companies were willing and eager to maintain their cozy relationship with government officials by making changes to their products.

The spirit of co-operation reduced the element of friction to a minimum. Oftentimes it was the case that a picture could be made helpful [from the perspective of the CPI] by a change in title or elimination of a scene, and in no instance did a producer fail to make the alterations suggested. . . . During its [the CPI's] existence . . . more than eight thousand motion pictures were reviewed.[15]

A similar dynamic existed during World War II. In June of 1942, President Franklin D. Roosevelt signed Executive Order 9182 authorizing the creation of the Office of War Information (OWI).[16] The OWI's mission was to create—through a variety of media, including film—information programs surrounding the conflict. Like the CPI before it, the OWI sought to garner public support for the government's wartime activities.

As part of its activities, the OWI formed the Bureau of Motion Pictures (BMP) to "coordinate the production of entertainment features with patriotic, morale-boosting themes and messages about the 'American way of life,' the nature of the enemy and the allies, civilian responsibility on the home front, and the fighting forces themselves."[17] OWI director Elmer Davis, a well-known journalist, discussed the important function of film and propaganda during the war and reaffirmed the points made by Creel some twenty years earlier. "The motion picture is the most powerful instrument of propaganda in the world, whether it tries to be or not. The easiest way to inject a propaganda idea into most people's minds is to let it go through the medium of an entertainment picture when they do not realize that they are being propagandized."[18]

From the outset, the OWI and the BMP sought to make films that would not only appeal to American and foreign audiences but also foster support for U.S. war efforts.[19] War was by no means a new topic for cinema, but before the creation of the OWI and the BMP, the treatment of the subject looked radically different. In mid-1942, for example, Hollywood studios were either considering or producing 213 films that dealt with war in some capacity. Despite the focus on war, the OWI was displeased with *how* Hollywood portrayed war and America's role in conflict. According to historians Clayton Koppes and Gregory Black, "disturbing to the OWI, Hollywood had simply grafted the war to conventional mystery and action plots or appropriated it [the war] as a backdrop for frothy musicals and flippant comedies. Interpretation of the war remained at a rudimentary level: the United States was fighting because it had been attacked, and it would win."[20] To remedy this perceived deficiency, the OWI created the "Government Information Manual for the Motion Picture Industry" (GIMMPI). The GIMMPI and the OWI exist, state the manual, "to assist the motion picture industry in its endeavor to inform the American people, via the screen, of the many problems attendant on the war program."[21]

The GIMMPI is a remarkably clear example of the government's commitment to the use of propaganda. Throughout the more than 150 pages, the OWI looked to use the film industry to disseminate purposely biased information to the American public to promote U.S. government political causes. By suggesting how various aspects of the war "might be dramatized," the OWI sought to limit dissent and any questioning of U.S. wartime activities.[22] The manual instructed filmmakers on how they ought to transmit and frame a number of issues related to the war, including the behavior of civilians (discussed in more detail below), with the explicit goals of cultivating fear of the enemy and coordinating citizens around government initiatives. Core propaganda techniques—appeals to authority, to patriotism, and to an "us versus them" mentality figure prominently throughout.

One particularly illustrative example of how the OWI sought to alter the messages received by the American public comes from a chapter in the GIMMPI related to the "home front," or the civilian population as it pertains to the military and the war effort as a whole.[23] The chapter discusses seven topics related to the home front that film producers should emphasize and provides guidance on how these topics should be portrayed. The manual states that films should push civilians to cooperate with civilian defense authorities, primarily by volunteering and obeying any orders coming from government. The chapter also encourages film studios to impress on the populace that *they* [the civilian population] are responsible for preventing inflation, though it doesn't explain how this is the case. The manual makes clear that participating in government war programs is "American" and patriotic. "In war-time," it reads, "every cent he [the civilian] spends on a luxury should have gone toward defense of his country. He must buy bonds. This is an *investment* in freedom—investment for his future security. He must pay his taxes promptly and cheerfully—pay in advance if he can afford it."[24]

Continuing, the chapter advises the film industry to portray rationing as necessary and patriotic. The manual makes clear that questioning these programs or the nature of the threat from abroad is un-American and aligns the dissenter with the enemy.

Every individual must be made to see the immediacy of the danger to *him*. Thus, when he is asked to make sacrifices, to give up certain pleasures or comforts, he considers it in the light of necessary and vital contributions to victory rather than as irksome restrictions. . . . The grumbler, the hoarder, the law-evader is an unwitting enemy. . . . We expect [the men at the front] to risk their lives. For our part we can do no less than make the few sacrifices asked of us [by the government].[25]

The effort to delineate a clear "us versus them" is evident in the OWI's instructions on how film studios should depict those seeking to evade the government's strict controls on rationed goods. The policies of the U.S. government, according to the manual, are just and necessary. Individuals looking to receive more than their "fair share" of goods, or those turning to black markets for goods and services, are to be portrayed as enemies of the war effort and, therefore, enemies of America.

They [those attacking the United States from within] are the buyers and sellers of "The Black Market." They are the bootleggers and purchasers of tires, gasoline, steel and irreplaceable critical materials, who evade the rationing laws and rules designed to assure the United States of sufficient military and industrial strength to win the battle for its existence and for the preservation of the rights of free men. . . . *They must be shown! They must learn that they are enemies of their nation!*[26]

There is nothing clever or smart or funny in getting around laws that were enacted to safeguard the country. . . . Our job—and particularly the job of motion pictures—is to shame the bootlegger and his customer out of existence. . . . *The bootlegger and his customer must be shown as what they are—Axis friends and our enemies.*[27]

The manual also encourages threat inflation by instructing film studios to portray the enemy as cunning and well equipped, both physically and mentally. The enemy is not to be portrayed as a bumbling caricature but instead as intelligent, worthy, and wholly threatening to the American way of life. Furthermore, the manual promotes the idea of ubiquitous domestic threats as well as the simple "us versus them" dichotomy to encourage film studios to assist in quashing any questioning or criticism of war-related policies.

But he [the enemy] is also in every town and every home in America, disguised as waste, inefficiency, disunity, insecurity, [and] ill-health, plotting to weaken the home front and thereby to weaken the production front and the fighting front—to decrease the total striking power of the nation.[28]

An unknown number of Axis agents are operating today in the United States, aided and abetted by Axis sympathizers and, worse yet, by loyal Americans who mistake rumor-mongering for honest criticism and thus give currency to Axis-inspired whispering campaigns.[29]

The manual also provides studios with the government-approved portrayals of waste and conservation efforts, manpower mobilization, Red Cross blood donation, black market operations, and nursing. The manual explicitly addresses how to portray the U.S. Armed Forces to children, stating that motion pictures "wield an incalculable influence on school-aged youngsters."[30] Ironically, the OWI's instructions include a section on how to depict the dangers of propaganda, stating that the "enemy" looks to spread false information and rumors that would demoralize the American populace and disrupt American cohesion.[31]

Like its predecessor, the CPI, the OWI was disbanded in 1945 following the end of the war. This did not mean that the government would cease
its work with the film industry, which continued during the Cold War. In
1949 the creation of the DOD came with the simultaneous formation of
the Motion Picture Production Office (MPPO), headed by Donald Baruch.
Baruch—who had produced four off-Broadway plays in the 1930s and
completed stints at Hal Roach Studios, MGM, and Paramount—worked
during the war as an officer in the Army/Air Force Office of Public Information.

According to military historian Lawrence Suid, "the office received
the mandate to take over the cooperation process from the individual [military branches] and supervise the details of assistance, thereby
regulating the armed forces' zealous pursuit of film roles."[32] Suid goes
on to note that "throughout the 1950s each [military branch] had virtually a blank check to provide assistance [to Hollywood studios]. . . .
Filmmakers received as much help on any movie as a service's public
affairs office . . . decided served its best interest."[33] In discussing the
role Baruch played in the film industry over the next four decades, the
National Archives state that "Baruch reviewed movie and television
scripts to make recommendations on whether or not the DoD should
agree to cooperate with proposed [projects] that sought military assistance for their production."[34]

The purpose of the relationship was clear from the DOD's perspective. Projects receiving support from the DOD were to portray the agency
and those involved with it in a positive light. Negative portrayals would
not be supported. DOD Instruction 5410.15, dated November 3, 1966,
outlines six principles "governing assistance to non-government audio-
visual media."[35] The first is particularly relevant and demonstrates how
officials sought to use popular cinema as a means to convey positive
messages about U.S. government activities. It states the project will
"benefit the DOD or otherwise be in the national interest," be based
on "authenticity of the portrayal of military operations, historical incidents, persons or places depicting the true nature of military life," and
be in "compliance with accepted standards of dignity and propriety in
the industry."[36]

Under Baruch's leadership, the entanglements between the DOD and major Hollywood studios remained strong. Hundreds of films, from *20,000 Leagues under the Sea* (1954) to *Indiana Jones and the Last Crusade* (1989) utilized the MPPO in order to obtain assistance for their projects. In exchange for the DOD's personnel and material, members of the film industry relinquished autonomy over their projects, making changes at the behest of Baruch and his office. Suid's analysis indicates that from the time Baruch assumed his position in 1949 until his retirement in 1989, the DOD sponsored dozens of films, including thirteen features by Columbia Pictures, seven MGM productions, eleven films by Paramount, fifteen by Twentieth Century Fox, fifteen by Universal Studios, and sixteen by Warner Brothers. Of the films sponsored, the army participated in the production of fifty-two films, and the Navy provided support for thirty-six. The Marines cooperated on twenty-seven projects, and the Air Force was involved with twenty.[37]

Most of these films received what Suid refers to as "complete cooperation," meaning the films were able to use military personnel, equipment, locations, and technical advice. Another nine received "limited cooperation," with access to locales, some personnel, and technical advice. Two films received "courtesy cooperation" and received technical advice or combat footage. Of the films Suid examined from this period, request for military involvement was denied in twenty-four cases and was not requested in twenty-five.[38] Unsurprisingly, many of the films that received cooperation related directly to contemporary U.S. foreign policy, namely the Korean War, the Vietnam War, and the Cold War more broadly.

What is equally interesting, however, are those films addressing these conflicts that did *not* receive DOD support despite requests for assistance. Films like *Apocalypse Now, The Bedford Incident, Blue Thunder, Coming Home, The Deer Hunter, Fail Safe, Go Tell the Spartans, Platoon, Rolling Thunder, Seven Days in May, WarGames,* and *War Hunt* were all denied DOD support. Although these films addressed the same issues as those that received cooperation, they differ in that each is either critical of the aforementioned U.S. policies, shows the DOD or military personnel in an unflattering light, or otherwise portrays conflict in ways unpleasing to the DOD.

One of the films that attained major critical and financial success, *Platoon*, was denied any and all support from the DOD. The film's director, Oliver Stone, followed a script he wrote in 1975 based on his combat experiences in Vietnam. A confidential memo from the army's public affairs staff dated June 28, 1984, reads, "We have reviewed the script . . . the Army cannot support it as written. . . . The script presents an unfair and inaccurate view of the Army. There are numerous problem areas in the script. They include: the murder and rape of innocent Vietnamese villagers by U.S. soldiers, the coldblooded murder of one U.S. soldier by another, rampant drug abuse, the stereotyping of black soldiers and the portrayal of the majority of soldiers as illiterate delinquents."[39]

Despite claims by the DOD that such actions were unfair or inaccurate, such atrocities absolutely occurred. In March 1968, for example, Army soldiers brutally murdered civilians, including men, women, and children, in the Vietnamese village of My Lai. Some of the women and girls were raped before their executions. Afterward, the soldiers burned the village, destroyed food stores and livestock, and tainted the water supply.[40] Drug use among servicemen was a major problem during the Vietnam War. In fact, in 1971 the DOD reported that 51 percent of the armed forces had smoked marijuana. Some 31 percent has used drugs like LSD, mescaline, or hallucinogenic mushrooms. Another 28 percent had used drugs like cocaine and heroin.[41] With respect to literacy, in 1966 secretary of defense Robert McNamara announced a plan for the military to recruit men who had been rejected for service based on their Armed Forces Qualification Test (AFQT) and to enlist some one hundred thousand low-literacy recruits per year. These men would come to be known as "McNamara's Moron Corps."[42]

Issues of racism and discrimination were very much relevant in the lives of black soldiers in Vietnam. Reflecting on watching films on Vietnam, Wallace Terry, the Vietnam correspondent for *Time* magazine between 1967 and 1969, said, "I find it amusing to see a Vietnam movie and the white guys are popping their fingers to black music. That just didn't happen. This is revisionism."[43]

The silver screen was not the only entertainment genre to seek the assistance of Baruch and the MPPO. Numerous television shows submitted proposals, scripts, and other materials to the office and made changes in order to obtain the DOD's assistance. To give but one example, Warner Brothers contacted Baruch in 1977 for assistance on the production of "Trouble in Paradise" for the Wonder Woman Series. Responding to the request from the studio, Baruch outlined the specific changes he required before assistance would be granted. In the letter, dated July 26, Baruch outlined four script changes.

No objections are interposed to Navy assisting by making available the bridge of a destroyer for filming sequences provided the following script changes are accomplished:

1. Page 2—delete the jokes during the transmission between aircraft and show facility, i.e., "Tell Sparks I said to stop drinking on the job. Unless I happen to be there."

2. Page 3—delete reference to that was just a cover. Also delete reference to *neutron*, suggest "nuclear" instead.

3. Page 4—delete or rewrite exchange with Southern, Diana, and Atkinson to drop references to neutron bomb and its awesomeness but necessary to maintain our country's defense.

4. Page 60—delete "neutron" in Atkinson's speech.[44]

The letter concludes with a note at the bottom, "Advised, by phone, Richard Vane, location manager, Warner Bros.; he saw no problem and would get changes made [to the script]."[45]

Other examples abound. In addition to assisting with entertainment for adult audiences, the DOD also influenced a variety of children's programs including American classics like *Lassie* (1954–1973, also known as *Jeff's Collie* and *Timmy and Lassie*). Seeking assistance, producers of the show wrote the DOD in 1961. In the proposed episode, Lassie, the canine heroine, saves the day by uncovering the mystery of a crashed military aircraft. In the original version of the script, an army L-19 reconnaissance aircraft crashed as the result of a correctable design flaw. "We suggest the L-19 be depicted as having encountered unpredictable icing conditions which weighted the wings," Major William Ellington of the Pentagon Film Office wrote to producers. "The latter condition [as opposed to a design flaw] could be interpreted as causing the mysterious sound oscillations which could only be heard by Lassie." He continued, "If you find that you are able to make the suggested changes, we feel that we will be able to offer you full [DOD] cooperation."[46] According to Robb, "the producers [of Lassie] not only made the changes, but they adopted Major Ellington's proposed dialogue, virtually word for word."[47]

In his analysis of the DOD's involvement with Hollywood, Robb highlights how the entanglements between the DOD and major producers of film and television projects resulted in fundamental changes to the entertainment products consumed by the American public. Writing on the aforementioned episode of *Lassie*, for example, Robb notes that the objections of the military—and the desire for military cooperation—all but completely sterilized the critical message of the show.

The new dialogue written by the military did two things. It not only provided a new explanation for the crash—unpredictable icing (no one to blame), but it also changed the whole point of the original story, which was *not* that Lassie solved a mystery, but rather, that in solving the mystery, she had saved lives—her whole reason for being.

The last line in the synopsis for the original script says that "Lassie solves the mystery and no lives will be endangered because of it." But that last part was taken out by the military. In the script approved by the army, Lassie is still a good detective, but she is no longer a hero because no lives have been saved by her actions.

Is this a proper role for the military—to make Lassie look less heroic so that the military will look better instead? Don't they have anything better to do with taxpayers' money?[48]

The relationship between the military and Hollywood would continue throughout the Cold War. Baruch retired in 1989, and Phil Strub assumed his role. Based on the films studied by Suid—from 1990 to 2001—the DOD continued to provide support for a number of studios including Disney, DreamWorks, HBO, MGM, Paramount, Showtime, Sony, Touchstone Pictures, Twentieth Century Fox, Universal Studios, and Warner Brothers. The Army would provide support to most films, followed by the Navy, Marines, and the Air Force. Of the films reviewed, seventeen received "full cooperation," one "limited cooperation," and five "courtesy cooperation." DOD assistance was not requested or required for twelve films, and support was denied for eight projects.[49] With the long history of entanglements between the U.S. military and the entertainment industry, the stage was set for Hollywood to play a central role in propaganda dissemination following the 9/11 attacks.

HOLLYWOOD AND THE PENTAGON POST-9/11

The War in Iraq and the War on Terror

As history indicates, Hollywood and government officials—particularly within the DOD—have mutually benefitted from collaboration. Given the long history of their relationship, it makes sense that this would continue following the 9/11 attacks.[50] Just as the DOD sought to use their influence to frame the portrayal of conflicts like World War II, Vietnam, and the Cold War, so, too, have officials looked to influence studios to offer a favorable portrayal of the Iraq War and the war on terror. Just as the DOD looked to cultivate "American" ideals and the notion of American exceptionalism before 9/11, such tactics continued to be employed after the attacks.

The DOD saw Hollywood as a means to spread the messages of just and righteous war while reinforcing the necessity of a range of government activities, both domestically and abroad. After the attacks, officials quickly connected with major Hollywood players in an effort to disseminate such ideas to the broader public. In November 2001, for example, President Bush's senior advisor and deputy chief of staff Karl Rove met with the chairman of the Motion Picture Association of America (MPAA) Jack Valenti and other industry insiders, including the chair of Paramount Pictures's film division, in Beverly Hills, California.[51] Then White House spokesman Ari Fleischer said that a number of major television and film studios were expected to attend, including CBS television, Viacom, Showtime, DreamWorks, HBO, and MGM. Speaking of the meeting, Fleischer stated, "across America every community is looking to pitch in [after the attacks], Hollywood included, and this White House is pleased."[52] Karl Rove echoed these sentiments, saying that "these people [in Hollywood production studios], like every other American, feel strongly about the events of 11 September and the need to see this war through to its victorious conclusion."[53]

Though officials were careful to state that they were not interested in dictating content, Rove offered the executives and industry representatives in attendance a seven-point message from the White House. While the specifics differed from what the BMP offered to film studios during World War II, there were certainly parallels. Film studios should portray events surrounding current policy in particular ways to the American public and foreign audiences. The position of the U.S. government is good, noble, and serves the broader public interest, and supporting these ends requires supporting the government's policies.

Rove presented seven points to industry representatives: (1) the war is against terrorism, not Islam, (2) Americans must be called to national service, (3) Americans should support the troops, (4) the war on terror is global and, as such, requires a global response, (5) the war on terror is a war against evil, (6) American children must be reassured, and (7) the narrative behind the war effort should be accurate and honest.[54] It is clear from statements of industry leaders who participated in the meeting that major producers of film and television were not just willing to assist officials with their message—they would also be very careful to adopt their proposed guidelines for framing content (and later their edits).

From the outset, film studios worked closely with officials to transmit and frame the messages in major entertainment to align with the goals of the Bush administration. Screenwriter, director, and producer Bryce Zabel stated this idea clearly, noting how support for the war on terror became synonymous with being "American." "What we are excited about is neither propaganda nor censorship," he said. "The word I like is advocacy. We are willing to volunteer to become advocates for the American message."[55] This "volunteerism" and "advocacy," however, came at the price of relinquishing autonomy in the creation of film and television projects to become an informal propaganda arm of the U.S. government.

The studios would offer control and editorial power to primarily one individual—Phil Strub. As noted above, Strub assumed the role of director of entertainment media for the DOD after Baruch's retirement in 1989. Strub's involvement with film studios from the late 1980s to at least the late 2010s is critical for understanding the scale and scope of the interactions between film studios and the DOD in the post-9/11 period.

The film *Windtalkers,* discussed at the beginning of this chapter, is but one of many films made possible through cooperation with (and capitulation to the demands of) the DOD. In fact, Strub and his team would have a hand in more than 130 films between 2001 and 2017 alone. (A list of these films is included in the appendix.)[56] In addition to these films, Strub's office also had a hand in nearly one thousand television programs between 2004 and 2011, including shows like *The 700 Club, American Chopper, America's Next Top Model,* the *Country Music Awards, Ellen, Extreme Makeover: Weight Loss Edition, Grey's Anatomy, Ice Road Truckers, Iron Chef, Man vs. Food,* the *Miss America Pageant, MTV's True Life, Myth Busters, NCIS, Say Yes to the Dress, Snoop Dogg's Father Hood, The Price Is Right,* and *Wheel of Fortune,* among others.[57]

The dynamics at play during the post-9/11 period represent a continuation of the historical entanglement of Hollywood and the DOD. Just as earlier films were altered at the behest of the DOD to fit their desired narrative, films in the post-9/11 period were no different. Officials have been quick to push back against the idea that they unduly influence Hollywood. The suggestions of the DOD, they argue, are merely that—suggestions. If a studio doesn't want to make the suggested change, they can simply part ways with the DOD. This is captured clearly in a statement from Phil Strub, "There is no way we are going to go in and to steamroll anyone's vision [for a project]. They will just tell us to drop dead and go away."[58]

The reality is often much different than this statement suggests. In fact, many studios have come to *rely* on DOD support in order to successfully complete film projects. Without the DOD's blessing (and offer of equipment and personnel), some projects become financially untenable such that studios decide to alter the underlying messages of their work. The result is that films, which may have once had a critical or thoughtful message related to U.S. foreign policy, instead promote an uncritical or wholly positive view of the activities of the U.S. government. This may be clearly observed in examining films related to the war in Iraq. As discussed (see chaps. 3 and 4), the Bush administration went to great lengths to garner support for the war both before the invasion and afterward. It should come as no surprise, then, that Strub and other officials were keen to offer assistance to films that portrayed the war and occupation positively while rebuffing those projects that failed to show the war as necessary and noble.

Writing on the contemporary relationship between Hollywood and the Pentagon, journalist Julian Barnes noted that "Army officials are eager to work with filmmakers making serious movies about Iraq—the kind of pictures that have the power to shape the public's view of the war and its warriors."[59] In the same article, Barnes quotes Paul Haggis, the writer and director of the Iraq War film *In the Valley of Elah*. The film, starring Charlize Theron and Tommy Lee Jones, follows a retired army sergeant (Jones) searching for his son after his return from Iraq. After submitting the script for the film to the DOD, producers received twenty-one pages of objections to the film. Haggis stated that producers told him the pro-testations of the DOD meant they wouldn't support the project. In a clear illustration of the influence that the DOD attempts to exert over the film industry, Haggis said, "If they [the DOD] had reasonable input I would have taken it. But I am not there to do publicity for the Army. I am there to do a movie as I see true."[60] He said of the DOD's involvement with *In the Valley of Elah*, "They [the DOD] are trying to put the best spin on what they are doing. Of course, they want to publicize what is good. But it doesn't mean it's true."[61]

Throughout the war on terror, particularly with respect to the wars in Iraq and Afghanistan, the DOD sought to influence Hollywood in a delib-erate effort to frame and transmit messages to the public with the goal of influencing public attitudes regarding US government policies. Speaking in an interview on National Public Radio in 2008, Julian Barnes discussed the importance of pro-American war films for the U.S. government.

The Iraq war movies are very important to the military. They don't like how the war is being portrayed, particularly how the soldiers are being portrayed. And many people, not everyone, but many people within the military think that if they can persuade Hollywood to present a more nuanced picture of a soldier who served in Iraq, that it will affect public attitudes toward soldiers.[62]

The host of the program then asked Barnes about the number of films the DOD was involved in related to Iraq and Afghanistan at that time, pointing to how the Pentagon worked to "control the message about the war in Iraq" using some of the propaganda tactics discussed in earlier chapters. Barnes responded,

Well, the military would say no. I mean, they would say, look, we're just trying to get a more multidimensional picture out there, that we're just striving for accuracy. We're not trying to censure anyone. We're not trying to spin anyone. Hollywood directors, though, some of them have a different view. They think that the military is trying to push a positive view of the Iraq war, or a positive view of how they're treating soldiers.[63]

It's reasonable to think officials in the DOD would be hesitant to offer assistance to film studios producing entertainment that reflects badly on the military or the U.S. government's foreign policy. This means that even if they aren't explicitly intending to produce propaganda, the government's involvement in the entertainment industry will naturally lead to a pro-military and pro-U.S. foreign policy bias.

Transformers: More Than Meets the Eye

Beyond specific conflicts, the DOD also utilizes its relationship with Hollywood to advance a positive general portrayal of the military to both Americans and foreigners. This is perhaps best illustrated by an unlikely set of films—*Transformers* (2007) and *Transformers: Revenge of the Fallen* (2009). These films don't portray any real-world conflict but are instead based on the Hasbro children's toys from the 1980s. The films, products of collaboration between Paramount, di Bonaventura, and DreamWorks, tell the simple story of an American teenager Sam Witwicky (Shia LeBeouf).

Threatened by evil alien robots—the Decepticons—Sam, his love interest Mikaela Banes (Megan Fox), and a group of good alien robots—the Autobots—join forces with the U.S. military in a battle between good and evil. Together, Sam, Mikaela, the Autobots, and the DOD defeat the Decepticons, saving America and the world—all while showcasing a cornucopia of military hardware and nearly every branch of the U.S. Armed Forces.

Production on the two films was only possible as the result of intensive support from the DOD. Ian Bryce, one of the producers of *Transformers*, concisely captures the nature of the relationship between the DOD and film studios. "Without the superb military support we've gotten on this film, it would be an entirely different looking film. We want to cooperate with the Pentagon to show them off in the most positive light, and the Pentagon likewise wants to give us the resources to be able to do just that."[64]

The films' director, Michael Bay, expressed similar sentiments. "I was dead set on getting military cooperation," he said. "I've worked with the Department of Defense on several projects . . . so I already knew many of their ground rules." The statements by Bryce and Bay make clear what is known throughout Hollywood—Pentagon cooperation requires an unquestioningly positive portrayal of the U.S. military.

Transformers and *Transformers: Revenge of the Fallen* are particularly germane examples of the DOD-Hollywood relationship in that these films represent the largest collaboration between the two groups in history. The films received assistance from four of the five branches of the military (only the Coast Guard was absent from the films). Tanner Mirrlees, a communications and digital media studies scholar, discusses the films within the broader context of "militainment"—military advertisement packaged as benign entertainment. He notes that both films offer "special thanks" in their credits to a cadre of individuals within the Pentagon hierarchy and the film liaison offices as well as the "men and women of the U.S. Armed Forces."[65] He further highlights how nearly every military role—including those of extras—was played by military personnel—with the idea of turning "real heroes" returning from combat in Iraq into "reel heroes."

Those DOD members not on screen worked as active crewmembers, coordinating action shots and training cast and crew.[66] The films utilize and show off a variety of high-priced military hardware including the A-10 Thunderbolt II, AC-130 Gunship, Boeing VC-25, C-17 Globemaster III, CV-22 Osprey, C-130 Hercules, F-117 Nighthawk, F-22 Raptor, and the MQ-1 Predator—the unmanned aerial vehicle (UAV or "drone") utilized most extensively in the war on terror. *Revenge of the Fallen* also included the use of six F-16s, two Bradley tanks, 10 armored Humvees, two M-1 Abrams tanks, an M-270 Multiple Launch Rocket System, and a Sikorsky UH-60 Black Hawk helicopter.[67]

Mirrlees highlights precisely how these films benefit both the DOD and Hollywood producers, noting how the films paint a positively glowing picture of the U.S. Armed Forces and highlight contemporary military tactics as the pinnacle of military prowess.

These films make the DoD's personnel—from the top to the bottom of its hierarchy—look great and convey a "support the brass" and the "support the troops" message. The Secretary of Defense Keller (played by . . . Jon Voight) is smart, decisive, capable, and willing to adapt to new threats and battle circumstances easily. Upon learning that the threat to the world is not a traditional territorial state actor like Russia, China, or North Korea, but extraterrestrial robots, Keller responds calmly and reasonably, following procedures and sometimes adapting them as needed. The "boots on the ground" force is a multicultural team of special operations soldiers led by William Lennox (Josh Duhamel) and Robert Epps (Tyrese Gibson). Throughout [the films], these soldiers are depicted as smart, heroic, and committed to DoD to the extreme; they fight a technologically superior alien enemy flexibly, bravely, selflessly, and sacrifice themselves for the security of America and the human race. . . . These soldiers are victorious. . . . These films also depict DoD's doctrine of Network Centric Warfare (NCW).[68]

In addition, the themes of unity, obedience, and American exceptionalism are prominent throughout both films. Mirrlees, quoting Phil Strub, notes that, "Strub decries 'the enduring stereotype of the loner hero [soldier] who must succeed by disobeying orders, going outside the rules by being stupid,' so he was likely pleased with [the films'] depiction of soldiers working as a networked team to achieve victory."[69] Mirrlees continues, "Both [films] communicate American exceptionalism—the idea that the United States has a unique role to play in the world, to lead and shape it, to protect the world from threats to it. . . . [The films] portray . . . real countries like China and Russia . . . and then . . . fictional robot aliens . . . as the basis for legitimization of American military power and operations. . . . These films depict the United States as an exceptional military power, but one that is needed, a force for global good."[70]

Military cooperation on the *Transformers* franchise meant for the studios exactly what it meant for D. W. Griffith in the early 1900s—huge cost savings and access to equipment and personnel that would otherwise mean a less impressive (and probably less profitable) film. In return for positive portrayal of the military, filmmakers receive access to military hardware, personnel, and advice at little to no cost. Discussing the involvement of the Armed Forces in the *Transformers* franchise, journalist Peter Debruge noted that the production companies (with respect to *Transformers* and other films) don't "pay location fees or military personnel salaries though servicemen can take time off to serve as extras. . . . With a bit of creativity from the commanders involved, some maneuvers have actually been designated as training exercises and offered at no cost to filmmakers."[71] Captain Bryon McGarry, deputy director of the air force public affairs office, recalled one such exercise of F-16s simulating a low-level attack. "The flyover was very much the type of training the Air National Guard out of Kirkland AFB [Air Force Base] does every day. Only that day, Michael Bay and his cameras had a front row seat to the air power show."[72]

In his concluding remarks on the *Transformers* films as a form of militainment, Mirrlees identifies the films as works of propaganda. "The DoD uses public monies to create its own media and entertainment products that put it in a positive light and encourages private media to do the same. . . . DoD's assistance to T [*Transformers*] and TRF [*Transformers: Revenge of the Fallen*] are examples of federally funded propaganda."[73] Though the military vehemently denies that its involvement with film projects involves propaganda, it is difficult to take these claims seriously given the historical relationship between the military and Hollywood and the fact that the DOD's involvement is predicated on presenting preapproved information in a manner intended to advance the interests of the American government and military.

CONCLUSION

The Pentagon's involvement in the film industry is little more than propaganda packaged as mass entertainment. The DOD unapologetically favors and provides special treatment and assistance to those films that portray the U.S. military and its activities in a positive light while shunning those who do not. Phil Strub has been remarkably candid in his bias with respect to deciding which films will be offered support and which will not.

"I will plead guilty to bias in favor of the military. I wouldn't be able to look myself in the mirror and go to work every day if I didn't believe the military is a force for good. If a script comes to us portraying the military as a malign force, we won't provide support."[74]

The DOD's influence in film and television is particularly troubling from the perspective of checks and balances on government behavior and power. Media, in its various forms, has the capacity to play a critical role in mitigating propaganda by providing information and offering alternative perspectives to correct for information asymmetries between citizens and the government. Furthermore, genres like film and television provide an avenue through which new ideas reach the citizenry. The entanglements between the DOD and the entertainment industry undermine these functions of film and television by making Hollywood an informal public relations arm of the U.S. military. More troubling is that the role of government in shaping and influencing the information and messaging presented to the public is largely covert except for a brief mention in television and film credits.

Based on their long historical relationship, there is little doubt that the DOD will continue to provide assistance to film and television in exchange for influence over content.[75] The importance of these continued interactions cannot be understated. As highlighted by international relations scholar Mark Lacy,

the cinema becomes a space where "common sense" ideas about global politics and history are (re)produced and stories about what is acceptable behavior from states and individuals are naturalised and legitimated. It is a space where myths about history and the origins of the state are told to a populist audience. One can think of contemporary war films . . . that rewrite history into one where historical and moral ambiguity are replaced with certainty."[76]

In the American context, such revisions to both historical and current events will continue to occur at the behest of film liaison offices inside the DOD.

The Power of the Propagandized

Throughout history, governments have employed propaganda to influence and manipulate citizens. Present-day America is no different. As discussed in previous chapters, the post-9/11 "war on terror," which is entering its twentieth year with no end in sight, has been intertwined with government propaganda from the start. The ubiquity of government propaganda has both short-term and long-term consequences for a free society.

In the short-term, propaganda contributes to the adoption and persistence of policies that are not in the interests of many citizens. If the policies were in their interests, then the political elite would seek their genuine consent by making their case with an accurate presentation of the relevant information, and citizens would happily acquiesce. The use of propaganda by the state indicates that officials do not believe citizens will grant consent if provided with unbiased and complete information, meaning that policies purporting to serve the best interests of the citizenry may have the opposite effect.

In the long term, the institutionalized use of government propaganda threatens the foundations of a free society. As the Hoover Commission reported in 1949,

Whether the immediate purpose of Government propaganda is good or bad, the fact remains that individual liberty and free institutions cannot long survive when the vast powers of Government may be marshaled against the people to perpetuate a given policy or a particular group of office holders. Nor can freedom survive if all Government policies and programs are sustained by an overwhelming government propaganda.[1]

This runs counter to the idea that propaganda may be used in a noble manner to further the interests of citizens who may lack the knowledge or will to do so on their own.[2] As the Commission noted, even *if* we assume that propaganda is used benevolently, it still threatens liberty by empowering state actors at the expense of the citizenry.

Further, there is reason to believe that the first-best case of benevolent propaganda rarely holds. As economist Roger Koppl notes, "while the interests of participants in the entangled deep state [his term for the U.S. national security state] often conflict, members of the deep state share a common interest in maintaining the status quo of the political system independently of democratic processes."[3] Appreciating that those in power wish to maintain their privileged position in conjunction with the corrosive effects on the foundations of a society of self-governing citizens makes clear the long-term threat posed by propaganda. This is especially troublesome in liberal democratic societies because the use of state propaganda runs parallel to the operation of political institutions predicated on the rhetoric of openness, transparency, citizen governance, and consent.

Given the immediate and long-term problems associated with propaganda, the central challenge facing the American people today is as follows. The national security state imbues government officials with substantial powers. Officials can use these powers to pursue their own interests by advancing a culture of militarism. Checking this power is difficult because of the secrecy that permeates all corners of the security state. The severe information asymmetries between the American people and their government incentivizes the dissemination of state propaganda that is biased toward achieving the goals of those in power.

What can be done to overcome this challenge? In this concluding chapter, we critically consider four potential solutions to overcoming the information asymmetries that allow those in government to use propaganda. In doing so, we discuss the limitations of each solution as well as the conditions under which each alternative is likely to be effective.

SOLUTION I: GOVERNMENT LAWS

Self-constraint by those in power is one way to limit the deleterious effects of government propaganda. This involves members of the U.S. government passing and enforcing laws intended to check the behaviors of current and future officials. In the past, those in government passed some laws intended, at least in word, to limit the domestic use of state propaganda.[4]

Antipropaganda Statutes

In 1919, Congress passed a law (5 U.S. Code § 3107) restricting the use of "publicity experts" by federal agencies to influence policy. Specifically, the law stated that "appropriated funds may not be used to pay a publicity expert unless specifically appropriated for that purpose."[5] In that same year, Congress also passed another law (18 U.S. Code § 1913) intended to prevent agencies from using budget appropriations to influence government policy and limit the ability of agencies to use government funds to lobby members of Congress and the general public for favorable treatment. The statute stated that "No part of the money appropriated by any enactment of Congress shall, in the absence of express authorization by Congress, be used directly or indirectly to pay for any personal service, advertisement, telegram, telephone, letter, printed or written matter, or other device, intended or designed to influence in any manner a Member of Congress, a jurisdiction, or an official of any government, to favor, adopt, or oppose, by vote or otherwise, any legislation, law, ratification, policy, or appropriation."[6]

In 1948, Congress passed the U.S. Information and Educational Exchange Act (Public Law 80-402), also known as the Smith-Mundt Act. The act allowed the U.S. State Department to use congressional appropriations to broadcast information to foreign audiences. In response to the concerns of some senators regarding the negative effects of government propaganda at home, the act included a provision restricting the domestic dissemination of materials distributed abroad.

On the heels of the U.S. Senate's payola investigation in the 1950s and 1960s, Congress passed a law (47 U.S. Code § 317) requiring radio broadcasters to disclose funding sources. The statute states that "all matter broadcast by any radio station for which any money, service or other valuable consideration is directly or indirectly paid, or promised to or charged or accepted by, the station so broadcasting, from any person, shall, at the time the same is so broadcast, be announced as paid for or furnished, as the case may be, by such person."[7] The idea behind the law was that listeners would be able to identify the sponsor of a broadcast, including the government, which would provide context to the content being aired.

Finally, in 2000 Congress passed the Information Quality Act (Public Law 106-554), also known as the Data Quality Act. This act requires that the Office of Management and Budget (OMB) issue general guidance to federal agencies for "ensuring and maximizing the quality, objectivity, utility, and integrity" of publicly disseminated information.[8] It also requires each federal agency to establish guidelines for information quality and clear mechanisms for correcting information when there is a disjoint between the information disseminated and OMB guidelines. The purpose of this statute is to ensure that members of the public are provided with accurate and reliable information from federal agencies.

In principle, these laws place some parameters on the dissemination of information by U.S. government agencies. However, there are several key issues with these laws that limit their effectiveness in preventing the members of the government from disseminating propaganda as it pertains to matters of national security.

The Weakness of Government-Created Law

Currently, there is no single federal agency with the responsibility of overseeing the communication activities of other federal agencies to ensure that they are using congressional appropriations appropriately.[9] Absent mechanisms of proactive oversight, members of Congress must wait for a complaint to be filed and then work through the Government Accountability Office (GAO), which determines whether to pursue an investigation. Even if the GAO does decide to investigate a complaint, however, it lacks the power to impose penalties. Instead, the GAO must refer cases to the Department of Justice (DOJ), which determines whether to impose punishment. Since the DOJ is a federal executive department, the implication is that punishment for the dissemination of propaganda ultimately "requires executive branch action, and when it comes to propaganda, the executive branch has demonstrated little interest in punishing wayward executive agencies."[10] This reality significantly undermines the effectiveness of the aforementioned statutes in protecting citizens from the use, and abuse, of government propaganda.

There are additional issues. The notions of "propaganda" and "publicity expert" are not concretely defined in existing statutes and are determined on an ad hoc basis by the GAO. The result is that "thus interpreted, the laws prohibiting the hiring of publicity experts and the expenditure of appropriated funds on publicity and propaganda place very few limits on agency public relations activities. GAO findings of agency wrongdoing have been infrequent."[11] The lack of concrete definitions results in a significant amount of discretion on the part of the GAO as the enforcer of these laws. The interpretation of the language is so elastic that it is easy to make the case that government agencies rarely, if ever, engage in the production and dissemination of propaganda. In the rare instances where agencies are accused of engaging in propagandizing, they can use the broad and ill-defined language of the statutes as a defense of their actions.

Similar issues of definition and interpretation affect newer legislation, such as the Information Quality Act. The requirements of the act apply to information that is deemed "influential" for "important" public policy. But what constitutes "influential" and "important" is left ill-defined, granting significant scope for interpretation by both the agencies affected by the law and those enforcing the law.[12]

The ineffectiveness of the most recent legislation should not be surprising, as the earlier antilobbying statute (18 U.S. Code § 1913), passed in 1919, has been rendered entirely useless. To date, no one has been indicted under the law. The reality is that "the GAO has, in effect, held that an agency may lobby the public to support a program, a proposed reform, or to encourage the public to adopt a particular viewpoint."[13] This interpretation of the law creates an environment conducive to the dissemination of government propaganda. It has also set a precedent whereby subsequent legislation is viewed as toothless.

In the case of the Smith-Mundt Act, the language of the original statute relates to the activities of the U.S. Department of State. Since the Department of Defense (DOD) was not explicitly identified in the original act, it was unclear whether the law applied to its activities. Its inapplicability to the DOD was made clear in 2012, when Congress passed the Smith-Mundt Modernization Act (H.R. 5736).[14] In addition to lifting many of the constraints on the Department of State to broadcast information domestically, the act clearly states that the provisions "shall apply only to the Department of State and the Broadcasting Board of Governors and to no other department or agency of the Federal Government."[15] The result is that DOD activities are not subject to the law, granting space for those in the agency to propagandize the American public.

Taken together, the result is that the domestic statutes related to government-produced information are ineffective in protecting the public from the pernicious effects of state propaganda. In practice, government actors are legally able to disseminate symbols, images, and claims with little to no fear of legal recourse. This goes for agencies across the government, including those that constitute the national security state, which have an incentive to take advantage of significant information asymmetries to pursue their own goals.

There is no reason to believe that new, additional laws will change the status quo. When considering how to constrain the U.S. government's propaganda activities, Kevin Kosar, an analyst with the Congressional Research Service, wonders whether new laws would lead to less propaganda by government agencies. He concludes that "absent an infusion of antipropaganda prosecutorial zeal into the DOJ, the answer would appear to be 'not likely.'" He goes on to note that "executive agencies have an interest in aggressively promoting themselves and have shown themselves willing to do so in spite of the plain language of the law (inadequate though it may be) and Congress's wishes."[16]

Anthony de Jasay, a philosopher and economist, noted that a constitution is like "a chastity belt whose key is always within the wearer's reach."[17] This is certainly the case for those in the national security state, where existing incentives encourage maintaining and extending entrenched power while avoiding democratic deliberation and other constraints on that power. The main takeaway is that Americans cannot rely on government self-constraint to limit the dissemination of propaganda.

SOLUTION 2: WHISTLEBLOWERS

Whistleblowing, which refers to an insider revealing an organization's wrongdoings, can ameliorate the negative effects of propaganda and political opportunism.[18] The pervasive secrecy of the national security state enables those in power to engage in self-interested behaviors at the expense of those they supposedly represent. In disclosing information regarding the actions of government officials, whistleblowers play a key role in bridging the information gap between those in power and the citizenry. In doing so, whistleblowers reveal the partial, biased, or inaccurate information contained in state-produced propaganda.

From this perspective, whistleblowing can be understood as a "fire alarm," alerting citizens and legislators to opportunistic behavior by political actors.[19] This type of fire alarm is especially important given the aforementioned weaknesses in state-provided law pertaining to propaganda, including the absence of a dedicated agency to actively patrol the activities of other agencies for violations of existing statutes. In government agencies, there are three main barriers to external monitors—citizens, watchdog groups, and oversight committees—gaining information to prevent abuses of power. Whistleblowing helps to overcome each of the three.

The first barrier is the ability of outsiders to understand the internal operations of the agency and the nuances of the processes through which bureaucratic outcomes emerge. Outside monitors often lack basic information regarding the day-to-day operations of an agency, making monitoring difficult. Because whistleblowers are embedded in the daily operations of the bureau, they are better able to differentiate between normal operations and abuses.

The second barrier is that external monitors are often dependent on agencies to self-report information about their activities. This allows bureaucrats to strategically control the content and timing of information flows to serve their interests. Whistleblowers can mitigate this problem by revealing information that otherwise would be delayed, downplayed, or kept secret by bureaucrats.

The third barrier is that a large portion of the information related to national security state activities is classified and not available for review.[20]

Only a small number of members of Congress, for example, might have access to certain information regarding the government's surveillance activities. Even then, the information under consideration is that produced by the bureau, as previously discussed. In this case, whistleblowers serve as a means of revealing information regarding political opportunism to the public and legislators who otherwise would be excluded from accessing this information.

Because of these three barriers, whistleblowers are especially crucial for checking the national security state, where officials possess monopoly control over information pertaining to highly clandestine activities. This role was succinctly captured by former U.S. attorney general Eric Holder in relation to the Edward Snowden revelations, when he noted that "we can certainly argue about the way in which Snowden did what he did, but I think that he actually performed a public service by raising the debate that we engaged in and by the changes that we made."[21] A key part of whistleblower effectiveness in providing this "public service" is the incentives they face to reveal information when they observe potential opportunism.

Laws Related to Whistleblower Protection

The effectiveness of whistleblowers will depend on their ability to reveal information to relevant parties. The channels of communication can be internal—that is, reporting wrongdoing through procedures within government—or external—that is, revealing information to the media or public. Over the past century, the members of the U.S. government have enacted laws to create internal channels for whistleblowers to report wrongdoing.

The Lloyd–La Follette Act of 1912 gave federal employees the ability to communicate information directly to Congress instead of having to obtain supervisor permission to do so. The intention was to facilitate the transfer of information to Congress while removing the ability of supervisors to strategically block employees from reporting on activities that were potentially damaging to the bureau or its leaders. The Civil Service Reform Act of 1978 established the Merit Systems Protection Board (MSPB), a quasi-judicial agency, to discourage retaliation against federal employees for coming forward with information about wrongdoing. This allows federal employees who believe they are mistreated to file an appeal with the MSPB, who investigates the claim. The Whistleblower Protection Act of 1989 clarified the procedures for reporting potential retaliation for engaging in whistleblowing.

Despite these laws, there are numerous historical cases where whistleblowers related to the national security state chose to forgo internal channels and publicly sound the alarm on government opportunism (e.g., Daniel Ellsberg, Mark Felt, Thomas Tamm, Thomas Drake, and Edward Snowden). These whistleblowers brought information directly to the public via the media. In order to understand why some whistleblowers choose external versus internal channels to reveal information, it is important to understand the incentives facing whistleblowers, which are shaped by the unique rules governing the national security state.

The aforementioned whistleblower protection laws do not apply to a significant portion of the national security state, which is instead covered by the following legislation. The Intelligence Community Whistleblower Protection Act of 1998 established a chain of command for reporting misconduct to Congress related to classified information. The whistleblower first reports the wrongdoing to the agency's inspector general, who reports it to the agency head, who then determines whether to share the information with Congress. One issue with this process is that if the agency head is involved in opportunism, or if the agency head wants to protect their agency from negative publicity, they can strategically withhold information from Congress.

Because the Intelligence Community Whistleblower Protection Act did not offer protection against retaliation, President Obama signed Presidential Policy Directive 19 (PPD-19) in 2012. PPD-19 prohibits retaliation against whistleblowers and requires security agencies to implement policies for employees to file claims of retaliation.[22] It is important to note that the protections apply to intelligence community employees but not to contractors, who make up a large portion of people employed by the security state.[23]

The protections offered by PPD-19 involve perverse incentives. According to one report, "under PPD-19, the initial review of an improper retaliation allegation occurs within the agency wherein the whistleblower allegedly faced retaliation. This could raise questions regarding the initial review's impartiality, and thus effectiveness at achieving accurate results."[24] An external review process by a three-member inspector general panel does exist if an employee believes the internal review process is unfair. However, the panel's final decision, which is not binding, is reported to the head of the agency where the whistleblower resides, resulting in the same fairness issues as the initial internal review.

There is further evidence of the weakness of existing mechanisms intended to protect those using internal whistleblowing channels. In February 2018, journalist Kevin Poulsen published an article discussing a report by the Office of the Inspector General of the Intelligence Community regarding retaliation against whistleblowers.[25] The report, which has not been publicly released, reviewed 190 cases of supposed retaliations against internal whistleblowers across six intelligence agencies, including the CIA and the NSA. In only one instance did the agencies find in favor of a whistleblower who claimed retaliation for revealing perceived wrongdoing through formal, internal channels. Moreover, according to Poulsen, the review process in that one case took a total of 742 days.

Parallel to the dysfunctions with formal rules is strong norms of secrecy, patriotism, and loyalty, which disincentivize whistleblowing in the national security state. As Daniel Ellsberg notes, "the mystique of secrecy in the universe of national security, even beyond the formal apparatus of classification and clearances, is a compelling deterrent to whistleblowing and thus to effective resistance to gravely wrongful or dangerous policies. In this realm, telling secrets appears unpatriotic, even traitorous."[26] In conjunction with problematic formal protections, this deep-seated culture discourages revealing wrongdoing and weakens internal whistleblowing as a means of checking those in the national security state.

Laws Related to Leaking Information

Four key federal statutes shape the incentives facing whistleblowers pertaining to the handling and transfer of classified information.[27] The first is the federal law (8 U.S.C. § 641) regarding the theft of public money, property, and records. While this law, which dates back to 1875, was not intended to deal with matters of national security, it has been used that way by the U.S. government. The text of the law prohibits the theft or misuse of a "thing of value," which has been interpreted by government officials to include government information leaked to the press.[28] The U.S. government has relied on this law in several cases to charge national security leakers, including Daniel Ellsberg (1973), Samuel Morison (1985), and Jeffrey Sterling (2010).

The second is the Espionage Act passed in 1917.[29] The law, which was initially intended to prohibit interference with military operations and recruitment during World War I, has been amended on several occasions to expand the scope of what is covered.[30] For potential whistleblowers, the relevant aspect of the law can be found in Section 793, which makes it a crime to engage in activities "for the purpose of obtaining information respecting the national defense with intent or reason to believe that the information is to be used to the injury of the United States."[31] Violations of the law carry penalties ranging from fines, to imprisonment, to death.[32]

Before 2009, the U.S. government used the Espionage Act rarely. Those charged under the act included Daniel Ellsberg and Anthony Russo (1973), Samuel Morison (1985), and Lawrence Franklin (2005). The charges against Ellsberg and Russo were dismissed, while Morison and Franklin were convicted. Under President Obama, however, the use of the Espionage Act to punish whistleblowers expanded dramatically, with eight people charged during his administration—Shamai Leibowitz (2009), Thomas Drake (2010), Stephen Jin-Woo Kim (2010), Chelsea Manning (2010), Donald Sachtleben (2012), Jeffrey Sterling (2010), John Kiriakou (2012), and Edward Snowden (2013).

The third piece of relevant legislation is the Atomic Energy Act of 1954 (42 U.S.C. § 2011–2021). This law operates in a similar spirit to the Espionage Act to limit the public dissemination of information related to national security. The focus of this law is on information specifically related to the U.S. government's atomic weapons or nuclear materials. To date, this law has not been invoked in cases related to individuals leaking national security information.

The final piece of legislation is the Intelligence Identities Protection Act of 1982 (50 U.S.C. §§ 421–426), which makes it a crime to intentionally reveal the identity—either directly or through the sharing of classified information—of a covert intelligence agent of the U.S. government. The law disincentivizes whistleblowing because its language is so broad that it could potentially be used to prosecute "not only the malicious publicizing of agents' names but also the efforts of legitimate journalists to expose any corruption, malfeasance, or ineptitude occurring in American intelligence agencies."[33] To date, the act has been invoked once in a whistleblowing case. In 2012, John Kiriakou, who was initially charged under the Espionage Act, pled guilty to violating the Intelligence Identities Protection Act in exchange for the other charges being dropped.[34]

Together, these laws are intended to disincentivize the public dissemination of information related to national defense and security.[35] One effect of these mandates, however, is to weaken the effectiveness of whistleblowers as a means of checking political opportunism and the use of state-produced propaganda.

SOLUTION 3: THE MEDIA

The media refers to the various private people and organizations that report news. In its role as the "Fourth Estate," a free media can potentially play a key role in countering the negative effects of government propaganda in two ways.

First, by communicating information to the public, the media can help ameliorate the information asymmetries inherent in democratic politics by fostering transparency. This can serve as a counter to government-disseminated information, including propaganda, which might be selective, biased, misleading, or false.

Second, free and competitive media allows for the contestability of ideas and information. This serves as a potential internal check on other members of the media—with each media outlet checking the reporting of others—while also offering an array of perspectives and viewpoints regarding the activities of the government. With technological advances, the cost of participating in media falls, thus increasing the number of media sources and increasing the contestation of ideas and information. Contestability may weaken the deleterious effects of government-produced propaganda by offering an alternative narrative to the public. As Brian Anse Patrick and A. Trevor Thrall note, "even during times of greatest official control over information, the existence of a diverse marketplace of news providers offers the greatest chance for an informed public capable of deliberating matters of war and peace."[36]

The effectiveness of media in these dual roles is determined by the degree of autonomy from government influence and the legal structure in which members of the media operate.[37]

Factors Influencing Media Effectiveness

The independence, or autonomy, of media from government interference is central to whether it is able to communicate information to the public. The government can limit autonomy through a variety of channels. In some instances, the government might outright censor the media, preventing its members from revealing information. In other cases, political gatekeepers might limit access to information, conflict zones, or to certain key decision makers based on which members of the media have, in the past, provided favorable coverage.

Or, related to whistleblowing, the government might take steps to limit the flow of information from those inside organizations to the members of the media. This influence directly affects the types of stories covered as well as the way they are communicated to the populace. If members of the media are unable to access and review information, they cannot disseminate it publicly, and the information asymmetries between political officials and the citizenry will persist.

Issues of autonomy are closely tied to the legal arrangement governing the relationship between the media and government. If the law allows those in government to delay or limit the public dissemination of information, then government actors can strategically conceal or reveal information to align with their own narrow interests.

Legal Statutes Affecting the Media

The first major U.S. court case involving the national security state and the media occurred in 1971 when the *New York Times* sought to publish the Pentagon Papers.[38] President Nixon sought to use his executive authority to stop the media from publishing classified information. In *New York Times Co. v. United States* (1971), the Supreme Court weighed the freedom of speech of the press against the power of the government to maintain secrecy in the name of national security.[39] They decided that the media—the *New York Times* and the *Washington Post*—could publish the classified Pentagon Papers without government censorship.

While the decision reinforced the precedent that government censorship of the media was unconstitutional, the case left open the legality of post-publication punishment of journalists and those that provide information to the media. "In *dicta*, some of the justices indicated that the newspapers could or should be prosecuted under the Espionage Act, even if the government could not prevent publication."[40] Since the Supreme Court's finding in that case, the courts have failed to reach any kind of comprehensive consensus on the relationship between government's control of information and the press.[41]

Members of the media often rely on those internal to government agencies as a crucial source of information. As a result, the four main legal statutes pertaining to the leaking of information discussed above (see "Laws Related to Leaking Information") also matter for journalists. To date, the U.S. government has not charged a member of the media under the federal law (8 U.S.C. § 641), or under the Espionage Act. However, as discussed in the previous section on whistleblowing, the government *has* charged media sources who provided information to journalists. This matters for two reasons.

First, there is the possibility that members of the media could be charged under the Espionage Act in the future, which may make some hesitant to critically report on the activities of the national security state. Indeed, although not formally charged under the Espionage Act to date, members of the media have certainly been affected by the government's enforcement of the law.

Consider the case of Donald Sachtleben, a former FBI agent, who was charged under the Espionage Act for leaking classified documents about a foiled terrorist plot in Yemen to the Associated Press. Sachtleben was only identified as a suspect in the case after the U.S. government secretly accessed the phone records of reporters at the Associated Press.[42] The ability of the government to secretly seize the communications of journalists raises a host of legal issues related to media independence and freedom.

Second, whistleblowers often choose to publicly reveal wrongdoing and typically use the media as the mechanism to disclose information regarding government misconduct. The use of the Espionage Act to punish whistleblowers adversely affects the ability of insiders, who believe that members of the government are engaged in malfeasance, to publicly share information. This weakens the effectiveness of both whistleblowers and the media as a check against political abuse.

To date, the Atomic Energy Act of 1954 has been invoked by the government once, in 1979, to secure an injunction to prevent the publication of a story in the *Progressive* detailing the process of making a hydrogen bomb.[43] Finally, the Intelligence Identities Protection Act of 1982 has been invoked once in the context of the media. In 2003, the DOJ investigated journalist Robert Novak, who published the name of CIA officer Valerie Plame, to see whether he had violated the law.[44] No charges were filed.

Together, these four federal statutes serve as the legal architecture influencing the behavior of both sources of information (whistleblowers) as well as members of the media as it pertains to the activities of the national security state. Even though these laws have rarely been invoked against members of the media directly, they have been used against information sources who serve as a crucial input in allowing the media to serve as a check on political propaganda. Moreover, even though these laws have not been used to target members of the media directly, they remain on the books and could be invoked in the future to try to limit media's ability to reveal the realities of national security state operations.

Media Complicity

To be an effective check, the media must be willing to critically report on the government and reveal instances of political malfeasance. Members of the media, however, may be hesitant to do so in matters of national security. Media complicity with the security state can take several forms.

In some instances, editors may hesitate to publish information critical of the government's war efforts. Consider the case of journalist James Risen, who wrote a story for the *New York Times* that was critical of the Bush administration's intelligence regarding the Iraqi government's possession of weapons of mass destruction and connection to al-Qaeda.

Risen writes that "the story ran, but it was badly cut and buried deep inside the paper. I wrote another one, and the same thing happened. I tried to write more, but I started to get the message. It seemed to me that the Times didn't want these stories."[45] Editors may choose to engage in such behaviors either at the request of government officials or because they do not want to anger political gatekeepers whom they rely on for information.

In other cases, members of the media actively embrace and broadcast government-produced war propaganda in an unquestioning manner. They do so to stay in the good graces of the political elite while bolstering their own resume by having privileged access to political decision makers and the associated "behind the scenes" access to war. Chris Hedges, a former foreign correspondent for the *New York Times*, notes that during the Gulf War, "television reporters happily disseminated the spoon-fed images that served the propaganda effort of the [U.S.] military and the state."[46] He goes on to note that this propaganda "did little to convey the reality of war" and instead was intended "to make us [the U.S. populace] feel good about our nation and ourselves."[47] As these quotes indicate, the members of the independent media often become willing participants in disseminating the government's war-related propaganda.

This is not always a matter of narrow self-interest for purposes of career advancement. A sense of patriotism and nationalism can also contribute to members of the media being biased toward their government's war effort. The famous broadcast journalist Walter Cronkite captured this dynamic when commenting on American media reporting during World War II and the Vietnam War, noting,

I think it was about as objective as we can expect in a war time situation where journalists are covering the military of their own country. I wouldn't expect a reporter to be anything less than understanding of their own troops in action. The temptation to use the word "we" is almost inescapable. It was the same situation in the second world war, in Vietnam. When we're down in the trenches with the troops, we're part of that operation.[48]

As this suggests, even if pro-government bias and self-censorship is not intentional, it is bound to happen given that members of the media are also members of the society whose government is engaged in war. In this scenario, the unifying, patriotic effects of war can diminish, if not out-right undermine, the ability of media to check political propaganda and opportunism.

It is because of war's tendency to unify that media complicity with the state is likely to be greatest during times of conflict. As Chris Hedges argues, "the state spends tremendous time protecting, explaining, and promoting the cause. And some of the most important cheerleaders of the cause are the reporters. This is true in nearly every war."[49] Problem-atically, times of war are also the time when there is significant slack in constraints on government power and where checks on abuses of that power are of crucial importance.[50] For this reason, the media will often be limited in its effectiveness as a check on government-produced, war-time propaganda and its perverse effects on policy and society.

SOLUTION 4: CITIZEN INOCULATION

In his essay "The Power of the Powerless," Václav Havel, a Czech politi-cal dissident, future president of Czechoslovakia, and first president of the Czech Republic, explored the relationship between the communist regime and the citizenry. To illustrate the nature of this relationship, Havel pro-vides the example of a grocer who displays a propaganda sign reading "Workers of the world, unite!" in his shop. The grocer does so not be-cause he supports the regime or what it stands for but rather out of fear of the repercussions for not publicly signaling his support for the state.

Havel employs this example to highlight a core tension between the state and the individual living under the ruling regime. In order to avoid punishment, citizens must not only embrace a lie—their support for the ruling regime—but also perpetuate that lie by publicly signaling their support and acquiescence to the state. The cumulative effect is the en-trenchment and extension of state power over the lives of the citizenry. As Havel writes,

Individuals need not believe all these mystifications, but they must behave as if they did, or they must at least tolerate them in silence, or go along well with those who work with them. For this reason, however, they must *live within a lie*. They need not accept the lie. It is enough for them to have accepted their life with it and in it. For by this very fact, individuals confirm the system, fulfill the system, make the system, *are* the system.[51]

For our purposes, Havel's essay is important for two reasons.

First, it reiterates the various roles of propaganda and its harmful effects. The state employs propaganda to directly influence consumers of the government's message. At the same time, the state is able to use the citizenry, such as the grocer who displays the poster, to publicly disseminate propaganda and reinforce the messages contained therein. Together, the dual role of the citizenry—as a consumer and disseminator of propaganda—contributes to what Havel calls a broader "panorama of everyday life" that "reminds people where they are living and what is expected of them. It tells them what everyone else is doing, and indicates to them what they must do as well, if they don't want to be excluded, to fall into isolation, alienate themselves from society, break the rules of the game, and risk the loss of their peace and tranquility and security."[52]

Second, as the title of his essay suggests, Havel argued that ordinary members of society—those typically perceived as being powerless—possess significant power in their relationship with the state. Because everyday people are both victims *and* supporters of the system, they possess the power to remove their support. To illustrate this, Havel imagines what would happen if the grocer refrained from participating in the system by removing the propaganda poster and refraining from acts that legitimize the regime. Such small acts can potentially have significant effects. As Havel notes,

By breaking the rules of the game, he [the grocer] has disrupted the game as such. He has exposed it as a mere game. He has shattered the world of appearances, the fundamental pillar of the system. He has upset the power structure by tearing apart what holds it together. He has demonstrated that living a lie is living a lie. He has broken through the exalted facade of the system and exposed the real, base foundations of power. He has said that the emperor is naked. And because the emperor is in fact naked, something extremely dangerous has happened: by his action, the greengrocer has addressed the world. He has enabled everyone to peer behind the curtain. He has shown everyone that it is possible to live within the truth. Living within the lie can constitute the system only if it is universal.[53]

As this crucial insight makes clear, ordinary people are *the* most important mechanism for limiting the pernicious effects of state-produced propaganda.

Although Havel was focused on what he called a post-totalitarian regime, his insights can be extended to all types of governments, including democratic governments, that employ propaganda. Across all regimes, the populace is the ultimate target of the state's propaganda. The power of the citizenry is demonstrated by the very fact that those in government—both in the past and present—invest significant resources in crafting and disseminating propaganda to convince the populace of the necessity and legitimacy of state actions. Those in power would not expend this effort unless they required consent from the citizenry to pursue their desired ends.

Ultimately, this means that it is up to the members of the populace as to whether they choose to accept or reject the messages communicated through government propaganda. Inoculation against the deleterious effects of state-produced propaganda can only occur under certain conditions and with certain commitments by citizens.

Conditions for Citizen Effectiveness

For people to combat the negative effects of state-produced propaganda, they first need to internalize Havel's core insight regarding the nature of power relations in society. Many believe that the power in society comes from the state itself. However, as Havel made clear, while ordinary people can be victims of state power, they are often supporters of the very system that victimizes them. A similar point was made by political scientist Gene Sharp, who noted that a government's power is "determined by the degree of obedience and cooperation given by the subjects" and that this "obedience remains essentially voluntary," which means that "*all government is based on consent.*"[54] Like Havel, Sharp's point is that people have the choice to be free and need to decide whether to exercise their power in relation to the state, which includes the ability to reject state propaganda.

Second, citizens must be willing to bear the cost of exercising this power. The burden on citizens to be active, self-governing participants in politics is a costly one in ordinary, day-to-day politics. This burden is even greater in matters of national security, given the extreme secrecy surrounding the state's activities. The political elite leverage these information asymmetries to shape the message communicated to citizens. These include perpetuating fear through threat inflation while advancing a culture of militarism through the myth that a massive national security state apparatus is necessary for order and people's safety and freedom.

The same asymmetries that make citizen monitoring of politicians so difficult, however, are also what make citizen involvement so crucial to the maintenance of a free society. As discussed, the members of government are unlikely to restrain themselves, and there are limits on the effectiveness of whistleblowers and the media as constraints on government power. Even where whistleblowing and the media are effective, they are ultimately inputs into self-governance, which requires an engaged citizenry that cares about limiting unscrupulous political behaviors.

When citizens are disengaged or disinterested, the information provided by whistleblowers and the media will fall on deaf ears, the result being the persistence of political opportunism and the erosion of liberty due to the corrosive effects of state propaganda. As the economist Joseph Schumpeter put it, "without the initiative that comes from immediate responsibility, ignorance will persist in the face of masses of information however complete and correct."[55] This suggests that citizens must not only recognize the power they possess over the state but also feel the "immediate responsibility" to exercise that power in order for it to be effective.

Third, people must appreciate the realities of politics and the role that propaganda plays in all political systems, including democracy. For citizens to constrain government, they must appreciate that democratic politics offers those in power significant space to pursue their own ends. People do not need to understand all the nuances and pathologies of democratic politics or the national security state. They do, however, need to understand the risks to freedom that exist when large amounts of discretionary power are concentrated in the hands of a small number of people, especially when those same people possess monopoly control over information related to clandestine activities. These realities are defining features of the U.S. national security state.

Many Americans view the activities of the U.S. security state as central to protecting their liberties and freedoms. As documented in previous chapters, the members of the security state invest significant resources in producing propaganda to reinforce this belief. But the activities of the security state also pose a significant threat to the very liberties the government purports to protect.[56] As Robert Higgs notes, the state's national security power is best understood as a "master key" because it "opens all doors, including the doors that might otherwise obstruct the government's invasion of our most cherished rights to life, liberty, and property."[57] By priming citizens to accept expansions in state power, government-produced propaganda hastens the process through which these doors are opened. A crucial aspect of citizen inoculation against government propaganda is an awareness of this reality. Unless people have some sense of the nature of politics, regardless of political party, and the incentives facing those that operate in that system, they will remain easy targets for state-produced propaganda.

The activities of the national security state, including the production and dissemination of propaganda, are couched in democratic rhetoric and rituals. The result is that while these behaviors appear to be part of the democratic process, they erode those very institutions as the relationship between the state and the citizenry is turned on its head. Instead of the political elite viewing the citizenry as the source of their power, they instead come to view people as an annoyance preventing them from achieving their desired ends. Given this view, those in power feel comfortable, if not justified, employing propaganda to influence and manipulate the citizenry as a way of overcoming the barrier they represent. This is the very opposite of governance by a self-governing citizenry that is at the core of a free society.[58]

Citizen inoculation against state propaganda requires thinking through the answers to crucial questions related to militarism, such as those put forth by retired lieutenant colonel (USAF) William Astore:

How is the dominant military power of which U.S. leaders so casually boast to be checked? How is the country's almost total reliance on the military in foreign affairs to be reined in? How can the plans of the profiteers and arms makers to keep the good times rolling be brought under control?[59]

To answer these questions, Astore argues that people must take the national security state off its pedestal and apply a critical eye toward the realities of how government operates. This involves realizing that militarism is a choice and that citizens possess the power to curtail efforts by government actors to expand their influence through the dissemination of propaganda. It is up to each person to decide whether and how they choose to exercise the power they possess.

Those concerned with a free society would be wise to consider the words of journalist Frank Chodorov, who warned of the corrosive effects of war and propaganda on a free society. To combat these nefarious effects, he argued, "we [the people] must train our minds as an athlete trains his body, against the inevitable conflict with the powerful propaganda that will be used to destroy our sanity. Now, before it is too late, we must learn to think peace in the midst of war."[60] This mental training begins with an appreciation of the role that propaganda plays in the policies and activities of America's national security state that threaten individual freedom in the very name of protecting it.

DOD-Sponsored Film Projects 2001–2017

Act of Valor (2012)

Afghan Knights (2007)

Aloha (2015)

An American Girl (2008)

Annapolis (2006)

Antwone Fisher (2002)

The A-Team (2010)

Avatar (2009)

The Avengers (2012)

Basic (2003)

Batman Vs Superman: Dawn of Justice (2016)

Battle of Los Angeles (2011)

Battleship (2012)

The Bear (2010)

Behind Enemy Lines (2001)

Beneath the Flesh (2009)

Big Miracle (2012)

Black Hawk Down (2001)

Bridge of Spies (2015)

Bruno (2008)

Buffalo Soldiers (2001)

Bullets, Fangs, and Dinner at 8 (2015)

Captain America: The First Avenger (2011)

Captain America: The Winter Soldier (2014)

Captain Phillips (2013)

Cat Run 2 (2014)

Closing the Ring (2007)

Contagion (2008)

The Day After Tomorrow (2004)

The Day The Earth Stood Still (2008)

Dear John (2010)

Déjà Vu (2006)

Devil's Playground (2010)

Die Another Day (2002)

Dirty Bomb (2012)

The Dry Land (2010)

Eagle Eye (2008)

Elizabethtown (2005)

End of Watch (2012)

Everybody Loves Whales (2012)

Expendable Assets (2016)

Fantastic Four 2 (2007)

Fighter Pilot: Operation Red Flag (2004)

The Finest Hours (2016)

The Five Year Engagement (2012)

Flag of My Father (2011)

Flags of Our Fathers (2007)

Flight (2012)

Fort Bliss (2014)

Fort McCoy (2011)

Freezer Burn (2007)

Frost/Nixon (2008)

Fury (2014)

G.I. Joe: Rise of Cobra (2009)

Godzilla (2014)

Good Kill (2014)

The Great Raid (2005)

The Green Dragon (2001)

The Guardian (2006)

Hearts in Atlantis (2001)

Heroes (2006)

Hidden Figures (2016)

The Hulk (2003)

I Am Legend (2007)

Independence Day: Resurgence (2016)

The Invisible War (2013)

In the Pursuit of Happiness (2010)

Iron Man (2008)

Iron Man 2 (2010)

Jurassic Park III (2001)

The Last Full Measure (forthcoming)

Legends of Flight (2010)

Life Flight (2013)

Lone Survivor (2013)

The Lucky One (2012)

The Lucky Ones (2008)

Machines (2003)

Major Movie Star (2008)

Man of Steel (2013)

Master and Commander (2003)

Max (2015)

Megan Leavey (2017)

Memorial Day (2012)

The Messenger (2009)

Moneyball (2011)

The Mummy (2017)

Northfork (2003)

Nowhere Safe (2005)

Over There (2018)

Pacific Rim (2013)

Pearl Harbor (2001)

Race to Space (2001)

Reel Steel (2011)

Sabotage (2014)

Safe House (2012)

San Andreas (2015)

Serbian Scars (2009)

The Shepherd (2008)

A Soldier's Gift (2015)

Space Command (2016)

Spare Parts (2015)

Star Spangled Banner (2013)

Stealth (2005)

Stranger Tides (2011)

Subconscious (2015)

Suicide Squad (2016)

Sully (2016)

Sum of All Fears (2002)

Taken by Force (2010)

Tears of the Sun (2003)

Terminator: Genisys (2015)

Terminator: Salvation (2009)

Thank You for Your Service (2015)

Thirteen Days (2001)

Transformers (2007)

Transformers: Dark of the Moon (2009)

Transformers: The Last Knight (2017)

Transformers: Revenge of the Fallen (2011)

Tropic Thunder (2008)

Tugger (2005)

Turkey Shoot (2014)

2 Guns (2013)

Unaccompanied Minors (2006)

Unbroken (2014)

United 93 (2006)

USS Indianapolis: Men of Courage (2016)

The Visiting (2007)

War for the Planet of the Apes (2017)

War of the Worlds (2005)

Warrior (2011)

We Were Soldiers (2002)

Whiskey Tango Foxtrot (2016)

Windtalkers (2002)

Source: *Alford and Secker* (2017), 195–204.

Notes

PREFACE

1. Whitlock 2019.
2. Quoted in Whitlock (2019).
3. Davis 2012a. See also Davis 2012b, 2019.
4. Donovan 1970; Bacevich 2005.

CHAPTER I

1. Brewer 2009, 3–13.
2. For a firsthand account of the operation of the CPE, see Creel 1920.
3. Axelrod 2009.
4. See Winkler (1978) for a detailed discussion of the OWI.
5. Roosevelt 1942.
6. Writer's War Board 1942, 5.
7. Howell 1997, 795.
8. Howell 1997, 796–97.
9. United States Information Agency 1998, 5. For more on the operations and influence of the USIA, see Elder (1968), Snyder (1995), and Osgood (2006).
10. See Wilford (2009) for a discussion of the history and activities of Operation Mockingbird.
11. Sessions 2016, 248.
12. Fulbright 1971, 33–34.
13. Fulbright 1971, 35–38.
14. Fulbright 1971, 149–50.
15. Andrzejewski 2015, 7.
16. Andrzejewski 2015, 20.
17. Paul and Matthews 2016. The authors limit their discussion of the "firehose of falsehood" model to Russian propaganda internationally. But the same characteristics they highlight as part of this model also apply to the U.S. government domestically and abroad.
18. Fulbright 1971, 29.
19. Fellows 1959.
20. Irwin 1936, 3.
21. https://www.lexico.com/definition/propaganda.
22. Marlin 2013, 12.
23. Jowett and O'Donnell 1986, 7. For a review of various definitions of *propaganda* across disciplines, see Jowett and O'Donnell (1986, 2–7).
24. Nelson and Izadi 2009, 338.
25. Stanley 2015, 11.
26. Nelson and Izadi 2009, 338.
27. Mearsheimer 2011, 20.

28. See Marlin (2013, 4–13) for a review of the various definitions of *propaganda*.

29. On some of the important differences between private advertising and government advertising, see Schumpeter (1950: 263), Wagner (1976) and DiLorenzo (1988, 67–68). As Wagner (1976, 96) puts it, "The absence of alternative suppliers of credence services [services for which consumers cannot observe qualities after purchase], suppliers which exist in the private market, serves to strengthen the selling position of the government. Advertising, then, serves essentially a reassuring and reinforcing function within the structure of the monopolistic state." The implication is that "the function of public advertising is to maintain public acquiescence in social patterns in which instances of felt discomfort are attributable to government action, but the picture portrayed nonetheless is one that calls for the provision of still more public services" (Wagner 1976: 97).

30. Norton 2017, 543.

31. Brewer 2009, 7.

32. Fulbright 1971, 22.

33. Crawford 2019.

34. On the topic of whether America is safer from terrorist threats, see Mueller and Stewart (2021) and DePetris (2019).

35. Our list has some overlap, but also some differences, with that presented by Black (2001, 133–34).

36. Sapolsky (2017, 387–424) explores the neurobiological foundations of the "us versus them" dichotomy which helps explain why governments so often rely on this technique for manipulation. We thank Yahya Alshamy for raising this point.

37. Bush 2001a.

38. Bush 2003b.

39. Patrick and Thrall 2007, 102.

40. Jacoby 2000, 751. See also Edelman 1993; Rochefort and Cobb 1994; Chong and Druckman 2001; Hiebert 2003.

41. Brewster 2009.

42. Friedell 1969; Lewis 1969; Chwe 2001.

43. Porter 1994, 12, italics in original.

44. Robin 2004, 2.

45. Higgs 2006b; Coyne and Hall 2018, 21–25.

46. Higgs 2006b, 447–48.

47. Berger and Luckmann 1966, 87.

48. MacArthur 1965, 333.

49. Stanley 2016.

50. Higgs 1987.

51. On the differences between "hegemonic propaganda theory," which holds that political leaders enjoy unparalleled power to directly control opinions, with "classical propaganda theory," which holds that propaganda is situational and context specific and encourages the receiver to select a particular opinion among a range of acceptable options at a particular time and place, see Patrick and Thrall (2007) and the literature cited therein. Our analysis is closer to the classical theory in that it places the ultimate power in the hands of the citizenry.

52. Patrick and Thrall 2007, 101–2.

53. This is consistent with political science scholarship that finds that "Americans' foreign policy attitudes are structured, meaningful, and accessible" (Kushner Gadarian 2010, 1048).

54. See Sharp (2012), 7–32 and the references therein.

55. As Hayek (1961) noted, commercial advertising is one influence on consumer tastes, but it does not solely determine those tastes. The consumers of information ultimately determine what they believe and desire.

56. Yanagizawa-Drott 2014, 1947.

57. Utley 2018.

58. Stanley 2015, 11.

59. Stanley 2015, 11.

60. Ostrom 1991; Boettke 2018; Aligca, Boettke, and Tarko 2019.

61. Mearsheimer 2011, 91.

62. Donovan 1970, 25–26, emphasis in original.

63. Vagts 1937, 15.

64. Tocqueville (1835–1840) 1988: 285; Coyne and Hall 2018.

65. Fulbright 1971, 14.

66. Bacevich 2005, 1.

67. Bacevich 2005, 225.

68. Coyne and Hall 2018.

69. Orwell 1968: 139.

70. See Higgs 1987, 2006a, 2012; Coyne and Hall 2018.

71. Lippmann 1922; Lasswell 1927, 1938; Bernays 1928; Ponsonby 1928; Doob 1935; Knight 1936; Arendt (1951) 1973, 1972; Ellul 1973 Altheide and Johnson 1980; Jowett and O'Donnell 1986; Herman and Chomsky 1988; Smith 1989; Nelson 1996; Sproule 1997; Pratkanis and Aronson 2001; Chomsky 2002; Cunningham 2002; Gentzkow and Shapiro 2004; Patrick and Thrall 2004, 2007; Strömberg 2004; Eisensee and Strömberg 2007; DiMaggio 2008; Brewer 2009; Gerber, Karlan, and Bergan 2009; Olken 2009; DellaVigna and Gentzkow 2010; Enikolopov, Petrova, and Zhuravskaya 2011; Marlin 2013; DellaVigna et al. 2014; Selgin 2014; Yanagizawa-Drott 2014; Adena et al. 2015; Schuessler 2015; Stanley 2015; Little 2017, Zollmann 2017; Seagren and Henderson 2018; Testa 2018.

72. For an accessible introduction to political economy, see Holcombe (2016). For more advanced treatments, see Mueller (2003), Rowley and Schneider (2004), and Reksulak, Razzolini, and Shughart (2014).

73. Eggertsson 1990; North 1990; Furubotn and Richter 1997; Menard and Shirley 2005.

74. On the connection between political economy and institutional economics, see Boettke, Haeffele-Balch, and Storr (2016).

75. Buchanan 1979.

76. Exceptions include Seagren and Henderson (2018) and Schuessler (2015), who incorporate political economy insights.

77. Sunstein 2005; Kaufmann 2006; Mueller 2006; Thrall and Cramer 2009; Goodman 2013; Unger 2013; Preble and Mueller 2014; Porter 2015; Levine 2018.

78. Thrall and Cramer 2009, 6–9.

79. Schuessler 2015, 24.

80. In this regard we follow Schuessler (2015), 24–25.

CHAPTER 2

1. See Buchanan (1975) for this rendering of the protective state.

2. See, for example, Ferejohn (1986).

3. Dunne 1995, 409.

4. Holcombe 2005.

5. On the centrality of the principal-agent problem in democratic politics, see Barro (1973), Ferejohn (1986), Besley (2006), and Higgs (2018).

6. See Buchanan (1954), Miller (1999), and Wagner and Yazigi (2014) for an analysis of the key differences between individual choice in private markets versus choice in political settings.

7. On rational ignorance see Downs (1957), Bohanon and Van Cott (2002), Heckelman (2003), Gelman, Silver, and Edlin (2012), Somin (2013), and Brennan (2016).

8. Somin 2013. For specific examples from foreign policy, see U. Friedman (2012) and G. Friedman (2014).

9. We thank Diana Thomas for raising this point. On the role of systematic biases in democratic politics, see Caplan (2007).

10. "During any six-year period (say, from November 1994 through November 2000), each voter is allowed to vote twice for a president/vice president team, four times for a U.S. representative, and a maximum of three times for a U.S. senator" (Boudreaux 1996, 117).

11. Higgs 2012, 34–46.

12. A hawkish position regarding U.S. foreign policy was rewarded by voters in the 2004 presidential election (see Kushner Gadarian 2010). This voter response may be, at least partially, a product of the post-9/11 government propaganda that framed the Bush administration as being "tough" against the supposed existential terrorist threat. As Kushner Gadarian (2010, 1061) notes, the "trustee model" of government, whereby citizens forgo close representation so that those in power can protect them from threats, "becomes problematic when leaders artificially create crises to maintain power, provide false information about the consequences of policy, or cynically portray their foreign policy positions in elections." We thank Yahya Alshamy for raising this point.

13. See Higgs (1987) on the "ratchet effect" and Coyne and Hall (2018) on the "boomerang effect" of government crises and intervention on the growth of government.

14. Higgs 2012, 44–46.

15. On the logic of interest groups, see Olson (1965). Becker (1983) discusses the legislature as a political marketplace.

16. Melman 1970, 1974; Higgs 2006a; Duncan and Coyne 2013a, 2013b, 2015; McCartney and McCartney 2015.

17. Mueller 2006.

18. Edelman 1985, 4.

19. Gates 2014.

20. Niskanen 1971, 1975, 2001.

21. Tullock 1965; Wagner 2007.

22. Whitlock and Woodward 2016.

23. Steinhauer 2015.

24. See Horton 2015.

25. Mearsheimer 2011, 57.

26. Koppl 2018, 230–1.

27. For a history of executive orders and the U.S. classification system, see Quist (2002, 44–77).

28. Executive Order No. 8381, January 2, 1938, "Defining Certain Vital Military and Naval Installations and Equipment," https://fas.org/irp/offdocs/eo/eo-8381.htm.

29. Executive Order No. 10290, September 24, 1951, "Prescribing Regulations

Establishing Minimum Standards for the Classification, Transmission, and Handling, by Department and Agencies of the Executive Branch, of Official Information Which Requires Safeguarding in the Interest of the Security of the United States," https://fas.org/irp/offdocs/eo/eo-10290.pdf.

30. Huard 1956, 179–90.
31. Setty 2012, 1567.
32. Goitein and Shapiro 2011, 4–5.
33. Aftergood 2009, 404.
34. For a discussion of experts and how the centralization and monopolization of information can result in mistakes and abuses, see Levy and Peart (2016) and Koppl (2018).
35. Huard 1956, 219.
36. Parks 1957–1958, 23–24.
37. Setty 2012, 1572; Cole 2003.
38. Setty 2012; 1574.
39. See Burr (2019) for a discussion of the present-day dysfunctions in the U.S. government's system of declassification.
40. Kristian 2017.
41. Carlson 2017.
42. Knox 2017.
43. Hedges 2002, 143.
44. Lippmann 1922, 43.
45. Lippmann 1922, 44.
46. See Kuran 1997; Little 2017.
47. Porter 1994; Bacevich 2005; Coyne and Hall 2018, 27, 111.
48. Quoted in Bailey (1997).
49. Dalberg-Acton 1907, 504.
50. On the selection mechanisms behind this tendency, see Hayek (1944), Higgs (1997), and Coyne and Hall (2016).
51. Mearsheimer 2011, 93.

<h2 style="text-align:center">CHAPTER 3</h2>

1. Gallup 2017.
2. Gallup 2017.
3. Gallup 2017.
4. Gallup 2017.
5. Gallup 2017.
6. Brewer 2009, 248.
7. See Hahn (2012b) for a more thorough examination of the history of U.S. involvement in Iraq.
8. United States Department of State 2017.
9. See Hahn 2012b, 59–60.
10. United States Department of State 1958.
11. Morris 2003.
12. Quoted in PBS (1990).
13. Dietrich 2011.
14. Hahn 2012a.
15. BBC News 2013.

16. ABC News 2008.

17. ABC News 2008.

18. Human Rights Watch 2002.

19. Human Rights Watch 2002.

20. Hahn 2012b, 77–78; Battle 2003.

21. White House 1983.

22. White House 1984.

23. Gompert, Binnendijk, and Lin 2014.

24. Gompert, Binnendijk, and Lin 2014.

25. Hahn 2012b, 121.

26. See Project for the New American Century, letter to President Clinton, January 26, 1998, https://www.noi.org/wp-content/uploads/2016/01/iraqclintonletter1998-01-26-Copy.pdf.

27. Clinton 1998b.

28. See "The Iraqi Liberation Act," Public Law 105–338 of the 105th Congress, 1998, https://www.gpo.gov/fdsys/pkg/STATUTE-112/pdf/STATUTE-112-Pg3178.pdf.

29. Bush 1999b.

30. Bush 1999a.

31. Quoted in Frontline (2008).

32. Quoted in Frontline (2008).

33. Quoted in Borger (2006).

34. Quoted in Frontline (2008).

35. Quoted in Frontline (2008).

36. Quoted in Frontline (2008).

37. James A. Baker III Institute for Public Policy 2001, 40.

38. Moran 2013.

39. Bush 2003d.

40. United States House of Representatives Committee on Government Reform 2004.

41. Quoted in *Meet the Press* (2006).

42. Benjamin 2002.

43. Benjamin 2002.

44. Director of Central Intelligence 2002.

45. Quoted in Frontline (2008).

46. Quoted in Frontline (2008).

47. Quoted in Frontline (2014).

48. Quote in Frontline (2005).

49. Powell 2003.

50. Brewer 2009, 243.

51. Program on International Policy Attitudes and Knowledge Networks 2003, 2.

52. Program on International Policy Attitudes and Knowledge Networks 2003, 3.

53. Program on International Policy Attitudes and Knowledge Networks 2003, 3.

54. Program on International Policy Attitudes and Knowledge Networks 2003, 4.

55. Bush 2002a.

56. Bush 2003d.

57. Cheney 2002a.

58. Quoted in Stein and Dickinson (2006), emphasis added.

59. United States House of Representatives Committee on Government Reform 2004, iii.

60. For a time line of the UN weapons inspections in Iraq, see CNN (2017).

61. United Nations Monitoring, Verification, and Inspections Commission 2003.

62. Director of Central Intelligence 2002.

63. ElBaradei 2003.

64. Wilson 2003.

65. Warrick 2003.

66. United States House of Representatives Committee on Government Reform 2004, 5.

67. United States House of Representatives Committee on Government Reform 2004,5.

68. United States House of Representatives Committee on Government Reform 2004, 11.

69. ElBaradei 2003.

70. Hammond 2012.

71. Quoted in CNN 2002.

72. Quoted in Barstow, Broad, and Gerth 2004.

73. Program on International Policy Attitudes and Knowledge Networks 2002.

74. *New York Times,* "Complete Results," September 8, 2002 (http://www.nytimes.com/packages/html/national/20020908_POLL/020908poll-results.html).

75. Ibid.

76. Western 2005, 119–20.

77. Larson and Savych 2005,149.

78. Newport 2002.

79. Saad 2002.

80. Program on International Policy Attitudes and Knowledge Networks 2002.

81. Quoted in Breslow 2016.

82. Bush 2002b.

83. Bush 2003a.

84. Bush 2003c.

85. Bush 2003a

86. Boucher 2003.

87. Carney 2011.

88. Brockes 2003.

89. United States Central Intelligence Agency 2020.

90. Brockes 2003.

91. Brewer 2009, 251.

92. Program on International Policy Attitudes and Knowledge Networks 2003: 8

93. Kohut, Doherty, and Gross 2004,11.

94. Gallup 2017.

95. Gallup 2017.

96. United States House of Representatives Committee on Government Reform 2004, 30.

CHAPTER 4

1. Patrick and Thrall 2007, 96.

2. Patrick and Thrall 2007, 96.

3. Patrick and Thrall 2007, 104.

4. McClellan 2008, 174

5. McClellan 2008, 175, emphasis added.

6. McClellan 2008, 142.

7. Brewer 2009, 242.

8. BBC News 2001b. In October 2002 the Coalition Information Center was renamed the Office of Global Communication.

9. Gordon and Miller 2002.

10. Quoted in Frontline (2006).

11. Quoted in Meet the Press (2002).

12. Quoted in Frontline (2006).

13. Quoted in Frontline (2006).

14. Project for Excellence in Journalism 2003.

15. Quoted in Brewer (2009), 252.

16. Purdum and Rutenberg 2003. The merits of embedded journalism have been hotly debated by journalists. See Project for Excellence in Journalism (2003) and Farrell (2010) for a more thorough discussion of this debate.

17. Quoted in Frontline (2006).

18. Quoted in Frontline (2006).

19. Quoted in Farrell (2010).

20. Barstow 2008.

21. Quoted in Barstow (2008).

22. Quoted in Barstow (2008).

23. Quoted in Barstow (2008).

24. Quoted in Barstow (2008).

25. McClellan 2008, 175.

26. McClellan 2008, 175.

27. Program on International Policy Attitudes and Knowledge Networks 2003, 12.

28. Program on International Policy Attitudes and Knowledge Networks 2003, 13.

29. Program on International Policy Attitudes and Knowledge Networks 2003, 16, emphasis in original.

30. Cheney 2002b.

31. The use of the American flag directly undermined the idea that the war was about "liberation" as opposed to "occupation." For a further discussion of this issue, see Brewer (2009), 257.

32. Brewer 2009, 257.

33. Quoted in Frontline (2008).

34. Quoted in Frontline (2008).

35. Quoted in Frontline (2008).

36. Quoted in Frontline (2008).

37. Quoted in Frontline (2008).

38. Quoted in Frontline (2008).

39. Quoted in United States Senate Democrats (2007).

40. Diamond 2004.

41. Woodward 2004,150.

42. GlobalPolicy.org 2004, 35.

43. GlobalPolicy.org 2004, 37.

44. GlobalPolicy.org 2004, 39.

45. Globalpolicy.org 2007, 6–8.

46. Globalpolicy.org 2007, 10.

47. Globalpolicy.org 2007, 6.

48. Globalpolicy.org 2007, 8.

49. Globalpolicy.org 2007, 10
50. Program on International Policy Attitudes and Knowledge Networks 2003, 8.
51. Program on International Policy Attitudes and Knowledge Networks 2003, 6.
52. Program on International Policy Attitudes and Knowledge Networks 2003, 6.
53. Brewer 2009, 253.
54. See Antiwar.com (2006) for a gallery of these images.
55. Hersh 2007.
56. Senate Select Committee on Intelligence 2014. For a firsthand account of torture at Abu Ghraib by a former interrogator, see Fair (2016).
57. Roberts 2002.
58. Brewer 2009, 247.
59. Program on International Policy Attitudes and Knowledge Networks 2003, 5.
60. Program on International Policy Attitudes and Knowledge Networks 2003, 6.
61. Gallup 2017.
62. See Kiely (2016).
63. Rivera 2011.
64. Haq 2015.

CHAPTER 5

1. National Hockey League 2014.
2. Esteban 2011.
3. McCain and Flake 2015, 64.
4. McCain and Flake 2015, 59–66.
5. Goodell 2016.
6. PBS 2002.
7. PBS 2002.
8. PBS 2002.
9. Quoted in Wakefield (1997), 22. The piece makes specific reference to the controversy surrounding the "work or fight" rule during the war and how it related to baseball. A complete discussion of this controversy is beyond the scope of this book. For a more complete accounting, see Kelly (2018).
10. PBS 2002.
11. Quoted in Wakefield (1997), 24.
12. Wakefield 1997, 37, 42.
13. For a more comprehensive discussion of these tensions in the interwar period, see L. Olson (2014).
14. Wakefield 1997, 70.
15. Wakefield 1997, 71.
16. Quoted in Wakefield (1997), 74.
17. Wakefield 1997, 74.
18. Lipsky 1985, 68–69.
19. Quoted in Der Derian and Shapiro (1989), 76
20. Lévi-Strauss 1962, 21, emphasis in original.
21. Guttmann 1986, 558.
22. Guttmann 1986, 559.
23. Guttmann 1986, 160.
24. Guttmann 1986, 160.

25. Guttmann 1986, 162.
26. Guttmann 1986, 163.
27. Robbie 2015.
28. Budowsky 2018.
29. Hester 2005, 46.
30. Lipsky 1981, 140.
31. Lipsyte 1975, 13.
32. Lipsyte 1975, 13.
33. Balbus 1975, 26.
34. Quoted in Broder (1991).
35. Quoted in Newsweek (1991).
36. Clinton 1998a.
37. Billings, Butterworth, and Turman 2012, 127.
38. Bairner 2001, xi..
39. Jones 2015.
40. Jones 2015.
41. Norman 2018.
42. Norman 2018. Football surpassed baseball in popularity in 1972 and the gap between the sports has widened ever since.
43. Harris Poll 2011.
44. Harris Poll 2011.
45. Rapaport 2018. The only top 20 broadcast that wasn't the Super Bowl was the series finale of M*A*S*H in 1983.
46. Gough 2020.
47. Scott 2016.
48. Segrave 2000, 51.
49. National Football League 2011.
50. Quoted in Fox Sports (2011).
51. Associated Press 2001.
52. Fox Sports 2011.
53. Brown 2004, 40.
54. Brown 2004, 40.
55. Brown 2004, 40.
56. Brown 2004, 40.
57. Quoted in Berkow (1991).
58. Real 1975, 36, 42.
59. Stossel 2001.
60. Quoted in Scott (2016), emphasis in original.
61. Billings, Butterworth, and Turman 2012, 133.
62. King 2008, 528.
63. Vinall 2003.
64. King 2008, 537.
65. Quoted in King (2008), 536.
66. King 2008, 536.
67. Montgomery 2003.
68. Montgomery 2003.
69. Montgomery 2003.

70. Quoted in Montgomery (2003).

71. Gabel 2008.

72. Bryant 2013.

73. McCain and Flake 2015, i.

74. McCain and Flake 2015, 5. The monetary accounting is further complicated by the structure of the NFL. While the league and its central office are one organization, the individual teams are their own private entities. It is unclear exactly how the DOD paid out various funds. One potential difficulty in calculating the precise magnitude of these payments relates to the tax status of the NFL and its teams. Until 2015, the league office of the NFL was considered tax exempt while the individual teams were not. Payments made to the NFL league office, for instance, may be easier to uncover because of reporting requirements than payments made to individual teams. We thank Alisha Harper for bringing this point to our attention.

75. Whitney 2019.

76. Quoted in Whitney (2019).

77. U.S. Army 2019, Facebook post, December 30, https://www.facebook.com/USarmy/posts/10157349611033558?__tn__=-R.

78. For a full accounting of Tillman's life during his time with the Cardinals and the wars in Iraq and Afghanistan, see Krakauer (2009).

79. Quoted in Farmer (2002).

80. Quoted in Krakauer (2009), 173.

81. Quoted in Krakauer (2009), 173.

82. Quoted in Krakauer (2009), 173.

83. Quoted in Krakauer (2009), 173.

84. Quoted in Stow (2017), 159.

85. Krakauer 2009, 248.

86. While back in the United States between overseas deployments, Pat spoke to a friend from Arizona State about a possible meeting with MIT linguist and well-known U.S foreign policy critic Noam Chomsky after his return from Afghanistan. Pat would be killed before such a meeting could take place. See Fish (n.d.).

87. Krakauer 2009, 349.

88. Quoted in Krakauer (2009). 320.

89. At the time of Pat Tillman's death, the rangers were separated into two distinct groups. Pat was in the first group. His brother Kevin was in the second. It quickly became common knowledge among Pat's group that his death was the result of friendly fire. This information remained unknown to the second group, including Kevin Tillman.

90. Adapted from Krakauer (2009), 268.

91. Krakauer 2009, 334.

92. Quoted in Krakauer (2009), 334.

93. Quoted in Krakauer (2009), 336.

94. Associated Press 2007. For a more detailed accounting of these investigations, see Army Regulation 15–6, "Investigation Guide for Informal Investigations," https://home.army.mil/riley/application/files/5515/1630/6429/15-6InvestigationOfficer.pdf.

95. Krakauer 2009, 339.

96. Quoted in Krakauer (2009), 337.

97. Quoted in Krakauer (2009), 340.

98. Krakauer 2009, 340.

99. Quoted in Krakauer (2009), 341. For more details on this specific incident, see 340–41.

100. Quoted in Krakauer (2009), 344. For more details on this specific incident, see 342–45.

101. Committee on Oversight and Public Reform 2008, 12.

102. Committee on Oversight and Public Reform 2008, 12.

103. Committee on Oversight and Public Reform 2008, 12.

104. Quoted in Krakauer (2009), 347–48.

105. See Gettleman (2004).

106. See Antiwar.com (2006) for a gallery of these images.

107. Krakauer 2009, 349–50.

108. Quoted in NBC News (2004).

109. Bush 2004.

110. Quoted in Krakauer (2009), 357.

111. Krakauer 2009, 359.

112. Krakauer 2009, 359.

113. Tillman 2007.

114. Campbell 2017.

115. Neuman 2017.

116. For a discussion of this controversy, see Mindock (2018).

117. Quoted in Schmitz (2017).

118. Pierce 2018.

CHAPTER 6

1. An image of this poster is available at https://c1.staticflickr.com/1/49/15232468656b1ec90c8.jpg.

2. Schneier 2009.

3. Bowen and Rodrigue (n.d.).

4. Port Authority of New York and New Jersey 2013.

5. Bowen and Rodrigue (n.d.).

6. For a more detailed summary of this deregulation and its implications, see Bailey (1985).

7. Team 2016.

8. Team 2016.

9. United States Department of Transportation 2018b.

10. McCabe 2013. A communist sympathizer, Ramirez Ortiz stated he wished to warn Castro of an assassination attempt by Dominican dictator Rafael Trujillo. Ramirez Ortiz would be jailed multiple times in Cuba before escaping back to the United States in 1975, only to be sentenced to twenty years in prison for the incident.

11. Engle 2011.

12. Federal Aviation Administration 2017.

13. United States Department of Transportation 2018a.

14. Engle 2011.

15. Meltzer 2015.

16. Meltzer 2015.

17. Meltzer 2015.

18. O'Connor 2016.

19. Beaven 2016.

20. Quoted in National Commission on Terror Attacks upon the United States (2004), 2.

21. See the National Commission on Terror Attacks upon the United States (2004).

22. For a more complete yet accessible accounting of the attacks, see Bergen (2018).

23. Bergen 2018.

24. See de Boer (1979) and Landes (1977) for examples.

25. Johnson 1976, 3–4.

26. Mueller and Stewart 2011, 40–41.

27. Mueller 2006, 2.

28. Mueller 2006, 2.

29. Saliba 2017.

30. Forrester, Weiser, and Forrester 2018.

31. Nowrasteh 2017.

32. Nowrasteh 2017.

33. Ritchie 2018.

34. World Bank 2018.

35. Data retrieved from the World Terrorism Database. Ambiguous cases of terrorism are included. Excluded from the analysis were the Las Vegas shooting in 2017 (while fuel tanks were hit by gunfire, they did not appear to be the intended target) and the bombing of a flight in 1982 en route to Honolulu, as the flight originated outside of U.S. airspace. Examples of non-U.S. targets within the United States include the Youth of the Star bombing of a Dominican airline in Miami in 1975, the detonation of a car bomb outside the El Al Airlines terminal in New York in 1973 targeting Israel, and others. Of the fifteen cases where the nationality of the target was not the United States, Israel and the former Soviet Union were the most frequent targets, followed by Venezuela and other countries.

36. United States Federal Bureau of Investigation 2018.

37. Roots 2003, 509.

38. Quoted in Smithsonian Magazine (n.d.)

39. Encyclopedia Britannica 2019b.

40. Ayers 2011.

41. United States Department of Homeland Security 2019, 13.

42. See Pekoske (2019).

43. "TSA by the Numbers," Factsheet, https://www.tsa.gov/sites/default/files/resources/tsabythenumbers_factsheet.pdf.

44. Bush 2001b.

45. Gowadia 2017.

46. Pekoske 2018.

47. United States Transportation Security Administration 2014.

48. "Surface Transportation," For Industry: Resources, https://www.tsa.gov/for-industry/surface-transportation.

49. Sural 2010. He is referring to an incident in which political reporter David Weigel refused a TSA pat down, stating, "If you touch my junk I'm going to have you arrested." See Lapidos (2010) for a discussion of the incident.

50. Sural 2010.

51. Sural 2010.

52. Mueller 2019, 2.

53. Mueller 2019, 2.

54. Mueller 2019, 2.

55. Mueller 2019, 4. It is worth noting that fatalities are not evenly distributed across each year. The number of deaths increased in 2015 and 2016 as a result of activity by the Islamic State in Iraq and Syria (known also as ISIS or IS). This is also an extreme outlier in terms of fatalities. In 2016 an ISIS-inspired gunman murdered forty-nine people at Pulse Nightclub in Orlando, Florida. Without this incident, the number of fatalities would be cut by half.

56. Mueller 2019, 76.

57. Mueller 2019, 79.

58. Quoted in Shannon (2002).

59. Yang 2001, 58.

60. Belluck and Chang 2001.

61. Mueller 2019, 50.

62. Meltzer 2015.

63. Mann 2011.

64. Quoted in Wilson (2017).

65. Wilson 2017.

66. For a detailed account of the plot, see Puhl (2011), 324–29.

67. Laville, Norton-Taylor, and Dodd 2006.

68. Puhl 2011, 319.

69. Chertoff 2006.

70. Gonzales 2006.

71. Puhl 2011, 333.

72. Mueller 2011, 317–18.

73. In the wake of COVID-19, the TSA quadrupled the carry-on allowance for liquid hand sanitizer to twelve ounces. See Fletcher (2020).

74. "Liquids Rule," Travel: Security Screening, https://www.tsa.gov/travel/security-screening/liquids-rule.

75. Quoted in Puhl (2011), 337.

76. Straub 2011, 381.

77. Quoted in Shepherd (2007).

78. Quoted in Schneier (2007).

79. Quoted in United States Attorney's Office Eastern District of New York (2007).

80. Straub 2011, 383.

81. Straub 2011, 378.

82. Straub 2011, 375.

83. Straub 2011, 378.

84. Straub 2011, 379.

85. Straub 2011, 382–83.

86. Anderson 2017.

87. Labott and Dougherty 2010.

88. Labott and Dougherty 2010.

89. Quoted in Harnden 2009.

90. Quoted in Harnden 2009.

91. CBC News 2009.

92. BBC News 2010.

93. Schecter and Ross 2010.

94. Schecter and Ross 2010.

95. Stewart and Mueller 2008, 155.

96. Schanzer 2018.

97. Quoted in Sforza (2010).

98. Quoted in United States Government Accountability Office (2017), 15.

99. Quoted in Sforza (2010).

100. Grabell 2016.

101. Grabell 2016.

102. Grabell 2016.

103. Stewart 2018.

104. United States Transportation Security Administration 2018.

105. Quoted in Schanzer (2018).

106. Stewart 2018; Winter 2018a.

107. Winter 2018b.

108. Quoted in Winter 2018b.

109. Electronic Privacy Information Center 2010.

110. Quoted in Knickerbocker (2010).

111. Quoted in Kravitz (2010).

112. Quoted in Schwartz (2009).

113. Quoted in Macedo (2010).

114. Kerley and Cook (2017).

115. Bradner and Marsh (2015).

116. United States Government Accountability Office 2010.

117. Quoted in Tien (2010).

118. Strickler 2010.

119. Quoted in Schwartz (2009).

120. Quoted in Schwartz (2009).

121. Quoted in Knox (2010).

122. United States Transportation Security Administration 2008.

123. Shahid 2010.

124. Electronic Privacy Information Center v. US Department of Homeland Security, 760 F. Supp. 2d 4 (D.D.C. 2011), https://www.courtlistener.com/opinion/2471526/electronic-privacy-v-us-dept-of-homeland-sec/.

125. Mellor 2010.

126. Ahlers 2013.

127. Competitive Enterprise Institute v. U.S. Department of Homeland Security (U.S. Court of Appeals, D.C. Cir. 2016), 8, https://epic.org/privacy/litigation/apa/tsa/bodyscanner/1639042-FTTUSA-Amicus-Brief.pdf.

128. Competitive Enterprise Institute v. U.S. Department of Homeland Security, 7.

129. Competitive Enterprise Institute v. U.S. Department of Homeland Security, 9.

130. Baskas 2011.

131. Associated Press 2011.

132. *The Week* 2010.

133. Quoted in Dominguez (2010).

134. NBC News 2014.

135. Johnson 2012.

136. Villafranca 2012.

137. Quoted in Johnson (2012).

138. Pittore 2011, 799.

139. It should be noted that Loewen's plot is considered to be more politically motivated than an act of a radical Islamic terrorist. Despite his "conversion," he was not a practicing Muslim, and no one in his family or friend group or the local Muslim community knew of his religion. He has been described as an "online Muslim only." See Pittore (2011), 789–90.

140. Pittore 2011, 789.

141. Pittore 2011, 797.

142. United States Federal Bureau of Investigation 2013.

143. United States Federal Bureau of Investigation 2013.

144. Williams 2019.

145. Richards et al. 2019, 17, 14.

146. Pittore 2011, 795.

147. Higgs 2006b, 447–48; Coyne and Hall 2018, 21–25.

CHAPTER 7

1. United States Central Intelligence Agency 2008.

2. Quoted in Robb (2004), 59.

3. Quoted in Robb (2004), 60.

4. Bingaman 2000, emphasis added.

5. Robb 2004, 63

6. Alford and Secker 2017, 195–220.

7. Quoted in Tarabay (2014).

8. Seelye 2002.

9. Dancis 2018.

10. Dancis 2018.

11. Dancis 2018.

12. Quoted in Fraser (2003, 40).

13. Creel 1920, 273.

14. Creel 1920, 273.

15. Creel 1920, 282.

16. See Winkler (1978) for a detailed discussion of the OWI.

17. Encyclopedia Britannica 2019a.

18. Koppes and Black 1977, 89.

19. Koppes and Black 1977, 88–89.

20. Koppes and Black 1977, 91.

21. United States Office of War Information 1942, 1.

22. United States Office of War Information 1942, 30.

23. Dictionary.com, s.v. "Home Front," http://www.dictionary.com/browse/home-front.

24. United States Office of War Information 1942, 36, emphasis in original.

25. United States Office of War Information 1942, 40–41, emphasis in original.

26. United States Office of War Information 1942, 114, emphasis in original.

27. United States Office of War Information 1942, 120, emphasis in original.

28. United States Office of War Information 1942, 73, emphasis in original.

29. United States Office of War Information 1942, 63.

30. United States Office of War Information 1942, 122.

31. United States Office of War Information 1942, 63.

32. Suid 2002, 136

33. Suid 2002, 136

34. Dancis 2018.

35. United States Department of Defense 1966, 3–4.

36. United States Department of Defense 1966, 3–4.

37. Suid 2002, 674–78.

38. Suid 2002, 674–78.

39. Anderson and Van Atta 1987.

40. Hersh 1972.

41. Janos 2018.

42. Vecchiarelli 2018.

43. Quoted in Maycock (2001).

44. Dancis 2018.

45. Dancis 2018.

46. Robb 2004, 303–5.

47. Robb 2004, 305.

48. Robb 2004, 305.

49. Suid 2002, 647–78.

50. It should be noted that information related to DOD involvement in the film industry post-9/11 is incomplete. We are limited in our analysis as the result of two issues. The first issue relates directly to the DOD's monopoly over this information and the agency's ability to grant or deny access to materials. The second issue relates to the information that has been released. While the DOD released information to historian Lawrence Suid, he has been largely unwilling to allow others to access that data. Since these files are now considered his private property and not that of the DOD, they are not subject to FOIA requests. For a more detailed accounting of these issues, see Alford (2016). We thank Matthew Alford and Tom Secker for clarification on these issues.

51. King 2001.

52. Quoted in King (2001).

53. Quoted in BBC News (2001a).

54. Cooper 2001.

55. Cooper 2001.

56. The films listed in the appendix are adapted from a more comprehensive list compiled by Alford and Secker (2017).

57. Alford and Secker 2017, 205–216.

58. Quoted in Barnes (2008).

59. Quoted in Barnes (2008).

60. Quoted in Barnes (2008).

61. Quoted in Barnes (2008).

62. Quoted in Raz (2008).

63. Quoted in Raz (2008).

64. Quoted in Turse (2008), 111–12.

65. Mirrlees 2017, 416.

66. Mirrlees 2017, 417.

67. Mirrlees 2017, 417–18.

68. Mirrlees 2017, 419.

69. Mirrlees 2017, 419.

70. Mirrlees 2017, 420.

71. Debruge 2009.

72. Quoted in Debruge (2009).

73. Mirrlees 2017, 427.

74. Quoted in Riesman (2012).

75. Secker n.d.

76. Lacy 2003, 614.

CONCLUSION

1. Quoted in Creel (1952), 149.

2. Mearsheimer 2011, 45–70.

3. Koppl 2018, 228.

4. See Kosar (2005) for more detail on the laws intended to constrain the executive branch.

5. Employment of publicity experts; restrictions, 5 U.S. Code § 3107, https://www.law.cornell.edu/uscode/text/5/3107.

6. Lobbying with appropriated moneys, 18 U.S. Code § 1913, https://www.law.cornell.edu/uscode/text/18/1913.

7. Announcement of payment for broadcast, 47 U.S. Code § 317, https://www.law.cornell.edu/uscode/text/47/317.

8. Public Law 106–554 of the 106th Congress, December 21, 2000, https://www.govinfo.gov/content/pkg/PLAW-106publ554/pdf/PLAW-106publ554.pdf.

9. Kosar 2005, 788.

10. Kosar 2005, 794.

11. Kosar 2005, 789.

12. Copeland and Simpson 2004, 6.

13. Kosar 2005, 790.

14. Hudson 2013.

15. H.R. 5736, 112th Congress, 2d Sess., May 10, 2012, https://www.congress.gov/112/bills/hr5736/BILLS-112hr5736ih.pdf. For more on the implications of removing the domestic dissemination ban contained in the Smith-Mundt Act, see Sager (2015).

16. Kosar 2005, 796.

17. de Jasay 1997, 3.

18. This and the subsequent subsections on whistleblowers draws on arguments first developed in Coyne, Goodman, and Hall (2019).

19. An existing literature on bureaucratic monitoring explores various issues with incentive alignment and compliance (see Moe 1985; McCubbins, Noll, and Weingast 1987, 1989; Huber and Shipan 2002; Lewis 2003) and identifies two alternative mechanisms for the congressional oversight of government bureaus—"police patrols" or "fire alarms" (see McCubbins and Schwartz 1984; Weingast 1984; Lupia and McCubbins 1994a, 1994b; Figueiredo, Spiller, and Urbiztondo, 1999; Wangenheim 2011). The "police patrol" option for congressional oversight involves legislators taking a random sample of an agency's behavior and monitoring for deviations. "Fire-alarm" oversight, in contrast, involves legislators waiting until there is a strong protest against bureaucratic behavior, which is then investigated and dealt with appropriately (see Coyne, Goodman, and Hall, 2019, 4).

20. On the overclassification of information, see Huard (1956), 219, Aftergood (2009),

404, and Goitein and Shapiro (2011), 4–5

21. Quoted in Bromwich (2016).

22. Some of these protections were formally codified in the Intelligence Authorization Act of Fiscal Year 2014 (Title VI).

23. Halchin 2015.

24. Perry 2014, 9.

25. Poulsen 2019.

26. Ellsberg 2013.

27. For an overview of the legislation related to national security information, see Elsea (2006) and Vladeck (2015).

28. See Silver (2008), 458–61, and Lutkenhaus (2014). The government's interpretation has been upheld by the courts in several cases, for example, Morissette v. United States (1952) and United States v. Morison (1988).

29. For an overview of the various aspects of the Espionage Act, see Mulligan and Elsea (2017).

30. Trudell 1986, 205–6; Silver 2008, 461–2.

31. Gathering, transmitting, or losing defense information, 18 U.S. Code § 793, https://www.law.cornell.edu/uscode/text/18/793.

32. The punishments for violating the law can be found in 18 U.S. Code § 794, gathering or delivering defense information to aid foreign government, https://www.law.cornell.edu/uscode/text/18/794, and 18 U.S. Code § 798, disclosure of classified information (https://www.law.cornell.edu/uscode/text/18/798).

33. Biden 1982.

34. Schmidt 2013.

35. For a discussion of the potential for narrow opportunism on the part of whistleblowers as well as a potential solution, see Rahill (2014) and Coyne, Goodman, and Hall (2019).

36. Patrick and Thrall 2004, 28.

37. For the economic and political economy analysis of the media and its potential as a check on political opportunism, see Sen (1984, 1999), Bartels (1993), Mondak (1995), Besley and Burgess (2002), Djankov et al. (2003), Coyne and Leeson (2004, 2009a, 2009b), McMillian and Zoido (2004), Sutter (2004), Mullainathan and Shleifer (2005), Besley and Prat (2006), Gentzkow and Shapiro (2006), and Leeson and Coyne (2005, 2007).

38. DuVal 2006; Silver 2008.

39. An important precedent to this case was *Near v. Minnesota* (1931), where the Supreme Court held that prior restraint, or prepublication censorship, violated freedom of speech as per the First Amendment.

40. Silver 2008, 452–43.

41. See DuVal (1986), 582. For a summary of the relevant case law that has emerged after *New York Times Co. v. United States* (1971), see Duval (1986), 582n7, and Silver (2008), 452–72.

42. Savage and Kaufman 2013.

43. *United States of America v. Progressive, Inc.* (1979). See Silver (2012), 470–71.

44. Elsea 2013, 7.

45. Risen 2018.

46. Hedges 2002, 143.

47. Hedges 2002, 143.

48. Quoted in Byrne (2003).

49. Hedges 2002, 146.
50. Higgs 1987, 2006b, 2012.
51. Havel 1985/1986, 31, emphasis in original.
52. Havel 1985/1986, 35–36.
53. Havel 1985/1986, 39–40.
54. Sharp 2012, 28, emphasis in original.
55. Schumpeter 1950, 262.
56. Higgs 1987; Coyne and Hall 2018.
57. Higgs 2015, 276.
58. Ostrom 1991; Boettke 2018; Aligica, Boettke, and Tarko 2019.
59. Astore 2018.
60. Chodorov 1938, 2.

References

ABC News. 2008. "List of Saddam's Crimes Is Long." *ABC News*, February 27. http://abcnews.go.com/WNT/IraqCoverage/story?id=2761722&page=1.

Adena, Maja, Ruben Enikolopov, Maria Petrova, Veronica Santarosa, and Ekaterina Zhuravskaya. 2015. "Radio and the Rise of the Nazis in Pre-War Germany." *Quarterly Journal of Economics* 130 (4): 1885–1939.

Aftergood, Steven. 2009. "Reducing Government Secrecy: Finding What Works." *Yale Law and Policy Review* 27 (2): 399–416.

Ahlers, Mike M. 2013. "TSA Removes Body Scanners Criticized as Too Revealing." CNN, May 30. https://www.cnn.com/2013/05/29/travel/tsa-backscatter/index.html.

Alford, Matthew. 2016. "The Political Impact of the Department of Defense on Hollywood Cinema." *Quarterly Review of Film and Video* 33 (4): 332–47.

Alford, Matthew, and Tom Secker. 2017. *National Security Cinema: The Shocking New Evidence of Government Control in Hollywood*. Scotts Valley, CA: CreateSpace.

Aligica, Paul Dragos, Peter J. Boettke, and Vlad Tarko. 2019. *Public Governance and the Classical-Liberal Perspective*. New York: Oxford University Press.

Altheide, David L. and John M. Johnson. 1980. *Bureaucratic Propaganda*. Boston: Allynand Bacon.

Anderson, Elisha. 2017. "Underwear Bomber Umar Farouk Abdulmutallab Sues over Treatment in Federal Prison." *Detroit Free Press*, October 22. https://www.freep.com/story/news/local/michigan/detroit/2017/10/22/underwear-bomber-suing-over-prison-treatment/788781001/.

Anderson, Jack, and Dale Van Atta. 1987. "Why the Pentagon Didn't Like 'Platoon.'" *Washington Post*, August 30. https://www.washingtonpost.com/archive/opinions/1987/08/30/why-the-pentagon-didnt-like-platoon/b638371d-0dbf-4810-9483-898fa8b68cfe/.

Andrzejewski, Adam. 2015. *The Department of Self-Promotion: How Federal Agencies PR Spending Advances Their Interests Rather Than the Public Interest, Fiscal Years 2007–2014: Oversight Study*. Open the Books. https://www.openthebooks.com/assets/1/7/OpenTheBooks_Oversight_Report_-_The_Department_of_Self-Promotion.pdf.

Antiwar.com 2006. "Abu Ghraib Abuse Photos." Antiwar.com, February 17. http://www.antiwar.com/news/?articleid=8560.

Arendt, Hannah. (1951) 1973. *The Origins of Totalitarianism*. New York: Harcourt.

———. 1972. *Crisis of the Republic*. New York: Harcourt Brace Jovanovich.

Associated Press. 2001. "Giants Took Visit to Heart." *ESPN*, September 23. http://www.espn.com.au/nfl/recap?gameId=210923012..

———. 2007. "Full Text of Tillman Memo to Top Generals: McChrystal Sent Message in Hopes of Sparing Bush 'Embarrassment.'" *NBC News*, August 3. http://www.

nbcnews.com/id/20113601/ns/us_news-military/t/full-text-tillman-memo-top-gener-als/#.Wz_fIq2ZPUp.

———. 2011. "Man Says He's Mishandled by Airport Screeners Again." *CBS Detroit*, July 23. https://detroit.cbslocal.com/2011/07/23/man-says-hes-mishandled-by-air-port-screener-again/.

Astore, William. 2018. "Taking War off Its Pedestal," *LobeLog*, February 7. https://lobelog.com/taking-war-off-its-pedestal/.

Axelrod, Alan. 2009. *Selling the Great War: The Making of American Propaganda*. New York: Palgrave Macmillan.

Ayers, Becky. 2011. "Ten Years of the TSA (Yes, It Seems Much Longer). *Forbes*, November 18. https://www.forbes.com/sites/realspin/2011/11/18/ten-years-of-the-tsa-yes-it-seems-much-longer/#2f651c821932.

Bacevich, Andrew. 2005. *The New American Militarism*. New York: Oxford University Press.

Bailey, Elizabeth. 1985. "Airline Deregulation in the United States: The Benefits Provided and the Lessons Learned." *International Journal of Transport Economics* 12 (2): 119–44.

Bailey, Ronald. 1997. "Origin of the Specious," *Reason*. http://reason.com/ar-chives/1997/07/01/origin-of-the-specious.

Bairner, Alan. 2001. *Sport, Nationalism, and Globalization: European and North American Perspectives*. New York: State University of New York Press.

Balbus, Ike. 1975. "Politics as Sports: The Political Ascendency of the Sports Metaphor in America." *Monthly Review: An Independent Socialist Magazine* 26 (10): 26–39.

Barnes, Julian E. 2008. "Calling the Shots on War Movies." *Los Angeles Times*, July 7. https://www.latimes.com/archives/la-xpm-2008-jul-07-na-armyfilms7-story.html.

Barro, Robert J. 1973. "The Control of Politicians: An Economic Model." *Public Choice* 14: 19–42.

Barstow, David. 2008. "Behind TV Analysts, Pentagon's Hidden Hand." *New York Times*, April 20. http://www.nytimes.com/2008/04/20/us/20generals.html.

Barstow, David, William J. Broad, and Jeff Gerth. 2004. "The Nuclear Card: The Alumi-num Tube Story—A Special Report; How White House Embraced Suspect Iraq Arms Intelligence." *New York Times*, October 3. http://www.nytimes.com/2004/10/03/washington/us/the-nuclear-card-the-aluminum-tube-story-a-special-report-how.html?_r=0.

Bartels, Larry. 1993. "Messages Received: The Political Impact of Media Exposure." *American Political Science Review* 87: 267–85.

Baskas, Harriet. 2011. "TSA Pat-Down Leaves Traveler Covered in Urine." *NBC News*, March 25. http://www.nbcnews.com/id/40291856/ns/travel-news/t/tsa-pat-down-leaves-traveler-covered-urine/#.W3Wxz63MzUp.

Battle, Joyce, ed. 2003. "Shaking Hands with Saddam Hussein: The U.S. Tilts toward Iraq, 1980–1984." National Security Archive. http://nsarchive.gwu.edu/NSAEBB/NSAEBB82/.

BBC News. 2001a. "Bush Adviser Meets Hollywood Execs." *BBC News*, November 12. http://news.bbc.co.uk/2/hi/entertainment/1651173.stm.

———. 2001b. "US Appoints Terror War Spin Doctor." *BBC News*, November 8. http://news.bbc.co.uk/2/hi/americas/1644763.stm.

————. 2010. "Boeing 747 Survives Simulated 'Flight 253' Bomb Blast." *BBC News*, March 5. http://news.bbc.co.uk/2/hi/in_depth/8547329.stm.

————. 2013. "Saddam's 1979 Baath Party Purge." *BBC News*, December 13. http://www.bbc.com/news/av/world-middle-east-25363857/saddams-1979-baath-party-purge.

Beaven, Katherine Alex. 2016. "Why the '80s and '90s Were the True Golden Age of Flying." *Oyster*, August 11. https://www.oyster.com/articles/54614-why-the-80s-and-90s-were-the-true-golden-age-of-flying/.

Becker, Gary. 1983. "A Theory of Competition among Pressure Groups for Political Influence." *Quarterly Journal of Economics* 98 (3): 371–400.

Belluck, Pam, and Kenneth Chang. 2001. "FBI Agent Testifies Shoe Bomb Could Have Brought Down Plane." *San Francisco Gate*, December 29. https://www.sfgate.com/news/article/FBI-agent-testifies-shoe-bomb-could-have-brought-2820765.php.

Benjamin, Daniel. 2002. "Saddam Hussein and Al Qaeda Are Not Allies." *New York Times*, September 30. http://www.nytimes.com/2002/09/30/opinion/saddam-hussein-and-al-qaeda-are-not-allies.html.

Bergen, Peter L. 2018. "September 11 Attacks." Britannica.com, updated September 10, 2020. https://www.britannica.com/event/September-11-attacks.

Berger, Peter L., and Thomas Luckmann. 1966. *The Social Construction of Reality*. New York: Anchor Books.

Berkow, Ira. 1991. "Sports of the Times; Once Again, It's the Star-Spangled Super Bowl." *New York Times*, January 27. https://www.nytimes.com/1991/01/27/sports/sports-of-the-times-once-again-it-s-the-star-spangled-super-bowl.html.

Bernays, Edward. (1928) 2005. *Propaganda*. New York: Ig.

Besley, Timothy. 2006. *Principled Agents? The Political Economy of Good Government*. Oxford: Oxford University Press.

Besley, Timothy, and Robin Burgess. 2002. "The Political Economy of Government Responsiveness: Theory and Evidence from India." *Quarterly Journal of Economics* 117: 1415–52.

Besley, Timothy, and Andrea Prat. 2006. "Handcuffs for the Grabbing Hand? Media Capture and Government Accountability." *American Economic Review* 96: 720–36.

Biden, Joseph R., Jr. 1982. "A Spy Law That Harms National Security." *Christian Science Monitor*, April 6. https://www.csmonitor.com/1982/0406/040622.html.

Billingsworth, Andrew C., Michael L. Butterworth, and Paul D. Turman. 2012. *Communication and Sport: Surveying the Field*. New York: Sage.

Bingaman, Jeff. 2000. "Honoring the Navajo Code Talker Act." *Congressional Record*, April 12. https://fas.org/irp/congress/2000_cr/s041200.html.

Black, Jay. 2001. "Semantics and Ethics of Propaganda." *Journal of Mass Media Ethics* 16 (2/3): 121–37.

Boettke, Peter. 2018. "Economics and Public Administration." *Southern Economic Journal* 84 (4): 938–59.

Boettke, Peter J., Stefanie Haeffele-Balch, and Virgil Henry Storr. 2016. *Mainline Economics: Six Nobel Lectures in the Tradition of Adam Smith*. Arlington, VA: Mercatus Center.

Bohanan, Cecil, and T. Norman Van Cott. 2002. "Now More than Ever, Your Vote Doesn't Matter." *Independent Review: A Journal of Political Economy* 6 (4): 591–95.

Borger, Julian. 2006. "Blogger Bears Rumsfeld's Post 9/11 Orders." *Guardian*, February 24. https://www.theguardian.com/world/2006/feb/24/freedomofinformation. september11.

Boucher, Richard. 2003. "Boucher Announces Coalition for Disarmament of Iraq: Countries to Offer Military, Post-Conflict Support." U.S. State Department, March 18. http://www.david-morrison.org.uk/other-documents/usstate-press-briefing-20030318.htm.

Boudreaux, Donald. J. 1996. "Was Your High School Civics Teacher Right After All? Donald Wittman's *The Myth of Democratic Failure.*" *Independent Review: A Journal of Political Economy* 1 (1): 111–28.

Bowen, John, and Jean-Paul Rodrigue. N.d. "Air Transport." *The Geography of Transport Systems.* https://transportgeography.org/?page_id=1765.

Bradner, Eric, and Rene Marsh. 2015. "Acting TSA Director Reassigned after Screeners Failed Tests to Detect Explosive Weapons." CNN, June 2. https://www.cnn.com/2015/06/01/politics/tsa-failed-undercover-airport-screening-tests/index.html.

Brennan, Jason. 2016. *Against Democracy.* NJ: Princeton University Press.

Breslow, Jason M. 2016. "Colin Powell: U.N. Speech 'Was a Great Intelligence Failure.'" PBS, *Frontline*, May 17. http://www.pbs.org/wgbh/frontline/article/colin-powell-u-n-speech-was-a-great-intelligence-failure/.

Brewer, Susan A. 2009. *Why America Fights: Patriotism and War Propaganda from the Philippines to Iraq.* New York: Oxford University Press.

Brockes, Emma. 2003. "What Can Eritrea Possibly Do to Help the U.S. in Iraq?" *Guardian*, March 19. https://www.theguardian.com/world/2003/mar/20/iraq.emmabrockes.

Broder, John M. 1991. "Schwarzkopf's War Plan Based on Deception." *Los Angeles Times*, February 28. http://articles.latimes.com/1991-02-28/news/mn-2834_1_war-plan.

Bromwich, Jonah Engel. 2016. "Snowden Leaks Illegal but Were 'a Public Service' Eric Holder Says." *New York Times*, May 31. https://www.nytimes.com/2016/06/01/us/holder-says-snowden-performed-a-public-service.html.

Brown, Robert. 2004. "Sport and Healing in America." *Society* 42 (1): 37–41.

Bryant, Howard. 2013. "Sports and Patriotism." *ESPN*, July 3. http://www.espn.com/espn/story/_/id/9449554/sports-patriotism.

Buchanan, James M.. 1954. "Individual Choice in Voting and the Market." *Journal of Political Economy* 62 (4): 334–43.

———. 1975. *The Limits of Liberty: Between Anarchy and Leviathan.* Chicago: Chicago University Press.

———. 1979. "Politics without Romance: A Sketch of Positive Public Choice Theory and Its Normative Implications." *IHS Journal, Zeitschrift des Instituts für Höhere Studien* 3: B1–B11.

Budowsky, Brent. 2018. "When American Patriotism Lit the Skies: The 'Miracle on Ice,' 1980 Olympics." *Hill*, February 10. http://thehill.com/opinion/international/373180-when-american-patriotism-lit-the-skies-the-miracle-on-ice.

Burr, William. 2019. "Trapped in the Archives: The U.S. Government's System for Declassifying Historical Documents Is in Crisis." *Foreign Affairs*, November 29. https://www.foreignaffairs.com/articles/2019-11-29/trapped-archives.

Bush, George W. 1999a. "A Distinctly American Internationalism." Speech at the Ronald Reagan Presidential Library, Simi Valley, California. November 19. https://www.mtholyoke.edu/acad/intrel/bush/wspeech.htm.

———. 1999b. "A Period of Consequences." Speech at the Citadel, South Carolina, September 23. http://www3.citadel.edu/pao/addresses/pres_bush.html.

———. 2001a. Address to a joint session of Congress and the nation. *Washington Post*, September 20. http://www.washingtonpost.com/wp-srv/nation/specials/attacked/transcripts/bushaddress_092001.html.

———. 2001b. Speech during the signing of the Aviation Security Bill. *Washington Post*, November 19. http://www.washingtonpost.com/wp-srv/nation/specials/attacked/transcripts/bushtext_111901.html.

———. 2002a. "The President's News Conference with President Vaclav Havel of the Czech Republic in Prague, Czech Republic." American Presidency Project, November 20. https://www.presidency.ucsb.edu/documents/the-presidents-news-conference-with-president-vaclav-havel-the-czech-republic-prague-czech.

———. 2002b. "State of the Union Address." CNN, January 29. http://edition.cnn.com/2002/ALLPOLITICS/01/29/bush.speech.txt/.

———. 2003a. "Letter to Congressional Leaders Reporting on the Commencement of Military Operations in Iraq." March 21. https://www.presidency.ucsb.edu/documents/letter-congressional-leaders-reporting-the-commencement-military-operations-against-iraq.

———. 2003b. "Remarks by the President to the Philippine Congress." U.S. Department of State, October 18. https://2001-2009.state.gov/p/eap/rls/rm/2003/25455.htm.

———. 2003c. "Saluting the Troops." CNN, September 12. http://www.cnn.com/TRANSCRIPTS/0309/12/se.01.html.

———. 2003d. "Text of President Bush's 2003 State of the Union Address." *Washington Post*, January 28. http://www.washingtonpost.com/wp-srv/onpolitics/transcripts/bushtext_012803.html.

———. 2004. "Remarks at the White House Correspondents' Association Dinner." American Presidency Project, May 1. http://www.presidency.ucsb.edu/ws/index.php?pid=64809.

Byrne, Ciar. 2003. "Cronkite: I believe in war censorship." *Guardian*, October 22. https://www.theguardian.com/media/2003/oct/22/pressandpublishing.broadcasting.

Campbell, Matt. 2017. "Trump Uses Pat Tillman—Killed by Friendly Fire—in Patriotism Feud with the NFL." *Kansas City Star*, September 25. https://www.kansascity.com/news/politics-government/article175266511.html.

Caplan, Bryan. 2007. *The Myth of the Rational Voter: Why Democracies Choose Bad Polices.* NJ: Princeton University Press.

Carlson, Stephen. 2017. "Report: 44,000 'Unknown' Military Personnel Stationed around the World." *Stars and Stripes*, December 7. https://www.stripes.com/report-44-000-unknown-military-personnel-stationed-around-the-world-1.501292.

Carney, Stephen A. 2011. *Allied Participation in Operation Iraqi Freedom.* Washington, DC: Center of Military History, United States Army. http://www.history.army.mil/html/books/059/59-3-1/CMH_59-3-1.pdf.

CBC News. 2009. "Bomb Could Have Blown Hole in Plane: Reports." *CBS News*, December 29. https://www.cbc.ca/news/world/bomb-could-have-blown-hole-in-plane-reports-1.809012.

Cheney, Richard. 2002a. "Press Conference by Vice President Dick Cheney and His Highness Salman bin Hamad Al Khalifa, Crown Price of Bahrain at Shaikh Hamad Palace." White House, March 17. https://georgewbush-whitehouse.archives.gov/vice-president/news-speeches/speeches/vp20020317.html.

———. 2002b. Speech to the Veterans of Foreign Wars National Convention, Nashville, Tennessee, August 22. https://www.theguardian.com/world/2002/aug/27/usa.iraq.

Chertoff, Michael. 2006. "Press Conference Regarding 2006 Transatlantic Liquids Explosives Plot." August 10. https://www.tsa.gov/news/press/speech/2006/08/10/press-conference-regarding-2006-transatlantic-liquids-explosives-plot.

Chodorov, Frank. 1938. "When War Comes," *Freeman*, November: 2.

Chomsky, Noam. 2002. *Media Control: The Spectacular Achievements of Propaganda.* New York: Seven Stories Press.

Chong, Dennis, and James N. Druckman. 2001. "Framing Theory." *Annual Review of Political Science* 10: 103–26.

Chwe, Michael. 2001. *Rational Ritual: Culture, Coordination, and Common Knowledge.* NJ: Princeton University Press.

Clinton, William J. 1998a. "Address before a Joint Session of the Congress on the State of the Union." American Presidency Project, January 27. https://www.presidency.ucsb.edu/documents/address-before-joint-session-the-congress-the-state-the-union-8.

———. 1998b. "Statement on the Signing of the Iraq Liberation Act of 1998." American Presidency Project, October 31. https://www.presidency.ucsb.edu/documents/statement-signing-the-iraq-liberation-act-1998.

CNN. 2002. "Top Bush Officials Push Case against Saddam." CNN, September 8. http://www.cnn.com/2002/ALLPOLITICS/09/08/iraq.debate/.

———. 2017. "Iraq Weapons Inspections Fast Facts." CNN, updated March 16, 2020. http://www.cnn.com/2013/10/30/world/meast/iraq-weapons-inspections-fast-facts/index.html.

Cole, David. 2003. "The New McCarythism: Repeating History in the War on Terror." *Harvard Civil Rights-Civil Liberties Law Review* 38: 1–30.

Committee on Oversight and Government Reform. 2008. "Misleading Information from the Battlefield: The Tillman and Lynch Episodes." H.R. Rep. No. 110–858. https://fas.org/irp/congress/2008_rpt/tillman.pdf.

Cooper, Marc. 2001. "Lights! Cameras! Attack! Hollywood Enlists." *Nation*, November 21. https://www.thenation.com/article/archive/lights-cameras-attack-hollywood-enlists/.

Copeland, Curtis W., and Michael Simpson. 2004. "The Information Quality Act: OMB's Guidance and Initial Implementation." CRS Report for Congress, August 19. https://fas.org/sgp/crs/RL32532.pdf.

Coyne, Christopher J., and Abigail R. Hall. 2016 "Empire State of Mind: The Illiberal Foundations of Liberal Hegemony." *Independent Review: A Journal of Political Economy* 21 (2): 237–50.

———. 2018. *Tyranny Comes Home: The Domestic Fate of U.S. Militarism.* Stanford, CA: Stanford University Press.

Coyne, Christopher J., Nathan Goodman, and Abigail R. Hall. 2019. "Sounding the Alarm: The Political Economy of Whistleblowing in the US Security State." *Peace Economics, Peace Science, and Public Policy* 25 (1): 1–11.

Coyne, Christopher J., and Peter T. Leeson. 2004. "Read All About It! Understanding the Role of Media in Economic Development." *Kyklos* 57: 21–44.

———. 2009a. "Media as a Mechanism of Institutional Change and Reinforcement." *Kyklos* 62 (1): 1–14.

———. 2009b. *Media, Development, and Institutional Change.* Cheltenham: Edward Elgar.

Crawford, Neta C. 2019. "United States Budgetary Costs and Obligations of Post-9/11 Wars through FY2020: $6.4 Trillion." 20 Years of War: A Costs of War Research Series, Brown University. https://watson.brown.edu/costsofwar/files/cow/imce/papers/2019/US%20Budgetary%20Costs%20of%20Wars%20November%202019.pdf.

Creel, George. 1920. *How We Advertised America: The First Telling of the Amazing Story of the Committee on Public Information That Carried the Gospel of Americanism to Every Corner of the Globe.* New York: Harper and Brothers.

———. 1952. *Congressional Attitudes Toward Informational Activities in the Federal Government.* Madison: University of Wisconsin–Madison.

Cunningham, Stanley B. 2002. *The Idea of Propaganda: A Reconstruction.* Westport, CT: Praeger.

Dalberg-Acton, John Emerich Edward. 1907. "Letter to Bishop Mandell Creighton, April 5, 1887." In *Historical Essays and Studies,* edited by John Neville Figgis and Reginald Vere Laurence, 503–5. London: Macmillan.

Dancis, Daniel. 2018. "With the Pentagon's Blessing: Hollywood, the Military, and Don Baruch." United States National Archives, *The Text Message,* March 1. https://textmessage.blogs.archives.gov/2018/03/01/with-the-pentagons-blessing-hollywood-the-military-and-don-baruch/.

Davis, Daniel L. 2012a. "Dereliction of Duty II: Senior Military Leaders' Loss of Integrity Wounds Afghan War Effort." February 6. Unclassified report. https://info.publicintelligence.net/USArmy-Dereliction-of-Duty-II.pdf.

———. 2012b."Truth, Lies, and Afghanistan." *Armed Forces Journal,* February 1. http://armedforcesjournal.com/truth-lies-and-afghanistan/.

———. 2019. "8 Years Ago I Warned the Government Lied about Afghanistan—Will Anyone Listen Now?" *National Interest,* December 22. https://nationalinterest.org/blog/skeptics/8-years-ago-i-warned-government-lied-about-afghanistan%E2%80%94will-anyone-listen-now-107696.

de Boer, Connie. 1979. "The Polls: Terrorism and Hijacking." *Public Opinion Quarterly* 43 (3): 410–18.

Debruge, Peter. 2009. "Film Biz, Military Unite for Mutual Gain." *Variety,* June 19. https://variety.com/2009/digital/features/film-biz-military-unite-for-mutual-gain-1118005186/.

de Jasay, Anthony. 1997. *Against Politics: On Government, Anarchy, and Order.* New York: Routledge.

DellaVigna, Stefano, Ruben Enikolopov, Vera Mironova, Maria Petrova, and Ekaterina Zhuravaskaya. 2014. "Cross Border Effects of Foreign Media: Serbian Radio and Nationalism In Croatia." *American Economic Journal: Applied Economics* 6 (3): 103–32.

DellaVigna, Stefano, and Matthew Gentzkow. 2010. "Persuasion: Empirical Evidence." *Annual Review of Economics* 2 (1): 643–69.

DePetris, Daniel R. 2019. "The War on Terror's Total Cost: $5,900,000,000,000." *National Interest*, January 12. https://nationalinterest.org/blog/skeptics/war-terrors-total-cost-5900000000000-41307.

Der Derian, James, and Michael J. Shapiro, eds. 1989. *International and Intertextual Relations: Postmodern Readings of World Politics*. New York: Lexington Books.

Diamond, John. 2004. "Prewar Intelligence Predicted Iraqi Insurgency." *USA Today*, October 24. https://usatoday30.usatoday.com/news/washington/2004-10-24-insurgence-intel_x.htm.

Dietrich, Christopher R. W. 2011. "'Arab Oil Belongs to Arabs': Raw Material Sovereignty, Cold War Boundaries, and the Nationalisation of the Iraq Petroleum Company, 1967–1973." *Diplomacy and Statecraft* 22 (3): 450–79.

DiLorenzo, Thomas J. 1988. "Competition and Political Entrepreneurship: Austrian Insights into Public-Choice Theory." *Review of Austrian Economics* 2 (1): 59–71.

DiMaggio, Anthony R. 2008. *Mass Media, Mass Propaganda: Understanding the News in the "War on Terror."* Lanham, MD: Lexington Books.

Director of Central Intelligence. 2002. "Iraq's Continuing Programs for Weapons of Mass Destruction." National Intelligence Estimate, April. http://nsarchive.gwu.edu/NSAEBB/NSAEBB129/nie.pdf.

Djankov, Simeon, Caralee McLiesh, Tatiana Nenova, and Andrei Shleifer. 2003. "Who Owns the Media?" *Journal of Law and Economics* 46: 341–82.

Dominguez, Robert. 2010. "Bad Timing: Video of TSA Pat-Down of 3-Year-Old Girl Resurfaces after Two Years." *Daily News*, November 17. Available online at: http://www.nydailynews.com/life-style/travel/bad-timing-video-tsa-pat-down-3-year-old-girl-resurfaces-years-article-1.456731.

Doob, Lenoard W. 1935. *Propaganda: Its Psychology and Techniques*. New York: Henry Holt.

Donlin, Eric Jay. 2008. *Leviathan: The History of Whaling in America*. New York: W. W. Norton.

Donovan, James A. 1970. *Militarism, U.S.A.* New York: Charles Scribner's Sons.

Downs, Anthony. 1957. *An Economic Theory of Democracy*. New York: Harper.

Duncan, Thomas K. and Christopher J. Coyne. 2013a. "The Origins of the Permanent War Economy," *Independent Review: A Journal of Political Economy* 18 (2): 219–40.

———. 2013b. "The Overlooked Costs of the Permanent War Economy: A Market Process Approach," *The Review of Austrian Economics* 26 (4): 413–431.

———. 2015. "The Revolving Door and the Entrenchment of the Permanent War Economy." *Peace Economics, Peace Science and Public Policy* 21 (3): 391–413.

Dunne, J. Paul. 1995. "The Defense Industrial Base." In *Handbook of Defense Economics*, vol. 1, edited by Keith Hartley and Todd Sandler, 399–430. New York: Elsevier Science.

DuVal, Benjamin S., Jr. 1986. "The Occasions of Secrecy." *University of Pittsburg Law Review* 47 (3): 579–674.

Edelman, Murray. 1985. *The Symbolic Uses of Politics*. Urbana: University of Illinois Press.

———. 1993. "Contestable Categories and Public Opinion." *Political Communication* 10: 231–42.

Eggertsson, Thrainn. 1990. *Economic Behavior and Institutions*. Cambridge, MA: Cambridge University Press.

Eisensee, Thomas, and David Strömberg. 2007. "News Droughts, News Floods, and U.S. Disaster Relief." *Quarterly Journal of Economics* 122 (2): 693–728.

ElBaradei, Mohamed. 2003. "Status of Nuclear Inspections in Iraq: An Update." International Atomic Energy Agency, March 7. https://www.iaea.org/newscenter/statements/status-nuclear-inspections-iraq-update.

Electronic Privacy Information Center. 2010. "Whole Body Imaging Technology and Body Scanners ('Backscatter' X-Ray and Millimeter Wave Screening)." epic.org, January. https://epic.org/privacy/airtravel/backscatter/.

Elder, Robert. 1968. *The Information Machine: The United States Information Agency and American Foreign Policy.* Syracuse, NY: Syracuse University Press.

Ellsberg, Daniel. 2013. "Secrecy and National Security Whistleblowing." *Huffington Post*, January 13. https://www.huffingtonpost.com/daniel-ellsberg/secrecy-and-national-secu_b_2469058.html.

Ellul, Jacques. 1973. *Propaganda: The Formation of Men's Attitudes.* New York: Random House.

Elsea, Jennifer K. 2006. *Protection of National Security Information.* Washington, DC: Congressional Research Service. https://fas.org/sgp/crs/secrecy/RL33502.pdf.

———. 2013. *Intelligence Identities Protection Act.* Washington, DC: Congressional Research Service. https://fas.org/sgp/crs/intel/RS21636.pdf.

Encyclopedia Britannica. 2019a. "Decline of the Hollywood Studios." Britannica.com. https://www.britannica.com/art/history-of-the-motion-picture/The-war-years-and-post-World-War-II-trends.

———. 2019b. "Transportation Security Administration." Britannica.com. https://www.britannica.com/topic/Transportation-Security-Administration.

Engle, Jane. 2011. "U.S. Aviation Security Timeline." *Los Angeles Times*, June 12. http://www.latimes.com/travel/la-tr-airline-safety-timeline-20110612-story.html.

Enikolopov, Ruben, Maria Petrova, and Ekaterina Zhuravskaya. 2011. "Media and Political Persuasion: Evidence from Russia." *American Economic Review* 111 (7): 3256–85.

Esteban. 2011. "9 Greatest Ceremonial Puck Drops in Hockey History." *TotalProSports*, July 11. http://www.totalprosports.com/2015/02/09/9-greatest-ceremonial-puck-drops-in-hockey-history/#12.

Fair, Eric. 2016. *Consequence: A Memoir.* New York: Henry Holt.

Farmer, Sam. 2002. "NFL Player Will Take Field for Army." *Los Angeles Times*, May 30. https://www.latimes.com/archives/la-xpm-2002-may-30-sp-tillman30-story.html.

Farrell, Stephen. 2010. "Embedistan." *New York Times*, June 25. https://atwar.blogs.nytimes.com/2010/06/25/embedistan-2/.

Federal Aviation Administration. 2017. "A Brief History of the FAA." January 4. https://www.faa.gov/about/history/brief_history/.

Fellows, Erwin W. 1959. "'Propaganda': History of a Word." *American Speech* 34 (3): 182–89.

Ferejohn John. 1986. "Incumbent Performance and Electoral Control." *Public Choice* 50 (1/3): 5–25.

Figueiredo, Rui J. P. de, Pablo T. Spiller, and Santiago Urbiztondo. 1999. "An Informational Perspective on Administrative Procedures." *Journal of Law, Economics, and Organization* 15: 283–305.

Fish, Mike. N.d.. "An (Un)American Tragedy." *ESPN.* http://www.espn.com/espn/eticket/story?page=tillmanpart3.

Fletcher, Brekke. 2020. "TSA Quadrupled Its Carry-On Allowance for Hand Sanitizer, But Where Can We Find Any?" CNN, March 15. https://www.cnn.com/travel/article/tsa-rule-change-hand-sanitizer/index.html.

Forrester, Jared A., Thomas G. Weiser, and Joseph D. Forrester. 2018. "An Update on Fatalities due to Venomous and Nonvenomous Animals in the United States (2008–2015)." *Wilderness and Environmental Medicine* 29: 36–44.

Fox Sports. 2011. "Tagliabue Recalls His 9/11 Experience." *Fox Sports,* September 9. https://www.foxsports.com/nfl/story/former-nfl-commissioner-paul-tagliabue-recalls-decision-to-cancel-games-after-9-11-090911.

Fraser, Matthew. 2003. *Weapons of Mass Distraction: American Empire and Soft Power.* Toronto: Key Porter Books.

Friedell, Morris. 1969. "On the Structure of Shared Awareness." *Behavioral Science* 14: 28–39.

Friedman, George. 2014. "The American Public's Indifference to Foreign Affairs." Forbes.com, February 19. http://www.forbes.com/sites/stratfor/2014/02/19/the-american-publics-indifference-to-foreign-affairs/#b83fc2716561.

Friedman, Uri. 2012. "8 Crazy Things Americans Believe about Foreign Policy." *Foreign Policy,* October 16. http://foreignpolicy.com/2012/10/16/8-crazy-things-americans-believe-about-foreign-policy/.

Frontline. 1990. "The Arming of Iraq." PBS, September 11. http://www.pbs.org/wgbh/pages/frontline/shows/longroad/etc/arming.html.

———. 2005. "Interviews: Vincent Cannistraro." PBS, December 12. http://www.pbs.org/wgbh/pages/frontline/bushswar/interviews/cannistraro.html.

———. 2006. "Interview with Tom Rosenstiel." PBS, October 16. http://www.pbs.org/wgbh/pages/frontline/newswar/interviews/rosenstiel.html.

———. 2008. "Bush's War." PBS, March 24–25. http://www.pbs.org/wgbh/frontline/film/bushswar/.

———. 2014. "Is There a Link between Al Qaeda and Iraq?" PBS. http://www.pbs.org/wgbh/pages/frontline/shows/gunning/etc/alqaeda.html.

Fulbright, J. William. 1971. *The Pentagon Propaganda Machine.* New York: Vintage Books.

Furubotn, Eirik G., and Rudolf Richter. 1997. *Institutions and Economic Theory: The Contribution of the New Institutional Economics.* Ann Arbor: University of Michigan Press.

Gabel, Peter. 2008. "Patriotism at the Ballpark." *Tikkun* 23 (4): 30–31.

Gallup. 2017. "Iraq." http://www.gallup.com/poll/1633/iraq.aspx.

Gates, Robert. 2014. "The Quiet Fury of Robert Gates." *Wall Street Journal,* January 7. http://www.wsj.com/articles/SB10001424052702304617404579306851526222552.

Gelman, Andrew, Nate Silver, and Aaron Edlin. 2012. "What Is the Probability Your Vote Will Make a Difference?" *Economic Inquiry* 50 (2): 321–26.

Gentzkow, Matthew A., and Jesse M. Shapiro. 2004. "Media, Education and Anti-Americanism in the Muslim World." *Journal of Economic Perspectives* 18 (3): 117–33.

———. 2006. "Media Bias and Reputation." *Journal of Political Economy* 114 (2): 280–316.

Gerber, Alan S., Dean Karlan, and Daniel Bergan 2009. "Does the Media Matter? A Field Experiment Measuring the Effect of Newspapers on Voting Behavior and Political Opinions." *American Economic Journal: Applied Economics* 1 (2): 35–52.

Gettleman, Jeffrey. 2004. "Enraged Mob in Fallujah Kills 4 American Contractors." *New York Times*, March 31. https://www.nytimes.com/2004/03/31/international/worldspecial/enraged-mob-in-falluja-kills-4-american.html.

GlobalPolicy.org. 2004. "Public Opinion in Iraq: First Poll Following Abu Ghraib Revelations." May 14–23. https://www.globalpolicy.org/images/pdfs/o6iiacss.pdf.

———. 2007. "Iraq Poll September 2007." https://www.globalpolicy.org/images/pdfs/09bbciraqipoll.pdf.

Goitein, Elizabeth, and David M. Shapiro. 2011. *Reducing Overclassification through Accountability*. New York: Brennan Center for Justice, New York University School of Law.

Gompert, David C., Hans Binnendijk, and Bonny Lin. 2014. *Blinders, Blunders, and Wars: What America and China Can Learn*. Santa Monica, CA: RAND Corporation. https://www.rand.org/pubs/research_reports/RR768.html.

Gonzales, Alberto. 2006. "Press Conference Regarding 2006 Transatlantic Liquids Explosives Plot." Transportation Security Administration, August 10. https://www.tsa.gov/news/press/speech/2006/08/10/press-conference-regarding-2006-transatlantic-liquids-explosives-plot.

Goodell, Roger. 2016. "Letter to Senators McCain and Flake." May 18. https://nfl-communications.com/Documents/2016%20Releases/Commissioner%20letter%20to%20Sen.%20McCain%20and%20Sen.%20Flake.pdf.

Goodman, Melvin A. 2013. *National Insecurity: The Cost of American Militarism*. San Francisco, CA: City Lights Books.

Gordon, Michael R., and Judith Miller. 2002. "Threats and Responses: The Iraqis; U.S. Says Hussein Intensifies Quest for A-Bomb Parts." *New York Times*, September 8. http://www.nytimes.com/2002/09/08/world/threats-responses-iraqis-us-says-hussein-intensifies-quest-for-bomb-parts.html.

Gough, Christina. 2020. "Total Revenue of All National Football League Teams from 2001 to 2016 (in Billion US Dollars)." *Statista*, October 9. https://www.statista.com/statistics/193457/total-league-revenue-of-the-nfl-since-2005/.

Gowadia, Huban. 2017. "Transparency at TSA." Transportation Security Administration, March 2. https://www.tsa.gov/news/testimony/2017/03/02/transparency-tsa.

Grabell, Michael. 2008. "History of the Federal Air Marshal Service." *ProPublica*, November 13. https://www.propublica.org/article/history-of-the-federal-air-marshal-service.

———. 2016. "The TSA Releases Data on Air Marshal Misconduct, 7 Years after We Asked." *ProPublica*, February 24. https://www.propublica.org/article/tsa-releases-data-on-air-marshal-misconduct-7-years-after-we-asked.

Guttmann, Allen. 1986. *Sports Spectators*. New York, NY: Columbia University Press.

Hahn, Peter. 2012a. "A Century of U.S. Relations with Iraq." *Origins: Current Events in Historical Perspective* 5(7). http://origins.osu.edu/article/century-us-relations-iraq.

———. 2012b. *Missions Accomplished? The United States and Iraq Since World War I*. New York: Oxford University Press.

Halchin, L. Elaine. 2015. *The Intelligence Community and Its Use of Contractors: Congressional Oversight Issues.* Washington, DC: Congressional Research Service. https://fas.org/sgp/crs/intel/R44157.pdf.

Hammond, Jeremy R. 2012. "The Lies That Led to the Iraq War and the Persistent Myth of 'Intelligence Failure.'" *Foreign Policy Journal,* September 8. https://www.foreign-policyjournal.com/2012/09/08/the-lies-that-led-to-the-iraq-war-and-the-persistent-myth-of-intelligence-failure/3/.

Haq, Husna. 2015. "Why Many Americans Hold False Beliefs about WMDs in Iraq and Obama's Birth Place." *Christian Science Monitor,* January 7. https://www.csmonitor.com/USA/Politics/Decoder/2015/0107/Why-many-Americans-hold-false-beliefs-about-WMDs-in-Iraq-and-Obama-s-birth-place-video.

Harnden, Toby. 2009. "Detroit Terror Attack: US Aviation Security System Failed, Napolitano Admits." *Telegraph,* December 28. https://www.telegraph.co.uk/news/worldnews/northamerica/usa/6901972/Detroit-terror-attack-US-aviation-security-system-failed-Napolitano-admits.html.

Harris Poll. 2011. "America's Sport—A Majority of Americans Watch NFL Football." *Harris Poll,* October 14. https://theharrispoll.com/new-york-n-y-october-14-2011-football-night-in-america-seems-at-first-to-be-a-presumptuous-name-for-nbc-to-call-their-pre-game-television-program-however-according-to-the-results-of-a-rece/.

Havel, Václav. 1985/1986. "The Power of the Powerless." *International Journal of Politics* 15 (3/4): 23–96.

Hayek, F.A . 1944. *The Road to Serfdom.* Chicago, IL: University of Chicago Press.

———. 1961. "The Non Sequitur of the 'Dependence Effect.'" *Southern Economic Journal* 27 (4): 346–48.

Heckelman, Jac C. 2003. "Now More Than Ever, Your Vote Doesn't Count: A Reconsideration." *Independent Review: A Journal of Political Economy* 7 (4): 599–601.

Hedges, Chris. 2002. *War Is a Force That Gives Us Meaning.* New York: Public Affairs.

Herman, Edward S., and Noam Chomsky. 1988. *Manufacturing Consent: The Political Economy of the Mass Media.* New York: Pantheon.

Hersh, Seymour M. 1972. "The Massacre at My Lai." *New Yorker,* January 22. https://www.newyorker.com/magazine/1972/01/22/coverup.

———. 2007. "The General's Report: How Antonio Taguba, Who investigated the Abu Ghraib Scandal, Became One of Its Casualties." *New Yorker,* June 25. http://www.newyorker.com/magazine/2007/06/25/the-generals-report.

Hester, Michael D. 2005. "America's #1 Fan: A Rhetorical Analysis of Presidential Sports Encomia and the Symbolic Power of Sport in the Articulation of Civil Religion in the United States." PhD diss., Georgia State University.

Hiebert, Ray Eldon. 2003. "Public Relations and Propaganda in Framing the Iraq War: A Preliminary Review." *Public Relations Review* 29 (3): 243–55.

Higgs, Robert. 1987. *Crisis and Leviathan: Critical Episodes in the Growth of American Government.* New York: Oxford University Press.

———. 1997. "Public Choice and Political Leadership." *Independent Review: A Journal of Political Economy* 1 (3): 465–67.

———. 2006a. *Depression, War, and Cold War: Studies in Political Economy.* New York: Oxford University Press.

———. 2006b. "Fear: The Foundation of Every Government's Power." *Independent Review: A Journal of Political Economy* 10 (3): 447–66.

———. 2012. *Delusions of Power: New Explorations of the State, War, and the Economy.* Oakland, CA: Independent Institute.

———. 2015. *Taking a Stand: Reflections on Life, Liberty, and the Economy.* Oakland, CA: Independent Institute.

———. 2018. "Principal-Agent Theory and Representative Government." *The Independent Review: A Journal of Political Economy* 22 (3): 479–80.

Holcombe, Randall G. 2005. "Political Entrepreneurship and the Democratic Allocation of Economic Resources." *Review of Austrian Economics* 15 (2/3): 143–59.

———. 2016. *Advanced Introduction to Public Choice.* Cheltenham: Edward Elgar.

Horton, Scott. 2015 *Lords of Secrecy: The National Security Elite and America's Stealth Warfare.* New York: Nation Books.

Howell, Thomas 1997. "The Writer's War Board: U.S. Domestic Propaganda in World War II." *Historian* 59 (4): 795–813.

Huard, Leo Albert. 1956. "The Status of the National Internal Security during 1955." *Georgetown Law Journal* 44 (2): 179–220.

Huber, John, and Charles Shipan. 2002. *Deliberate Discretion? The Institutional Foundations of Bureaucratic Autonomy.* Cambridge: Cambridge University Press.

Hudson, John. 2013. "U.S. Repeals Propaganda Ban, Spreads Government-Made News to Americans." *Foreign Policy*, July 14. http://foreignpolicy.com/2013/07/14/u-s-repeals-propaganda-ban-spreads-government-made-news-to-americans/.

Human Rights Watch. 2002. "Justice for Iraq." Human Rights Watch Policy Paper, December. https://www.hrw.org/legacy/backgrounder/mena/iraq1217bg.htm.

Irwin, Will. 1936. *Propaganda and the News: Or What Makes You Think So?* New York: McGraw-Hill.

Jacoby, William G. 2000. "Issue Framing and Public Opinion on Government Spending." *American Journal of Political Science* 44 (4): 750–67.

James A. Baker III Institute for Public Policy. 2001. "Strategic Energy Policy: Challenges for the 21st Century." *Baker Institute Policy Report* 15. https://scholarship.rice.edu/handle/1911/91544.

Janos, Adam. 2018. "G.I.s' Drug Use in Vietnam Soared—With Their Commanders' Help." *History.com*, updated August 19. https://www.history.com/news/drug-use-in-vietnam.

Johnson, Chalmers. 1976. "Perspectives on Terrorism." https://apps.dtic.mil/dtic/tr/fulltext/u2/a081201.pdf.

Johnson, James. 2012. "TSA Breaks Teens Insulin Pump during Forced Full-Body Scanner Examination." *Inquisitr*, May 9. https://www.inquisitr.com/233195/tsa-breaks-teens-insulin-pump-during-forced-full-body-scanner-examination/.

Johnson, Samuel. 1758. *The Idler: In Two Volumes.* London: J. Newbery.

Jones, Jeffrey M. 2015. "As Industry Grows, Percentage of U.S. Sports Fans Steady." *Gallup*, June 17. https://news.gallup.com/poll/183689/industry-grows-percentage-sports-fans-steady.aspx.

Jowett, Garth, and Victoria O'Donnell. 1986. *Propaganda and Persuasion.* Beverley Hills, CA: Sage.

Kauffman, Chaim. 2006. "Threat Inflation and the Failure of the Marketplace of Ideas: The Selling of the Iraq War." *International Security* 29 (1): 5–48.

Kelly, Matt. 2018. "On Account of War." National Baseball Hall of Fame. https://baseballhall.org/discover-more/stories/short-stops/1918-world-war-i-baseball.

Kerley, David and Jeffrey Cook. 2017. "TSA Fails Most Tests in Latest Undercover Operations at US Airports." *ABC News*, November 9. https://abcnews.go.com/US/tsa-fails-tests-latest-undercover-operation-us-airports/story?id=51022188.

Kieley, Eugene. 2016. "Yes, Trump Said Bush 'Lied.'" FactCheck.org, March 17. http://www.factcheck.org/2016/03/yes-trump-said-bush-lied/.

King, John. 2001. "White House Sees Hollywood Role in War on Terrorism." CNN, November 8. https://www.cnn.com/2001/US/11/08/rec.bush.hollywood/.

King, Samantha. 2008. "Offensive Lines: Sports-State Synergy in an Era of Perpetual War." *Cultural Studies: Critical Methodologies* 8 (4): 527–39.

Knickerbocker, Brad. 2010. "Pilots to Be Exempt from Airport Scanners, Intrusive Pat-Downs." *Christian Science Monitor*, November 19. https://www.csmonitor.com/USA/2010/1119/Pilots-to-be-exempt-from-airport-scanners-intrusive-pat-downs.

Knight, Bruce Winston. 1936. *How to Run a War.* New York: Alfred A. Knopf.

Knox, Olivier. 2017. "White House Hides Troop Numbers in Iraq, Syria, Afghanistan." *Yahoo News*, December 11. https://www.yahoo.com/news/white-house-hides-troop-numbers-iraq-syria-afghanistan-030637699.html.

Knox, Richard. 2010. "Protests Mount over Safety and Privacy of Airport Security." NPR, *Shots*, November 12. https://www.npr.org/sections/health-shots/2010/11/12/131275949/protests-mount-over-safety-and-privacy-of-airport-scanners.

Kohut, Andrew, Carroll Doherty, and Elizabeth Mueller Gross. 2004. "A Year after Iraq War: Mistrust of America in Europe Ever Higher, Muslim Anger Persists." *Pew Research Center*, March 16. http://www.people-press.org/2004/03/16/a-year-after-iraq-war/.

Koppes, Clayton R., and Gregory D. Black. 1977. "What to Show the World: The Office of War Information and Hollywood, 1942–1945." *Journal of American History* 64 (1): 87–105.

Koppl, Roger. 2018. *Expert Failure.* New York: Cambridge University Press.

Kosar, Kevin B. 2005. "The Law: The Executive Branch and Propaganda; The Limits of Legal Restrictions." *Presidential Studies Quarterly* 35 (4): 784–97.

Krakauer, Jon. 2009. *Where Men Win Glory.* New York: Anchor Books.

Kravitz, Derek. 2010. "Effectiveness of Airport Body Scanners Eyed." *Washington Post*, December 26. https://www.newsday.com/travel/effectiveness-of-airport-body-scanners-eyed-1.2570448.

Kristian, Bonnie. 2017. "The Fog of Troop Deployments." *The Week*, December 27. http://theweek.com/articles/742717/fog-troop-deployments.

Kuran, Timur. 1997. *Private Truths, Public Lies: The Social Consequences of Preference Falsification.* Cambridge, MA: Harvard University Press.

Kushner Gadarian, Shana. 2010. "Foreign Policy at the Ballot Box: How Citizens Use Foreign Policy to Judge and Choose Candidates." *Journal of Politics* 72 (4): 1046–62.

Labott, Elise, and Jill Dougherty. 2010. "State Department Failed to Confirm Terror Suspect's Visa." *CNN Politics*, January 8. http://www.cnn.com/2010/POLITICS/01/08/terror.suspect.visa/index.html.

Lacy, Mark J. 2003. "War, Cinema, and Moral Anxiety." *Alternatives: Global, Local, and Political* 28 (5): 611–36.

Landes, William M. 1977. "An Economic Study of U.S. Aircraft Hijacking, 1960–1976." Center for Economic Analysis of Human Behavior and Social Institutions, National

Bureau of Economic Research, Working Paper 210. https://www.nber.org/papers/w0210.pdf.

Lapidos, Juliet. 2010. "Does the TSA Ever Catch Terrorists? If They Do, for Some Reason They Won't Admit It." *Slate*, November 18. https://slate.com/news-and-politics/2010/11/does-the-tsa-ever-catch-terrorists.html.

Larson, Eric V., and Bogdan Savych. 2005. *American Public Support for U.S. Military Operations from Mogadishu to Baghdad.* Santa Monica, CA: RAND Corporation. http://www.rand.org/content/dam/rand/pubs/monographs/2005/RAND_MG231.pdf.

Lasswell, Harold D. 1927. "The Theory of Political Propaganda." *American Political Science Review* 21 (3): 627–31.

———. 1938. *Propaganda Technique in the World War.* New York: Peter Smith.

Laville, Sandra, Richard Norton-Taylor, and Vikram Dodd. 2006. "A Plot to Commit Murder on an Unimaginable Scale." *Guardian*, August 11. https://www.theguardian.com/uk/2006/aug/11/politics.usa1.

Leeson, Peter T., and Christopher J. Coyne. 2005. "Manipulating the Media." *Institutions and Economic Development* 1/2: 67–92.

———. 2007. "The Reformers' Dilemma: Media, Policy Ownership, and Reform." *European Journal of Law and Economics* 23: 237–50.

Levine, Daniel J. 2018. "Threat Inflation as Political Melodrama: ISIS and the Politics of Late Modern Fear." *Critical Studies on Security* 6 (1): 136–54.

Lévi-Strauss, Claude. 1962. *The Savage Mind.* Chicago, IL: University of Chicago Press.

Levy, David M., and Sandra J. Peart. 2016. *Escape from Democracy: The Role of Experts and the Public in Economic Policy.* New York: Cambridge University Press.

Lewis, David. 1969. *Convention: A Philosophical Study.* Cambridge, MA: Harvard University Press.

Lewis, David E. 2003. *Presidents and the Politics of Agency Design.* Stanford, CA: Stanford University Press.

Lippmann, Walter. 1922. *Public Opinion.* New York: Macmillan.

Lipsky, Richard. 1981. *How We Play the Game: Why Sports Dominate American Life.* Boston, MA: Beacon Press.

———. 1985. "The Political and Social Dimensions of Sport." In *American Sport Culture*, ed. Wiley Lee Umphlett, 68–75. Toronto: Associated University Press.

Lipsyte, Robert. 1975. *Sportsworld: An American Dreamland.* New York: Quadrangle/New York Times Book.

Little, Andrew T. 2017. "Propaganda and Credulity." *Games and Economic Behavior* 102: 224–32.

Lupia, Arthur, and Matthew D. McCubbins. 1994a. "Designing Bureaucratic Accountability." *Law and Contemporary Problems* 57:91–126.

———.1994b. "Learning from Oversight: Fire Alarms and Police Patrols Reconsidered." *Journal of Law, Economics, and Organization* 10: 96–125.

Lutkenhaus, Jessica. 2014. "Prosecuting Leakers the Easy Way: 8 U.S.C. § 641." *Columbia Law Review* 114 (5): 1167–1208.

MacArthur, Douglas. 1965. *A Soldier Speaks: Public Papers and Speeches of General of the Army Douglas MacArthur.* New York: Frederick A. Praeger.

Macedo, Diane. 2010. "New Scanners Kept Many Illegal or Dangerous Items off Planes This Year." *Fox News*, November 18. https://www.foxnews.com/us/tsa-new-scanners-kept-many-illegal-or-dangerous-items-off-planes-this-year.

Mann, Charles C. 2011. "Smoke Screening." *Vanity Fair*, December 20. https://www.vanityfair.com/culture/2011/12/tsa-insanity-201112.

Marlin, Randal. 2013. *Propaganda and The Ethics of Persuasion*. Orchard Park, NY: Broadview Press.

Maycock, James. 2001. "War within War." *Guardian*, September 14. https://www.theguardian.com/theguardian/2001/sep/15/weekend7.weekend3.

McCabe, Scott. 2013. "Crime History: Communist Sympathizer Commits First Airline Hijacking in U.S." *Washington Examiner*, April 30. https://www.washingtonexaminer.com/crime-history-communist-sympathizer-commits-first-airline-hijacking-in-us.

McCain, John, and Jeff Flake. 2015. "Tackling Paid Patriotism: A Joint Oversight Report." https://static.politico.com/98/a4/d61b3cae45f0a7b79256cf1da1e0/flake-report.45am.pdf.

McCartney, James, and Sinclair McCartney. 2015. *America's War Machine: Vested Interests: Endless Conflict*. New York: Thomas Dunne Books.

McClellan, Scott. 2008. *What Happened: Inside the Bush White House and Washington's Culture of Deception*. New York: Public Affairs Books.

McCubbins, Matthew D., Roger G. Noll, and Barry R. Weingast. 1987. "Administrative Procedures as Instruments of Political Control." *Journal of Law, Economics, and Organization* 3: 243–77.

———. 1989. "Structure and Process, Politics and Policy: Administrative Arrangements and the Political Control of Agencies." *Virginia Law Review* 75: 431–82.

McCubbins, Mathew D., and Thomas Schwartz. 1984. "Congressional Oversight Overlooked: Policy Patrols vs. Fire Alarms." *American Journal of Political Science* 28: 165–79.

McMillian, John, and Pablo Zoido. 2004. "How to Subvert Democracy: Montesinos in Peru." *Journal of Economic Perspectives* 18 (4): 69–92.

Mearsheimer, John J. 2011. *Why Leaders Lie: The Truth about Lying in International Politics*. New York: Oxford University Press.

Meet the Press. 2002. "Transcript of Interview with Vice-President Dick Cheney." NBC News, September 8. https://www.leadingtowar.com/PDFsources_claims_aluminum/2002_09_08_NBC.pdf.

———. 2006. "Transcript for Sept. 10." NBC News. September 10. http://www.nbcnews.com/id/14720480/ns/meet_the_press/t/transcript-sept/#.WTF_07SOrjI.

Mellor, Chris. 2010. "US Airport Body Scanners Can Store and Export Images." *Register*, January 12. https://www.theregister.co.uk/2010/01/12/tsa_body_scanners/.

Melman, Seymour. 1970. *Pentagon Capitalism: The Political Economy of War*. New York: McGraw-Hill.

———. 1974. *The Permanent War Economy: American Capitalism in Decline*. New York: Simon and Schuster.

Meltzer, Matt. 2015. "A Brief (And Totally Fascinating) History of Airport Security." *Thrillist*, July 14. https://www.thrillist.com/travel/nation/why-do-we-have-to-take-our-shoes-off-at-airport-security-history-of-the-tsa.

Menard, Claude and Mary M. Shirley, eds. 2005. *Handbook of New Institutional Economics*. Dordrecht: Springer.

Miller III, James C. 1999. *Monopoly Politics*. Stanford, CA: Hoover Institution Press.

Mindock, Clark. 2018. "Taking a Knee: Why Are NFL Players Protesting and When Did They Start to Kneel?" *Independent*, May 24. https://www.independent.co.uk/news/

world/americas/us-politics/taking-a-knee-national-anthem-nfl-trump-why-meaning-origins-racism-us-colin-kaepernick-a7966961.html.

Mirrlees, Tanner. 2017. "Transforming *Transformers* into Militainment: Interrogating the DoD Hollywood Complex." *American Journal of Economics and Sociology* 76 (2): 405–34.

Moe, Terry. 1985. "Control and Feedback in Economic Regulation." *American Political Science Review* 79: 1094–116.

Mondak, Jeffrey J. 1995. "Newspapers and Political Awareness." *American Journal of Political Science* 39:513–27.

Montgomery, David. 2003. "The NFL's New Turf." *Washington Post*, September 1. https://www.washingtonpost.com/archive/lifestyle/2003/09/01/the-nfls-new-turf/fd3e1160-7b16-4b8d-a7cd-df1dbef3e06c/?utm_term=.3fa651f777d9.

Moran, Terry. 2003. "Is Bush's Iraq Stance Rooted in Revenge?" *ABC News*, March 18. http://abcnews.go.com/US/story?id=90764&page=1.

Morris, Roger. 2003. "A Tyrant 40 Years in the Making." *New York Times*, March 14. http://www.nytimes.com/2003/03/14/opinion/a-tyrant-40-years-in-the-making.html.

Mueller, Dennis C. 2003. *Public Choice III*. Cambridge: Cambridge University Press.

Mueller, John,. 2006. *Overblown: How Politicians and the Terrorism Industry Inflate National Security Threats, and Why We Believe Them*. New York: Free Press.

Mueller, John, ed. 2019. *Terrorism Since 9/11: The American Cases*. Washington, DC: Cato Institute. https://politicalscience.osu.edu/faculty/jmueller/SINCE.pdf.

Mueller, John, and Mark G. Stewart. 2011. *Terror, Security, and Money: Balancing The Risks, Benefits, and Costs of Homeland Security*. New York: Oxford University Press.

———. 2021. "Terrorism and Bathtubs: Comparing and Assessing the Risk." *Terrorism and Political Violence* 33 (1): 138–63.

Mullainathan, Sendhil, and Andrei Shleifer. 2005. "The Market for News." *American Economic Review* 95 (4): 1031–53.

Mulligan, Stephen P., and Jennifer K. Elsea. 2017. *Criminal Prohibitions on Leaks and Other Disclosures of Classified Defense Information*. Washington, DC. Congressional Research Service. https://fas.org/sgp/crs/secrecy/R41404.pdf.

National Commission on Terrorist Attacks upon the United States. 2004. "The Aviation Security System and the 9/11 Attacks." Staff Statement No. 3. 2004. Available online at: https://govinfo.library.unt.edu/911/staff_statements/staff_statement_3.pdf.

National Football League. 2011. "NFL and the Military." National Football League, June 16. https://www.nfl.com/news/nfl-and-the-military-09000d5d8205a029.

National Hockey League. 2014. "Soldier Rappels to Drop Ceremonial Puck." https://www.youtube.com/watch?v=muG16je8OgQ/ (no longer posted).

NBC News. 2004. "Ex-NFL Star Tillman Makes 'Ultimate Sacrifice.'" *NBC News*, April 23. https://www.nbcnews.com/id/wbna4815441#.WoYZ8a3MygR.

———. 2014. "California Mom and TSA Settle Breast Milk Lawsuit for $75,000." *NBC News*, April 23. https://www.nbcnews.com/news/us-news/california-mom-tsa-settle-breast-milk-lawsuit-75-000-n88096.

Nelson, Richard Alan. 1996. *A Chronology and Glossary of Propaganda in the United States*. Westport, CT: Greenwood Press.

Nelson, Richard, and Foad Izadi. 2009. "Ethics and Social Issues in Public Diplomacy." In *Routledge Handbook of Public Diplomacy*, edited by Nancy Snow and Philip M. Taylor, 334–51. New York: Routledge.

Neuman, Scott. 2017. "Pat Tillman's Widow Pushes Back on Trump NFL Tweet." NPR, *The Two-Way*, September 26. https://www.npr.org/sections/thetwo-way/2017/09/26/553712302/pat-tillmans-widow-pushes-back-on-trump-nfl-tweet.

Newport, Frank. 2002. "Public Wants Congressional and U.N. Approval before Iraq Action." *Gallup News Service*, September 6. http://www.gallup.com/poll/6748/public-wants-congressional-un-approval-before-iraq-action.aspx.

Newsweek. 1991. "Anatomy of a Cakewalk." *Newsweek*, March 10. http://www.newsweek.com/anatomy-cakewalk-201550.

Niskanen, William A. 1971. *Bureaucracy and Representative Government*. Chicago, IL: Aldine-Atherton.

———. 1975. "Bureaucrats and Politicians." *Journal of Law and Economics* 18: 617–43.

———. 2001. "Bureaucracy." In *The Elgar Companion to Public Choice*, edited by William F. Shughart II and Laura Razzolini, 258–70. Cheltenham: Edward Elgar.

Norman, Jim. 2018. "Football Still Americans' Favorite Sport to Watch." *Gallup News*, January 4. https://news.gallup.com/poll/224864/football-americans-favorite-sport-watch.aspx.

North, Douglass C. 1990. *Institutions, Institutional Change, and Economic Performance*. Cambridge: Cambridge University Press.

Norton, Helen. 2017. "Government Speech and the War on Terror." *Fordham Law Review* 86 (2): 543–63.

Nowrasteh, Alex. 2017. "Fatalities and the Annual Chance of Being Murdered in a European Terrorist Attack." CATO Institute, June 21. https://www.cato.org/blog/european-terrorism-fatalities-annual-chance-being-murdered.

O'Connor, Lydia. 2016. "This Is What It Was Like to Go to the Airport before 9/11." *Huffington Post*, September 11. https://www.huffingtonpost.com/entry/airports-before-911_us_57c85e17e4b078581f11a133.

Olken, Benjamin A. 2009. "Do TV and Radio Destroy Social Capital? Evidence from Indonesian Villages." *American Economic Journal: Applied Economics* 1 (4): 1–33.

Olson, Lynne. 2014. *Those Angry Days: Roosevelt, Lindbergh, and America's Fight over World War II, 1939–1941*. New York: Random House.

Olson, Mancur. 1965. *The Logic of Collective Action*. Cambridge, MA: Harvard University Press.

Orwell, George. 1968. "Politics and the English Language." In *The Collected Essays, Journalism and Letters of George Orwell*, vol. 4, edited by Sonia Orwell and Ian Angos, 127–40. New York: Harcourt.

Osgood, Kenneth. 2006. *Total Cold War: Eisenhower's Secret Propaganda Battle at Home and Abroad*. Lawrence: University Press of Kansas.

Ostrom, Vincent. 1991. *The Meaning of Democracy and the Vulnerabilities of Democracies: A Response to Tocqueville's Challenge*. Ann Arbor: University of Michigan Press.

Parks, Wallace. 1957–1958. "Secrecy and the Public Interest in Military Affairs." *George Washington Law Review* 26: 23–77.

Patrick, Brian Anse, and A. Trevor Thrall. 2004. "Winning the Peace: Paradox and Propaganda after the Invasion of Iraq." *Global Media Journal* 2 (4): 1–29.

———. 2007. "Beyond Hegemony: Classical Propaganda Theory and Presidential Communication Strategy after the Invasion of Iraq." *Mass Communication and Society* 10 (1): 95–118.

Paul, Christopher, and Miriam Matthews. 2016. *The Russian "Firehouse of Falsehood" Propaganda Model: Why It Might Work and Options to Counter It.* Santa Monica, CA: RAND Corporation. https://www.rand.org/content/dam/rand/pubs/perspectives/PE100/PE198/RAND_PE198.pdf.

———. 2002. "Baseball: A Film by Ken Burns: Timeline." http://www.pbs.org/kenburns/baseball/timeline/.

Pekoske, David. 2018. "Examining the President's FY 2019 Budget Request for the Transportation Security Administration." Transportation Security Administration, April 12. https://www.tsa.gov/news/testimony/2018/04/12/examining-presidents-fy-2019-budget-request-transportation-security.

———. 2019. "Examining the President's FY 2020 Budget Request for the Transportation Security Administration." Transportation Security Administration, April 2. https://www.tsa.gov/news/testimony/2019/04/02/examining-presidents-fy-2020-budget-request-transportation-security.

Perry, Rodney M. 2014. *Intelligence Whistleblower Protections: In Brief.* Washington, DC: Congressional Research Service.

Pierce, Charles P. 2018. "Trump Has Made the NFL His Punching Bag: The League's Best Response Is Defiance." *Sports Illustrated*, July 9. https://www.si.com/donald-trump-nfl-anthem-policy-ireland-day-of-defiance.

Pittore, Niko. 2011. "Case 55: Wichita Airport." In *Terrorism Since 9/11: The American Cases*, edited by John Mueller. Washington, DC: Cato Institute. https://politicalscience.osu.edu/faculty/jmueller/55WAIR7.pdf.

Ponsonby, Arthur. 1928. *Falsehood in War-Time: Containing an Assortment of Lies Circulated throughout the Nations during the Great War.* London: Garland.

Port Authority of New York and New Jersey. 2013. "Port Authority's National Historic Landmark Building One Rededicated at Newark Liberty International Airport." Port Authority of New York and New Jersey Press Release, December 17. https://www.panynj.gov/press-room/press-item.cfm?headLine_id=255.

Porter, Bruce D. 1994. *War and the Rise of the State: The Military Foundations of Modern Politics.* New York: Free Press.

Porter, Patrick. 2015. *The Global Village Myth: Distance, War, and the Limit of Power.* Washington, DC: Georgetown University Press.

Poulsen, Kevin. 2019. "U.S. Intelligence Shuts Down Damning Report on Whistleblower Retaliation." *Daily Beast*, updated September 19. https://www.thedailybeast.com/us-intelligence-shut-downs-damning-report-on-whistleblower-retaliation.

Powell, Colin. 2003. "Transcript of Powell's U.N. Presentation." CNN, February 6. http://www.cnn.com/2003/US/02/05/sprj.irq.powell.transcript.09/index.html?iref=mpstoryview.

Pratkanis, Anthony R., and Elliot Aronson. 2001. *Age of Propaganda: The Everyday Use and Abuse of Persuasion.* New York: Freeman.

Preble, Christopher A., and John Mueller, eds. 2014. *A Dangerous World? Threat Perception and U.S. National Security.* Washington, DC: Cato Institute.

Program on International Policy Attitudes and Knowledge Networks. 2002. "PIPA-Knowledge Networks Poll: Americans on the Conflict With Iraq." http://www.pipa.org/OnlineReports/Iraq/IraqConflict_Oct02/IraqConflict%20Oct02%20quaire.pdf.

———. 2003. "Misperceptions, the Media and the Iraq War." http://web.stanford.edu/class/comm1a/readings/kull-misperceptions.pdf.

Project for Excellence in Journalism. 2003. "Embedded Reporters: What Are Americans Getting?" Pew Research Center, April 3. http://www.journalism.org/2003/04/03/embedded-reporters/.

Puhl, Tyler. 2011. "Case 20: Bombing Transatlantic Airliners." In *Terrorism Since 9/11: The American Cases*, edited by John Mueller. Washington, DC: Cato Institute. https://politicalscience.osu.edu/faculty/jmueller/SINCE.pdf.

Purdum, Todd S., and Jim Rutenberg. 2003. "A Nation at War: The News Media; Reporters Respond Eagerly to Pentagon Welcome Mat." *New York Times*, March 23. http://www.nytimes.com/2003/03/23/us/a-nation-at-war-the-news-media-reporters-respond-eagerly-to-pentagon-welcome-mat.html.

Quist, Arvin 2. 2002. *Security Classification of Information.* Vol. 1, *Introduction, History, and Adverse Impacts.* Oak Ridge, TN: Oak Ridge Classification Associates. https://fas.org/sgp/library/quist/.

Rahill, Patrick M. 2014. "Top Secret—The Defense of National Security Whistleblowers: Introducing a Multi-factor Balancing Test." *Cleveland State Law Review* 63: 237–67.

Rapaport, Daniel. 2018. "How Many People Watch the Super Bowl?" *Sports Illustrated*, February 4. https://www.si.com/nfl/2018/02/04/how-many-people-watch-super-bowl-viewership-ratings.

Raz, Guy. 2008. "Does the Military Wag Hollywood's Dog?" NPR, *Talk of the Nation*, July 10. https://www.npr.org/transcripts/92421139.

Real, Michael R. 1975. "Super Bowl: Mythic Spectacle." *Journal of Communication* 25 (1): 31–43.

Reksulak, Michael, Laura Razzolini, and William F. Shughart II, eds. 2014. *The Elgar Companion to Public Choice.* 2nd ed. Northampton, MA: Edward Elgar.

Richards, Lauren, Peter Molinaro, John Wyman, and Sarah Craun. 2019. "Lone Offender: A Study of Lone Offender Terrorism in the United States, 1972–2015." United States Federal Bureau of Investigation. https://www.fbi.gov/file-repository/lone-offender-terrorism-report-111319.pdf/view.

Risen, James. 2018. "The Biggest Secret: My Life as a New York Times Reporter in the Shadow of the War on Terror." *Intercept*, January 3. https://theintercept.com/2018/01/03/my-life-as-a-new-york-times-reporter-in-the-shadow-of-the-war-on-terror/

Ritchie, Hannah. 2018. "Is It Fair to Compare Terrorism and Disaster with Other Causes of Death?" *Our World in Data*, February 14. https://ourworldindata.org/is-it-fair-to-compare-terrorism-and-disaster-with-other-causes-of-death.

Rivera, Nick. 2011. "Ten Years Later, Belief in Iraq Connection with 9/11 Attack Persists." *Moderate Voice*, September 9. http://themoderatevoice.com/ten-years-later-belief-in-iraq-connection-with-911-attack-persists/.

Robb, David L. 2004. *Operation Hollywood: How the Pentagon Shapes and Censors the Movies.* New York: Prometheus Books.

Robbie, Kevin. 2015. "Miracle 1980: Cold War on Ice." *Thursday Review*, February 22. http://www.thursdayreview.com/MiracleHockeyUSA1980.html.

Roberts, Joel. 2002. "Daschle Fires Shot at Bush on War." Associated Press, February 28. http://www.cbsnews.com/news/daschle-fires-shot-at-bush-on-war/.

Robin, Corey. 2004. *Fear: The History of a Political Idea.* New York: Oxford University Press.

Rochefort, David A., and Roger W. Cobb. 1994. "Problem Definition: An Emerging Perspective." In *The Politics of Problem Definition*, edited by David A. Rochefort and Roger W. Cobb, 1–31. Lawrence: University Press of Kansas.

Roosevelt, Franklin D. 1942. "Executive Order 9182 Establishing the Office of WarInformation." American Presidency Project. https://www.presidency.ucsb.edu/documents/executive-order-9182-establishing-the-office-war-information.

Roots, Roger. 2003. "Terrorized into Absurdity: The Creation of the Transportation Security Administration." *The Independent Review: A Journal of Political Economy* 7 (4): 503–17.

Rowley, Charles K., and Friedrich Schneider, eds. 2004. *The Encyclopedia of Public Choice*. 2 vols. New York: Springer.

Saad, Lydia. 2002. "Top Ten Findings About Public Opinion and Iraq." *Gallup News*, October 8. http://www.gallup.com/poll/6964/top-ten-findings-about-public-opinion-iraq.aspx.

Sager, Weston R. 2015. "Apple Pie Propaganda? The Smith-Mundt Act before and after the Repeal of the Domestic Dissemination Ban." *Northwestern University Law Review* 109 (2): 511–46.

Saliba, Emmanuelle. 2017. "You're More Likely to Die Choking Than Be Killed by Foreign Terrorists, Data Show." *NBC News*, February 1. https://www.nbcnews.com/news/us-news/you-re-more-likely-die-choking-be-killed-foreign-terrorists-n715141.

Sapolsky, Robert M. 2017. *Behave: The Biology of Humans at Our Best and Worst*. New York: Penguin Press.

Savage, Charlie, and Leslie Kaufman. 2013. "Phone Records of Journalists Seized by U.S." *New York Times*, May 13. http://www.nytimes.com/2013/05/14/us/phone-records-of-journalists-of-the-associated-press-seized-by-us.html.

Schanzer, David H. 2018. "TSA's Air Marshal Program Is a Ridiculous Waste of Money." *The News and Observer*, August 9. https://www.newsobserver.com/opinion/article216362280.html.

Schecter, Anna, and Brian Ross. 2010. "Obama Orders Air Marshal Surge by Feb. 1: 'Race Against Time.'" *ABC News*, January 6. https://abcnews.go.com/Blotter/air-marshal-surge-race-time/story?id=9493323.

Schmidt, Michael S. 2013. "Ex-C.I.A. Officer Sentenced to 30 Months in Leak." *New York Times*, January 25. http://www.nytimes.com/2013/01/26/us/ex-officer-for-cia-is-sentenced-in-leak-case.html.

Schmitz, Melanie. 2017. "How the NFL Sold Patriotism to the U.S. Military for Millions." *Think Progress*, September 25. https://thinkprogress.org/nfl-dod-national-anthem-6f682cebc7cd/.

Schneier, Bruce. 2007. "Portrait of the Modern Terrorist as an Idiot." *Wired*, June 14. https://www.wired.com/2007/06/securitymatters-0614/.

———. 2009. "Beyond Security Theater." *Schneier on Security*, November 13. https://www.schneier.com/blog/archives/2009/11/beyond_security.html.

Schuessler, John M. 2015. *Deceit on the Road to War: Presidents, Politics, and American Democracy*. Ithaca, NY: Cornell University Press.

Schumpeter, Joseph A. 1950. *Capitalism, Socialism and Democracy*, 3rd ed. New York: Harper and Brothers.

Schwartz, John. 2009. "Debate Over Full-Body Scans vs. Invasion of Privacy Flare Anew after Incident." *New York Times*, December 29. https://www.nytimes.

com/2009/12/30/us/30privacy.html?mtrref=www.google.com&mtrref=undefined&a
ssetType=REGIWALL.

Scott, Shaun. 2016. "How the NFL Sells (and Profits from) the Inextricable Link between Football and War." *Sports Illustrated*, September 9. https://www.si.com/the-
cauldron/2016/09/09/remembering-september-11-nfl-football-warfare.

Seagren, Chad W., and David R. Henderson. 2018. "Why We Fight: A Survey of U.S.
Government War-Making Propaganda," *The Independent Review: A Journal of Political Economy* 23 (1): 69–90.

Secker, Tom. N.d. "Phil Strub Retired 6 Months Ago and No One Reported It." *Spy
Culture*. https://www.spyculture.com/phil-strub-retired-6-months-ago-and-no-one-
reported-it/.

Seelye, Katherine Q. 2002. "When Hollywood's Big Guns Come Right from the Source."
New York Times, June 10. https://www.nytimes.com/2002/06/10/us/when-holly-
wood-s-big-guns-come-right-from-the-source.html.

Segrave, Jeffrey O. 2000. "The Sports Metaphor in American Cultural Discourse." *Culture, Sport, Society* 3 (1): 48–60.

Selgin, George. 2014. "Operation Twist-the-Truth: How the Federal Reserve Misrepresents Its History and Performance." *Cato Journal* 34 (2): 229–63.

Sen, Amartya. 1984. *Poverty and Famines*. Oxford: Oxford University Press.

———. 1999. *Development as Freedom*. New York: Alfred A. Knopf.

Senate Select Committee on Intelligence. 2014. "Committee Study of the Central Intelligence Agency's Detention and Interrogation Program." Washington, DC: United
States Senate. http://i2.cdn.turner.com/cnn/2014/images/12/09/sscistudy1.pdf.

Sessions, Abigail. 2016. "Mockingbird, Operation (Late 1940s-1976)." In *The Central
Intelligence Agency: An Encyclopedia of Covert Ops, Intelligence Gathering, and
Spies*, edited by Jan Goldman, 247–49. Santa Barbara, CA: ABC-CLIO.

Setty, Sudha. 2012. "The Rise of National Security Secrets." *Connecticut Law Review*
44 (5): 1563–83.

Sforza, Teri. 2010. "Federal Air Marshal Program: 'A Total Waste of Money.'" *Orange
County Register*, February 5. https://www.ocregister.com/2010/02/05/federal-air-
marshal-program-a-total-waste-of-money/.

Shahid, Aliyah. 2010. "Feds Admit They Stored Body Scanner Images, Despite TSA
Claim the Images Cannot Be Saved." *New York Daily News*, August 4. https://www.
nydailynews.com/news/national/feds-admit-stored-body-scanner-images-tsa-claim-
images-saved-article-1.200279.

Shannon, Elaine. 2002. "Did Richard Reid Let Mom Know?" *Time*, May 23. http://
content.time.com/time/nation/article/0,8599,249418,00.html.

Sharp, Gene. 2012. *The Politics of Nonviolent Action, Part I: Power and Struggle*. Man-
chester, NH: Extending Horizons Books.

Shepherd, Ken. 2007. "AP: Foiled JFK Terror Plot Isn't Chilling, It's 'Chilling.'" *MRC
News Busters*, June 4. https://www.newsbusters.org/node/13628.

Silver, Derigan A. 2008. "National Security and the Press: The Government's Ability to
Prosecute Journalists for the Possession or Publication of National Security Information." *Communication Law and Policy* 13 (4): 447–83.

Smith, Ted D., ed. 1989. *Propaganda: A Pluralistic Perspective*. New York: Praeger.

Smithsonian Magazine. N.d.. "How 9/11 Drastically Altered U.S. Flight Security." https://www.smithsonianmag.com/videos/category/innovation/how-911-drastically-altered-us-flight-sec_1/.

Snyder, Alvin. 1995. *Warriors of Disinformation: American Propaganda, Soviet Lies, and the Winning of the Cold War*. New York: Arcade.

Somin, Ilya. 2013. *Democracy and Political Ignorance: Why Smaller Government Is Smarter*. Stanford, CA: Stanford University Press.

Sproule, J. Michael. 1997. *Propaganda and Democracy: The American Experience of Media and Mass Persuasion*. New York: Cambridge University Press.

Stanley, Jason. 2015. *How Propaganda Works*. Princeton, NJ: Princeton University Press.

————. 2016. "Beyond Lying: Donald Trump's Authoritarian Reality." *New York Times*, November 4. https://www.nytimes.com/2016/11/05/opinion/beyond-lying-donald-trumps-authoritarian-reality.html.

Straub, Bryan. 2011. "Case 23: JFK Airport." In *Terrorism since 9/11: The American Cases*, edited by John Mueller. Washington, DC: Cato Institute. https://politicalscience.osu.edu/faculty/jmueller/SINCE.pdf.

Stein, Jonathan, and Tim Dickinson. 2006. "Lie by Lie: A Timeline of How We Got into Iraq." *Mother Jones*, September/October. http://www.motherjones.com/politics/2011/12/leadup-iraq-war-timeline.

Steinhauer, Jennifer. 2015. "With Chairmanship, McCain Seizes Chance to Reshape Pentagon Agenda." *New York Times*, June 8. http://www.nytimes.com/2015/06/09/us/politics/mccain-uses-committee-post-to-press-for-defense-agenda.html?_r=0.

Stewart, Emily. 2018. "The Government Is Secretly Monitoring Ordinary US Citizens When They Fly." *Vox*, July 29. https://www.vox.com/2018/7/29/17627734/quiet-skies-tsa-flight-surveillance.

Stewart, Mark G., and John Mueller. 2008. "A Risk and Cost-Benefit Assessment of United States Aviation Security Measures." *Journal of Transportation Security* 1: 143–59.

Strickler, Laura. 2010. "TSA Body Scanners: Do They Even Work?" *CBS News*, November 17. https://www.cbsnews.com/news/tsa-body-scanners-do-they-even-work/.

Strömberg, David. 2004. "Radio's Impact on Public Spending." *Quarterly Journal of Economics* 119 (1): 189–221.

Stossel, Scott. 2001. "Sports: War Games." *American Prospect*, October 26. http://prospect.org/article/sports-war-games.

Stow, Simon. 2017. *American Mourning: Tragedy, Democracy, Resilience*. New York: Cambridge University Press.

Suid, Lawrence H. 2002. *Guts and Glory: The Making of the American Military Image in Film*. Lexington: University of Kentucky Press.

Sunstein, Cass. 2005. *Laws of Fear: Beyond the Precautionary Principle*. New York: Cambridge University Press.

Sural, Jeff. 2010. "Heightened TSA Security Is Necessary to Keep Us Safe." *US News and World Report*, December 20. https://www.usnews.com/opinion/articles/2010/12/20/heightened-tsa-security-is-necessary-to-keep-us-safe.

Sutter, Daniel. 2004. "News Media Incentives, Coverage of Government and the Growth of Government." *The Independent Review: A Journal of Political Economy* 8 (4): 549–67.

Tarabay, Jamie. 2014. "Hollywood and the Pentagon: A Relationship of Mutual Exploitation." *AlJazeera America*, July 29. http://america.aljazeera.com/articles/2014/7/29/hollywood-and-thepentagonarelationshipofmutualexploitation.html.

Team, Trefis. 2016. "The State of Air Travel in the U.S. Has Changed over the Years." *Forbes*, October 11. https://www.forbes.com/sites/greatspeculations/2016/10/11/the-state-of-air-travel-in-the-u-s-has-changed-over-the-years/#2eaf608529b6.

Testa, Patrick A. 2018. "Education and Propaganda: Tradeoffs to Public Education Provision in Nondemocracies." *Journal of Public Economics* 160: 66–81.

Thrall, A. Trevor, and Jane K. Cramer, eds. 2009. *American Foreign Policy and the Politics of Fear: Threat Inflation since 9/11.* New York: Routledge.

Tien, Lee. 2010. "Common Sense and Security: Body Scanners, Accountability, and $2.4 Billion Worth of Security Theater." *Electronic Frontier Foundation*, November 24. https://www.eff.org/deeplinks/2010/11/common-sense-and-security-body-scanners.

Tillman, Kevin. 2007. "Deliberate Acts of Deceit." *The Guardian*, April 24. https://www.theguardian.com/commentisfree/2007/apr/24/deliberateactsofdeceit.

Tocqueville, Alexis de. (1835–1840) 1988. *Democracy in America.* New York: Harper Perennial.

Trudell, Jereen. 1986. "The Constitutionality of Section 793 of the Espionage Act and Its Application to Press Leaks." *Wayne Law Review* 33: 205–28.

Tullock, Gordon. 1965. *The Politics of Bureaucracy.* Washington, DC: Public Affairs Press.

Turse, Nick. 2008. *The Complex: How the Military Invades Our Everyday Lives.* New York: Macmillan.

Unger, David C. 2013. *The Emergency State: America's Pursuit of Absolute Security at All Costs.* New York: Penguin Books.

United Nations Monitoring, Verification, and Inspections Commission. 2003. "Unresolved Disarmament Issues: Iraq's Proscribed Weapons Programmes." UNMOVIC Working Document, March 6. https://www.un.org/depts/unmovic/documents/UN-MOVIC%20UDI%20Working%20Document%206%20March%2003.pdf.

United States Attorney's Office, Eastern District of New York. 2007. "Four Individuals Charged in Plot to Bomb John F. Kennedy International Airport." Press release, June 2. https://www.justice.gov/archive/usao/nye/pr/2007/2007jun02.html.

United States Central Intelligence Agency. 2008. "Navajo Code Talkers and the Unbreakable Code." CIA, *News and Information.* https://www.cia.gov/news-information/featured-story-archive/2008-featured-story-archive/navajo-code-talkers/.

———. 2020. "Africa: Eritrea." CIA, World Factbook, updated October 9.https://www.cia.gov/library/publications/the-world-factbook/geos/er.html.

United States Department of Defense. 1966. "Delineation of DOD Audio-Visual Public Affairs Responsibilities and Policies." Instruction 5410.15, November 3.

United States Department of Homeland Security. 2019. "Transportation Security Administration Budget Overview." https://www.dhs.gov/sites/default/files/publications/19_0318_MGMT_CBJ-Transportation-Security-Administration_0.pdf.

United States Department of State. 1958. "5. National Security Council Report." In *Foreign Relations of the United States, 1958–1960, Near East Region; Iraq; Iran; Arabian Peninsula*, vol. 12. U.S. Department of State, Office of the Historian, January 24. https://history.state.gov/historicaldocuments/frus1958-60v12/d5.

United States Department of State. 2017. "The Baghdad Pact (1955) and the Central Treaty Organization (CENTRO)." United States Department of State Archive https://2001-2009.state.gov/r/pa/ho/time/lw/98683.htm.

United States Department of Transportation. 2018a. "Federal Aviation Act." https://www.congress.gov/115/plaws/publ254/PLAW-115publ254.pdf.

———. 2018b. "2017 Annual and December U.S. Airline Traffic Data." Bureau of Transportation Statistics. https://www.bts.dot.gov/newsroom/2017-annual-and-december-us-airline-traffic-data.

United States Federal Bureau of Investigation. 2013. "Kansas City Man Charged in Plot to Explode Car Bomb at Airport." FBI, Kansas City Division, press release, December 13. https://archives.fbi.gov/archives/kansascity/press-releases/2013/kansas-man-charged-in-plot-to-explode-car-bomb-at-airport.

———. 2018. "Murder." Uniform Crime Report, Crime in the United States, 2017. https://ucr.fbi.gov/crime-in-the-u.s/2017/crime-in-the--2017/topic-pages/murder.pdf.

United States Government Accountability Office. 2010. "TSA Is Increasing Procurement and Deployment of the Advanced Imaging Technology, but Challenges to This Effort and Other Areas of Aviation Security Remain." GAO, *Highlights*, March 17. https://www.gao.gov/assets/130/124211.pdf.

———. 2017. "Aviation Security: Actions Needed to Systematically Evaluate Cost and Effectiveness across Security Countermeasures." GAO, Report to Congressional Requesters, September. https://www.gao.gov/assets/690/687059.pdf.

United States House of Representatives Committee on Government Reform. 2004. "Iraq on the Records: The Bush Administration's Public Statements on Iraq." Minority Staff Special Investigations Division, March 16. http://web.archive.org/web/20060514140012/http://www.house.gov/reform/min/pdfs_108_2/pdfs_inves/pdf_admin_iraq_on_the_record_rep.pdf.

United States Information Agency. 1998. *United States Information Agency.* Washington, D.C.: United States Information Agency. http://dosfan.lib.uic.edu/usia/usiahome/overview.pdf. Accessed November 1, 2019 (no longer posted).

United States Office of War Information. 1942. *Government Information Manual for the Motion Picture Industry.* Washington, DC: Office of War Information. https://libraries.indiana.edu/collection-digital-archive-gimmpi.

United States Senate Democrats. 2007. "Report Comes Out on 'Prewar Intelligence Assessments on Post-war Iraq.'" May 25. https://democrats.senate.gov/2007/05/25/report-comes-out-on-prewar-intelligence-assessments-on-postwar-iraq/#.WVT9SzP-MzUo. Accessed May 2019 (no longer posted).

United States Transportation Security Administration. 2008. "TSA Launches Millimeter Wave Technology in Richmond." Press release, November 14. https://www.tsa.gov/news/releases/2008/11/14/tsa-launches-millimeter-wave-technology-richmond.

———. 2014. "If You See Something, Say Something™." Press release, July 28. https://www.tsa.gov/news/top-stories/2014/07/28/if-you-see-something-say-somethingTM.

———. 2018. *Facts about the "Quiet Skies"* (blog), August 22. https://www.tsa.gov/blog/2018/08/22/facts-about-quiet-skies.

Utley, Jon Basil. 2018. "The Lies Behind America's Interventions." *The American Conservative*, April 25. http://www.theamericanconservative.com/articles/the-pretty-little-lies-behind-americas-interventions/.

Vagts, Alfred. 1937. *A History of Militarism: Romance and Realities of a Profession.* New York: W. W. Norton

Vecchiarelli, Jennifer. 2018. "There Are No Names of 'Morons' on This Wall!" *Pro-Literacy*, May 25. https://proliteracy.org/Blogs/Article/345/There-Are-No-Names-of-Morons-on-This-Wall.

Villafranca, Omar. 2012. "TSA Agents Allegedly Strip-Search Woman, Fiddle with Feeding Tube." *NBCDFW*, July 18. https://www.nbcdfw.com/news/local/TSA-Agents-Allegedly-Strip-Search-Woman-Fiddle-With-Feeding-Tube-162985046.html.

Vinall, Casie. 2003. "Top Brass Launches Operation Tribute to Freedom to Honor Troops." *DOD News*, June 12. https://web.archive.org/web/20170930014816/http://archive.defense.gov/news/newsarticle.aspx?id=28876.

Vladeck, Stephen I. 2015. "Prosecuting Leaks under U.S. Law." In *Whistleblowers, Leaks, and the Media: The First Amendment and National Security*, edited by Paul Rosenzweig, Timothy J. McNulty, and Ellen Shearer, 29–42. Chicago, IL: American Bar Association.

Wagner, Richard. 1976. "Advertising and the Public Economy: Some Preliminary Ruminations." In *The Political Economy of Advertising*, edited by John Mueller, 81–100. Washington, DC: American Enterprise Institute.

———. 2007. *Fiscal Sociology and the Theory of Public Finance.* Cheltenham: Edward Elgar.

Wagner, Richard, and Deema Yazigi. 2014. "Form vs. Substance in Selection through Competition: Elections, Markets, and Political Economy." *Public Choice* 159 (3/4): 503–14.

Wakefield, Wanda Ellen. 1997. *Playing to Win: Sports and the American Military, 1989–1945.* New York: State University of New York Press.

Wangenheim, Georg von. 2011. "Production of Legal Rules by Agencies and Bureaucracies." In *Production of Legal Rules*, vol. 7 of *Encyclopedia of Law and Economics*, edited by F. Paris, 559–86. Massachusetts: Edward Elgar.

Warrick, Jo. 2003. "Some Evidence on Iraq Called Fake." *Washington Post*, March 8. https://www.washingtonpost.com/archive/politics/2003/03/08/some-evidence-on-iraq-called-fake/9b935f48-9124-4a69-9953-408001f768de/?utm_term=.18cd0b6cc2b5.

The Week. 2010. "Pat-Down Fury: The 5 Biggest TSA Horror Stories." *The Week*, November 22. http://theweek.com/articles/489105/patdown-fury-5-biggest-tsa-horror-stories.

Weingast, Barry R. 1984. "The Congressional-Bureaucratic System: A Principal Agent Perspective (with Applications to the SEC)." *Public Choice* 44: 147–91.

Western, Jo. 2005. "The War over Iraq: Selling War to the American Public." *Security Studies* 14 (1): 106–39.

White House. 1983. "National Security Decision Directive 114: Policy Toward the Iran-Iraq War." November 26. http://nsarchive.gwu.edu/NSAEBB/NSAEBB82/iraq26.pdf.

———. 1984. "National Security Decision Directive 139: Measures to Improve U.S. Posture and Readiness to Developments in the Iran-Iraq War." April 5. http://nsarchive.gwu.edu/NSAEBB/NSAEBB82/iraq53.pdf.

Whitlock, Craig. 2019. "At War with the Truth." *Washington Post*, December 19. https://www.washingtonpost.com/graphics/2019/investigations/afghanistan-papers/afghanistan-war-confidential-documents/.

Whitlock, Craig, and Bob Woodward. 2016. "Pentagon Buries Evidence of $125 Billion in Bureaucratic Waste." *Washington Post*, December 5. https://www.washingtonpost.com/investigations/pentagon-buries-evidence-of-125-billion-in-bureaucratic-waste/2016/12/05/e0668c76-9af6-11e6-a0ed-ab0774c1eaa5_story.html?utm_term=.22ea909d8c61.

Whitney, Briana. 2019. "Former Arizona Cardinals Player Says Pat Tillman Inspired Him to Enlist In Army." *CBS 5*, December 30. https://www.azfamily.com/news/features/former-arizona-cardinals-player-says-pat-tillman-inspired-him-to/article_88d26192-2b76-11ea-b7c8-cb1fec7fe2a3.html.

Wilford, Hugh. 2009. *The Mighty Wurlitzer: How the CIA Played America*. Cambridge, MA: Harvard University Press.

Williams, Pete. 2019. "FBI's 'Lone Wolf' Report Says Domestic Terrorists Are Rarely Isolated." *NBC News*, November 13. https://www.nbcnews.com/news/us-news/fbi-s-lone-wolf-report-says-domestic-terrorists-are-rarely-n1081741.

Wilson, Joseph C. 2003. "What I Didn't Find in Africa." *New York Times*, July 6. http://www.nytimes.com/2003/07/06/opinion/what-i-didn-t-find-in-africa.html.

Wilson, Julie. 2017. "Here's Why TSA Agents Make You Remove Your Shoes at the Airport." *ABC 11*, October 6. https://abc11.com/why-tsa-agents-make-you-remove-your-shoes-at-the-airport/2499196/.

Winkler, Allan. 1978. *The Politics of Propaganda: The Office of War Information, 1942–1945*. New Haven, CT: Yale University Press.

Winter, Jana. 2018a. "TSA Admits 'Quiet Skies' Surveillance Snared Zero Threats." *Boston Globe*, August 2. https://www.bostonglobe.com/metro/2018/08/02/tsa-says-quiet-skies-surveillance-snared-zero-threats/dsCm4BG3pq8v3xhi01zhLI/story.html.

———. 2018b. "Welcome to the Quiet Skies." *Boston Globe*, July 28. https://apps.bostonglobe.com/news/nation/graphics/2018/07/tsa-quiet-skies.

Woodward, Bob. 2004. *Plan of Attack: The Definitive Account of the Decision to Invade Iraq*. New York: Simon and Schuster.

World Bank. 2018. "Air Transport, Passengers Carried." https://data.worldbank.org/indicator/IS.AIR.PSGR?locations=US.

Writer's War Board. 1942. *Writers' War Board First Annual Report*. New York: Writers' War Board.

Yang, Jolie. 2011. "Case 1: The Shoe Bomber." In *Terrorism since 9/11: The American Cases*, edited by John Mueller. Washington, DC: Cato Institute. https://politicalscience.osu.edu/faculty/jmueller/SINCE.pdf.

Yanagizawa-Drott, David. 2014. "Propaganda and Conflict: Evidence from the Rwandan Genocide." *Quarterly Journal of Economics* 129 (4): 1947–94.

Zollmann, Florian. 2017. *Media, Propaganda and the Politics of Intervention*. New York: Peter Lang.

Index